Guide and Index to the Republic of Texas Donation Voucher Files 1879-1887 and Confederate Scrip Voucher Files 1881-1883 in the Texas General Land Office

By
Texas General Land Office

Edited by Robert de Berardinis

HERITAGE BOOKS
2008

HERITAGE BOOKS
AN IMPRINT OF HERITAGE BOOKS, INC.

Books, CDs, and more—Worldwide

For our listing of thousands of titles see our website
at
www.HeritageBooks.com

Published 2008 by
HERITAGE BOOKS, INC.
Publishing Division
100 Railroad Ave. #104
Westminster, Maryland 21157

Copyright © 2008 Robert de Berardinis

Other books by the author:
*Guide and Index to the Texas Confederate Audited Civil and Military Claims, 1861-1865
The Texas State Archives*, Edited by Robert de Berardinis

*Guide and Indexes to the Conserved and Microfilmed Harris County, Texas
Records of Oaths and Allegiance, Declarations of Intent,
and Final Naturalizations, 1886-1906*

Cover illustration is a detail from "Mrs. Eberle Firing Off Cannon" from
The Texas Scrap-Book (New York, 1875), *ex-libris*, the Editor.

The cover illustration was a depiction of the uprising of the citizens of Austin
attempting to stop the removal of land records of the General Land Office and the
Republic of Texas to Houston during the Mexican invasion of 1842. The Editor.

The seal of the Texas General Land Office supplied courtesy
of Jerry Drake, Archivist of the Texas General Land Office

All rights reserved. No part of this book may be reproduced or transmitted in any form or by any means,
electronic or mechanical, including photocopying, recording or by any information storage and retrieval system
without written permission from the author, except for the inclusion of brief quotations in a review.

International Standard Book Numbers
Paperbound: 978-0-7884-4764-8
Clothbound: 978-0-7884-7565-8

Table of Contents

Preface v

Republic of Texas Donation Vouchers, 1879–1887 1
   Guide to the microfilm 3
   Alphabetical Surname Index 5
   Numerical Listing 38

Confederate Scrip Vouchers, 1881–1883 71
   Guide to the microfilm 73
   Alphabetical Surname Index 75
   Numerical Listing 120

Preface

These two record sets at the Texas General Land Office can provide evidence of service in either the Texas Revolution or the Civil War on the Confederate side. In 1879, the Texas Legislature passed the first act establishing the Republic of Texas Donation grants of land and the terms by which veterans would be able to qualify. In 1881, there was further clarification of the terms. The documents submitted in support of the claim, when granted, constitute authentication "by notary or other qualified officer" as defined by Noel Stevenson on page 187 of *Genealogical Evidence* (revised edition, 1989). It does not require further substantiation by the researcher in a genealogical sense.

The documents submitted in a rejected claim are not necessarily defective. Some claims were rejected because the claimant died before the process was complete. The evidence submitted may be quite valid. At this point, when starting with a rejected claim, the researcher should attempt independent verification by a variety of source material now more easily available. Verification of service has been enhanced with the microfilm publication of several groups of documents at the General Land Office and State Archives. In some cases, these are extremely fragile documents no longer available to any researcher. An example would be the digitized files of the Texas Revolution and Republic Military Rolls at the Texas General Land Office.

Researchers may find additional material for service to the Republic of Texas in the introduction to *Guide and Index to the Texas Adjutant General Service Records, 1836–1935*.[1]

The Confederate Scrip Vouchers are another post-Reconstruction act. They were designed to lessen the burden of poverty visited upon many ex-Confederate soldiers by Reconstruction, especially the infirm, crippled, or their surviving families. Again, the same rules apply here as above with the accepted claims and rejected claims. Actually, the Confederate researcher has more documentary sources available to use in establishing independent verification of service. A starting guide would be this editor's "Primer on Texas Confederate Research" found later in this volume. Researchers will be given a variety of documentary collections to peruse, many with indexes, to establish verification of service.

Additionally, for researchers of the Texas Revolution and Republic Era as well as the Civil War, there are the invaluable bibliographies to source material compiled by Henry Putney Beers and Light Cummins. Researchers should avail themselves of the time to investigate the following:

---

[1] See introduction by Robert de Berardinis in Anthony Black & TSLAC Staff, *Guide and Index to the Texas Adjutant General Service Records, 1836–1935*, Robert de Berardinis, ed. (Westminster, Md.: Heritage Books, 2008).

1. Beers, Henry Putney. *Spanish & Mexican Records of the American Southwest: A Bibliographical Guide to Archive & Manuscript Sources*. Tucson: University of Arizona Press, 1979.
2. Beers, Henry Putney. *Guide to the Archives of the Government of the Confederate States of America*. Washington: National Archives, 1968.
3. Munden, Kenneth W., and Henry Putney Beers. *Guide to Federal Archives Relating to the Civil War*. Washington: National Archives, 1962.
4. Cummins, Light Townsend, and Alvin R. Bailey, Jr. *A Guide to the History of Texas*. New York: Greenwood Press, 1988.

The Editor

This book is dedicated to
Mary Smith Fay, CG, FASG,
Mentor, Friend, and Yenta

One of God's finer angels.

The Republic of Texas Donation Vouchers, 1879–1887

❧ Concordance to Claims ☙

❧ Alphabetical Surname Index ☙

❧ Numerical Listing ☙

Guide to the Rep. of Texas Donation Vouchers

The original documents are stored in the archives of the Texas General Land Office, the oldest national/state agency in Texas as it was founded in 1835. Microfilm of the originals is available at either the Texas General Land Office reading room in Austin or at Clayton Library in Houston. The concordance below gives the storage box number. All of the originals are now stored in mylar sleeves. Except for cases when the microfilm is not legible, copies made from the microfilm will only be available.

Correct complete citation for documents in the ROT Donation Vouchers

[Document], [Date of document], [Name of Claimant], File No. [File number], Box G 411, Texas General Land Office, *Republic of Texas Donation Voucher Files, 1879–1887.* (microfilm edition; Austin: Clayton Library Friends, 2003), roll [number].

Concordance

Box	File Numbers
G 411	1 through 49
G 412	50 through 99
G 413	100 through 147
G 414	148 through 199
G 415	200 through 247
G 416	248 through 299
G 417	300 through 344
G 418	345 through 399
G 419	400 through 451
G 420	452 through 499
G 421	500 through 550
G 422	551 through 599
G 423	600 through 650
G 424	651 through 699
G 425	700 through 746
G 426	747 through 799
G 427	800 through 850
G 428	851 through 899
G 429	900 through 948
G 430	949 through 999
G 431	1000 through 1045
G 432	1046 through 1099
G 433	1100 through 1149
G 434	1150 through 1191
G 435	1192 through 1233
G 436	1234 through 1270
G 437	1271 through 1327
G 438	1328 through 1390
G 439	1396 through 1452
G 440	1453 through 1506
G 441	1507 through 1562

Index to Rep. of Texas Donation Vouchers
Alphabetical Listing

Grantee's Name	File Number	Date/Description
	RDV 001000	
	RDV 000496	08/02/1881
ABBOTTS, LANCELOT	RDV 001282	REJECTED
ABLES, J S	RDV 000621	08/17/1881
ABLES, MARY ANN	RDV 001285	REJECTED
ABLES, MARY ANN, HARRISON	RDV 000234	07/14/1881
ADAMS, REBECCA	RDV 000125	11/18/1879
ADDISON, NATHANIEL	RDV 000683	08/20/1881
ALAMEDA, ALEMEDA, JOSE	RDV 000743	08/25/1881
ALAMEDA, JOSE	RDV 000184	05/22/1880
ALEXANDER, AREA	RDV 001127	01/14/1885
ALEXANDER, JANE G	RDV 000177	05/17/1880
ALEXANDER, JANE G, LYMAN W	RDV 000842	10/28/1881
ALLAN, CATHARINE, JAMES C	RDV 000766	10/21/1881
ALLBRIGHT, A F	RDV 000640	08/19/1881
ALLCORN, JULIA	RDV 000777	10/24/1881
ALLCORN, LYDIA, JAMES	RDV 000725	08/20/1881
ALLCORN, T J	RDV 001192	11/04/1885
ALLEN, BENJAMIN	RDV 000927	04/20/1882
ALLEN, ELIJAH	RDV 000064	09/12/1879
ALLEN, ELIJAH	RDV 000487	08/02/1881
ALLEN, ELISHA	RDV 000990	01/29/1883
ALLEN, GEORGE	RDV 000377	07/26/1881
ALLEN, JOHN	RDV 001078	11/15/1883
ALLEN, NANCY	RDV 001070	07/28/1883
ALLEN, WILLIAM	RDV 001198	12/24/1885
ALLEN, WILLIAMS	RDV 000163	05/13/1880
ALLEY, NANCY	RDV 001114	09/25/1884
ALMANAC, BRUNO	RDV 001284	REJECTED
ALSBURY, JUANA N	RDV 000183	05/19/1880
ALSBURY, Y, RODRIGUEZ, MARIA	RDV 000031	08/28/1879
AMASON, SARAH A	RDV 001271	05/05/1887
AMSLER, MARY, CHARLES	RDV 000845	10/28/1881
ANDERSON, E P, JOHN D	RDV 000731	08/25/1881
ANDERSON, HOLLAND	RDV 000328	07/20/1881
ANDERSON, HUGH	RDV 000388	07/26/1881
ANDERSON, HUGH	RDV 001283	REJECTED
ANDERSON, JOHN W	RDV 001002	01/30/1883
ANDERSON, MARY J	RDV 000051	09/05/1879
ANDERSON, MARY J, JOHN	RDV 000742	08/25/1881
ANDERSON, WASHINGTON	RDV 000691	08/19/1881
ANDREWS, MARTHA E	RDV 001264	11/30/1886
ANGLIN, MARY L, ABRAM	RDV 001033	04/07/1883

Republic of Texas Donation Vouchers-Alphabetical Listing

ANTHONY, RODNEY	RDV 001036	04/07/1883
ARCHER, ROSA	RDV 001279	06/06/1887
ARCHER, ROSA, JOHN A	RDV 000311	07/19/1881
ARIOLA, GUADALUPE	RDV 000155	05/11/1880
ARMSTRONG, CORDELIA, JAMES	RDV 000548	08/06/1881
ARMSTRONG, JAMES	RDV 000069	09/13/1879
ARMSTRONG, JAMES C	RDV 000598	08/11/1881
AROCHA, MACEDONIO	RDV 000193	06/26/1880
AROCHA, MACEDONIO	RDV 000951	04/26/1882
AROCHA, MACEDONIO	RDV 001280	REJECTED
ARRIOLA, ARIOLA, GUADALUPE	RDV 000259	07/15/1881
ASHWORTH, DELAIDE	RDV 001110	05/21/1884
ASHWORTH, DELAIDE, WILLIAM	RDV 001281	REJECTED
ASHWORTH, MARY, AARON	RDV 000912	04/19/1882
ATKINSON, MARGARET	RDV 000185	05/22/1880
ATKINSON, MARGARET, JESSE B	RDV 001151	01/23/1885
AUSTIN, ELIZABETH A, WILLIAM T	RDV 000219	07/14/1881
AUSTIN, N	RDV 000398	07/26/1881
AVERY, WILLIS	RDV 000405	07/28/1881
BAKER, JOHN B	RDV 000376	07/26/1881
BALCH, JOHN	RDV 000732	08/25/1881
BALLE, ANTONIO	RDV 000110	11/03/1879
BALLE, ANTONIO	RDV 000350	07/23/1881
BAMHART, JOSEPH	RDV 000270	07/16/1881
BANKS, REASON	RDV 000980	01/15/1883
BARCLAY, ANDERSON	RDV 000995	01/30/1883
BARKER, ALITIA	RDV 000055	09/09/1879
BARKER, ALITIA, WILLIAM	RDV 000461	08/02/1881
BARKLEY, CATHREN, RICHARD A	RDV 001287	REJECTED
BARNETT, MARY, THOMAS	RDV 001288	REJECTED
BARROW, BENJAMIN	RDV 001041	04/24/1883
BARROW, REUBEN	RDV 000776	10/21/1881
BARROW, REUBIN	RDV 001289	REJECTED
BARTLETT, JOSEPH C	RDV 000847	10/28/1881
BARTON, ELDER B	RDV 000964	05/06/1882
BASQUEZ, ANTOLINO	RDV 001304	NO DATE
BASQUEZ, ANTONIO	RDV 001290	07/15/1881
BASS, ARCHIBALD	RDV 000857	10/29/1881
BATES, SILAS H	RDV 000941	04/21/1882
BEATTY, VIRGINIA	RDV 001193	11/05/1885
BEATY, RACHAEL, JOHN B	RDV 000928	04/20/1882
BECK, JOHN	RDV 001277	06/06/1887
BECKNELL, JOHN	RDV 001176	07/30/1885
BECKNELL, MELINDA	RDV 001135	01/20/1885
BECKNELL, MELINDA L, WILLIAM A	RDV 001291	REJECTED
BEESON, JESSE	RDV 000706	08/25/1881
BEGLY, JOHN	RDV 001292	REJECTED
BELCHER, BARSHEBA, ISAM G	RDV 000785	10/24/1881
BELDIN, ELIZABETH, S C	RDV 001294	REJECTED

Republic of Texas Donation Vouchers-Alphabetical Listing

BELL, NANCY M, THOMAS B	RDV 001056	07/07/1883
BELL, PETER	RDV 001199	12/24/1885
BELL, SAM	RDV 001200	12/24/1885
BENNETT, JAMES	RDV 000581	08/08/1881
BENNETT, MILES	RDV 000855	10/28/1881
BENSON, ELLIS	RDV 000019	08/21/1879
BENSON, ELLIS	RDV 000429	07/29/1881
BERRY, A J	RDV 000203	10/20/1880
BERRY, ANDREW J	RDV 000874	11/12/1881
BERRY, HENRIETTA	RDV 001111	05/21/1884
BERRY, JOHN B	RDV 000563	08/08/1881
BERRY, N A	RDV 001270	02/16/1887
BERRY, S	RDV 000168	05/14/1880
BERRY, SEABORN	RDV 001295	REJECTED
BERRY, SEABORN	RDV 001296	REJECTED
BEST, LUCINDA	RDV 001168	03/14/1885
BEVINS, SEABORN	RDV 001298	REJECTED
BILLINGSLEY, ELIZ A, JESSIE	RDV 000590	08/11/1881
BIRD, DANIEL	RDV 000670	08/19/1881
BIRDWELL, GEORGE	RDV 001297	WITHDRAWN
BISHOP, W H	RDV 000008	08/13/1879
BISHOP, W H	RDV 000261	07/15/1881
BLAIR, L J, JOHN	RDV 000585	08/09/1881
BLAND, JOHN	RDV 000374	07/26/1881
BLAND, PRESTON	RDV 000734	08/25/1881
BLAND, SUSANNA	RDV 001122	10/03/1884
BLANTON, JACOB	RDV 001299	REJECTED
BLANTON, JACOB	RDV 001166	03/14/1885
BLEDSOE, GEORGE L	RDV 000436	07/29/1881
BLOODGOOD, LEVICY, WILLIAM	RDV 001049	05/15/1883
BLOUNT, S W	RDV 000252	07/15/1881
BLUNDELL, FRANCIS	RDV 000884	11/14/1881
BLUNDELL, FRANCIS	RDV 001300	NO DATE
BLUNDELL, SOLOMON	RDV 000748	08/25/1881
BLUNDELL, WILLIAM	RDV 000471	08/02/1881
BLUNDELL, WILLIAM	RDV 001301	NO DATE
BOON, N	RDV 001089	01/17/1884
BOONE, J W	RDV 000963	05/06/1882
BOONE, J W	RDV 001302	NO DATE
BOONE, NANCY, GARRETT E	RDV 000896	11/19/1881
BORDEN, JOHN P	RDV 000690	08/20/1881
BORDER, C E	RDV 001241	05/20/1886
BORDERS, STEPHEN A	RDV 001303	REJECTED
BOSTICK, S R	RDV 000221	07/14/1881
BOSTICK, SION R	RDV 000136	11/24/1879
BOWMAN, JAMES H	RDV 000106	10/28/1879
BOWMAN, JAMES H	RDV 000369	07/26/1881
BOWMAN, JOHN J	RDV 000780	10/24/1881
BOWMAN, N, JOSEPH	RDV 001068	07/28/1883

Republic of Texas Donation Vouchers-Alphabetical Listing

Name	Voucher	Date
BOX, LUCINDA	RDV 000060	09/11/1879
BOX, LUCINDA, JOHN	RDV 000992	01/30/1883
BOX, M E, STILWELL	RDV 001136	01/20/1885
BOYCE, ROBERT P	RDV 000498	08/02/1881
BRATTON, WILLIAM	RDV 001305	REJECTED
BRAY, JOHN L	RDV 001062	07/07/1883
BREEDING, CHARLOTTE	RDV 000144	01/22/1880
BREEDING, CHARLOTTE, W B	RDV 000447	07/29/1881
BREEDING, LOUISA, JOHN	RDV 000344	07/22/1881
BREWSTER, H P	RDV 000158	05/11/1880
BREWSTER, H P	RDV 000356	07/25/1881
BREWTON, DAVID	RDV 001071	11/15/1883
BRILL, SOLOMAN W	RDV 000216	07/14/1881
BRINGHAM, MARGARET	RDV 001084	11/16/1883
BRINGHURST, GEORGE H	RDV 000735	08/25/1881
BRISCOE, MARY J, ANDREW	RDV 000297	07/18/1881
BRITTRANG, THOMAS	RDV 001268	12/23/1886
BROOKS, G W	RDV 000318	07/19/1881
BROOKS, G W	RDV 001306	NO DATE
BROOKS, G W	RDV 000047	09/04/1879
BROOKS, GEORGE W	RDV 000205	02/26/1881
BROOKS, GEORGE W	RDV 000733	08/25/1881
BROOKS, GILBERT	RDV 000082	09/24/1879
BROOKS, GILBERT	RDV 000503	08/02/1881
BROWN, EDWARD	RDV 000396	07/26/1881
BROWN, EDWARD	RDV 001307	NO DATE
BROWN, HIRAM	RDV 001308	NO DATE
BROWN, HIRAM	RDV 000386	07/26/1881
BROWN, R R	RDV 000325	07/20/1881
BROWN, REUBEN R	RDV 000164	05/13/1880
BROWN, RICHARD	RDV 001011	02/10/1883
BROWN, RICHARD	RDV 001309	NO DATE
BROWN, WILLIAM S	RDV 001143	01/20/1885
BROWNING, H H	RDV 000120	11/14/1879
BROWNING, H H, GEORGE W	RDV 000763	10/21/1881
BROYLES, JOSEPH	RDV 000638	08/19/1881
BRUCE, WILLIS	RDV 000303	07/18/1881
BRUMMETT, HARRISON	RDV 000279	07/18/1881
BRUMMETT, HARRISON	RDV 001311	NO DATE
BRUNER, G C	RDV 000601	08/12/1881
BRUNTON, DAVID D	RDV 001312	NO DATE
BRUTON, ELISHA	RDV 001318	NO DATE
BRUTON, ELISHA	RDV 000285	07/18/1881
BRYAN, ANNA M, JOHN	RDV 000473	08/02/1881
BRYAN, ELIZABETH, CHRISTOPHER	RDV 000390	07/26/1881
BRYAN, MOSES AUSTIN	RDV 000510	08/02/1881
BRYAN, WILLIAM J	RDV 000946	04/26/1882
BUCKLEY, CATHERINE	RDV 001197	12/21/1885
BUCKLEY, TYRE	RDV 000038	08/30/1879

Republic of Texas Donation Vouchers-Alphabetical Listing

BUCKLY, TYRE	RDV 000424	07/28/1881
BUFFINGTON, A	RDV 000362	07/26/1881
BUMSTEAD, M W	RDV 000800	10/24/1881
BUNDICK, CLEMENTINE	RDV 000196	06/06/1880
BUNDICK, CLEMENTINE, THOMAS W	RDV 000610	08/17/1871
BUNTON, HERMINE, JOHN W	RDV 000249	07/15/1881
BUQUOR, P L	RDV 000962	05/05/1882
BURCH, JAMES	RDV 000669	08/19/1881
BURCH, VALENTINE	RDV 000773	10/21/1881
BURDITT, W B	RDV 000826	10/28/1881
BURDITT, WILLIAM B	RDV 000058	09/09/1879
BURK, SUSAN, BENJAMIN	RDV 001317	NO DATE
BURKE, ANNA, DAVID N	RDV 000304	07/18/1881
BURKE, ANNA MARIA	RDV 000030	08/27/1879
BURKE, SUSAN, BENJAMIN	RDV 000797	10/24/1881
BURLESON, AARON	RDV 000515	08/02/1881
BURLESON, JOSEPH	RDV 000093	10/01/1879
BURLESON, JOSEPH	RDV 000456	08/01/1881
BURLESON, MARILDA, AARON	RDV 000633	08/18/1881
BURLESON, NANCY B, JONATHAN	RDV 000925	04/19/1882
BURNAM, CAROLINE	RDV 000111	11/03/1879
BURNAM, CAROLINE, WILLIAM O	RDV 000460	08/02/1881
BURNAM, JESSE	RDV 001316	NO DATE
BURNS, JOSEPH	RDV 000143	01/06/1880
BURNS, JOSEPH	RDV 000451	07/29/1881
BURNSTEAD, M W	RDV 000135	11/24/1879
BURTON, STEPHEN H	RDV 001315	REJECTED
BUSTILLO, CLEMENTE	RDV 000063	09/11/1879
BUSTILLO, CLEMENTE	RDV 000457	08/01/1881
BUTLER, H M H	RDV 000998	01/30/1883
BUTLER, H W W	RDV 001314	REJECTED
BYARS, N T	RDV 001313	NO DATE
BYERLY, ADAM	RDV 000556	08/08/1881
BYERLY, ADAMS	RDV 000108	10/28/1879
BYERLY, WILLIAM	RDV 000555	08/08/1881
BYFIELD, LUCINDA, HOLMES	RDV 000820	10/28/1881
CABARUBIO, JULIAN	RDV 001320	REJECTED
CABASES, ALBENO	RDV 001038	04/11/1883
CABASOS, ALBINO	RDV 000039	09/13/1879
CADDEL, RHODA	RDV 000180	05/19/1880
CADENHEAD, JAMES G	RDV 001321	REJECTED
CAIN, WILLIAM	RDV 000678	08/19/1881
CAIN, WILLIAM	RDV 000145	01/24/1880
CALDEN, R J	RDV 000480	08/02/1881
CALLAHAN, JOHN H	RDV 001023	03/09/1883
CALLIHAN, J J	RDV 000134	11/22/1879
CALLIHAN, JOHANNA F, THOMAS J	RDV 000840	10/28/1881
CAMPBELL, A M, D W	RDV 000628	08/17/1881
CAMPBELL, ANGERINA, JOSEPH	RDV 000440	07/29/1881

Republic of Texas Donation Vouchers-Alphabetical Listing

CAMPBELL, CAROLINE M K D, RUFUS	RDV 000540	08/05/1881
CAMPBELL, JOHN	RDV 000569	08/08/1881
CAMPBELL, MILLIE	RDV 001152	01/24/1885
CANNON, WILLIAM J	RDV 000391	07/26/1881
CANTU, AGAPITO	RDV 001322	NO DATE
CANTUN, AGAPITO	RDV 001256	06/17/1886
CAREY, SETH	RDV 000652	08/19/1881
CARLETON, ELIZABETH, WILLIAM	RDV 000349	07/23/1881
CARLETON, ELIZABETH M	RDV 000096	10/04/1876
CARRELLO, MATIAS	RDV 001323	NO DATE
CARRO, MARCELIOUS	RDV 001219	01/09/1886
CARTWRIGHT, MATTHEW W	RDV 000266	07/16/1881
CARUTHERS, MARY, JOHN	RDV 000468	08/02/1881
CARUTHERS, WILLIAM	RDV 000968	05/08/1882
CARY, SETH	RDV 000083	09/24/1879
CASANOVA, REMEJIO	RDV 001324	NO DATE
CASIAS, GRAVIEL	RDV 000952	04/26/1882
CASILLAS, MATEO	RDV 000400	07/26/1881
CASILLAS, MATEO	RDV 000037	08/30/1879
CASTANON, LEWIS	RDV 000088	09/29/1879
CASTILLO, CAYETANO	RDV 001325	NO DATE
CASTILLO, FRANCIS	RDV 001326	REJECTED
CASTLEMAN, SOPHRONIA, JACOB	RDV 000635	08/18/1881
CAYCE, JOHN M	RDV 001177	07/30/1885
CAYCE, MARY F, HENRY P	RDV 000668	08/19/1881
CAYCE, SHADRACH	RDV 000263	07/15/1881
CERVANTES, AGAJITO	RDV 000895	11/17/1881
CHACON, ANTONIA	RDV 000033	08/28/1879
CHACON, ANTONIO RODRIGUEZ, CARLOS	RDV 000327	07/20/1881
CHAMBERLAIN, WILLARD	RDV 000727	08/25/1881
CHAMBLISS, S L	RDV 001319	NO DATE
CHAPMAN, CAROLINE, GEORGE W	RDV 000673	08/19/1881
CHARLES, ELIZABETH J	RDV 001098	05/08/1884
CHATHAM, THOMAS	RDV 000267	07/16/1881
CHAVES, LEANDRO	RDV 001327	NO DATE
CHERRY, CATHERINE	RDV 001158	01/24/1885
CHERRY, CATHERINE, SMITH R	RDV 001328	REJECTED
CHERRY, ELAN, WILLIAM	RDV 000915	04/19/1882
CHERRY, JOHN	RDV 001329	NO DATE
CHERRY, JOHN	RDV 000913	04/19/1882
CHERRY, LAURA, AARON	RDV 001044	04/24/1883
CHILDRESS, H M	RDV 000232	07/14/1881
CHILDRESS, H M	RDV 000128	11/21/1879
CHILDRESS, JOHN	RDV 001330	REJECTED
CHILDRESS, ROBERT	RDV 000262	07/15/1881
CHISOLM, MARY A, ENOCH P	RDV 001054	05/15/1883
CHISUM, JOHN	RDV 000868	10/29/1881
CHOATE, MARY	RDV 000201	07/12/1880
CHOATE, MARY, DAVID	RDV 000433	07/29/1881

Name	Voucher	Date
CLANTON, PATIENCE	RDV 001086	11/16/1883
CLAPP, ELI	RDV 000939	04/21/1882
CLARK, ABI, JOHN	RDV 001064	07/07/1883
CLARK, CAROLINE E, JAMES	RDV 000334	07/21/1881
CLARK, CAROLINE E, JAMES	RDV 001332	NO DATE
CLARK, ELIZABETH	RDV 001181	07/30/1885
CLARK, L H	RDV 001333	REJECTED
CLARK, SUSAN	RDV 001259	07/01/1886
CLARK, SUSAN, HENRY	RDV 001331	REJECTED
CLAYTON, JAMES	RDV 001335	NO DATE
CLEMONS, AUSTIN	RDV 001057	07/07/1883
CLEMONS, LEWIS C	RDV 000728	08/25/1881
CLEVELAND, ELIZA, J A H	RDV 001334	NO DATE
CLEVELAND, ELIZA J, J A H	RDV 000220	07/14/1881
CLOUD, REBECCA J, J W	RDV 000576	08/08/1881
COCHRAN, BETSY, THOMAS	RDV 000409	07/28/1881
COCKRELL, SIMON	RDV 001171	07/25/1885
COCKRELL, SIMON	RDV 001336	NO DATE
COLE, SIDNEY L, DAVID	RDV 000609	08/17/1871
COLEB, HOLLOWAY	RDV 001059	07/07/1883
COLLARD, J H	RDV 000802	10/30/1881
COLLARD, J S	RDV 000660	08/19/1881
COLLARD, L M	RDV 000646	08/19/1881
COLLEY, MARINDA, C C	RDV 000622	08/17/1881
COLLEY, MIRANDA	RDV 000057	09/09/1879
COLLINS, BELA	RDV 000796	10/24/1881
COLLINS, D J	RDV 001113	08/02/1884
COLLINSWORTH, S R, G M	RDV 000649	08/19/1881
CONE, SOPHRENIA E, HENRY H	RDV 000974	05/11/1882
CONLEE, M E, CONLEE, PRESTON	RDV 000217	07/14/1881
CONNELL, SARAH JANE, CONNELL, DAVID C	RDV 000218	07/14/1881
CONNELL, WILLIAM	RDV 000239	07/14/1881
CONTI, JULIAN	RDV 000072	09/13/1879
CONTI, JULIAN	RDV 000322	07/19/1881
COOK, JOSEPH THOMAS	RDV 000235	07/14/1881
COOK, JOSEPH THOMAS	RDV 001337	NO DATE
COOK, MARY J	RDV 000126	11/18/1879
COOK, MARY J	RDV 000871	10/29/1881
COOK, TEMPERENCE, HAMILTON	RDV 000348	07/23/1881
COOKE, COOK, F L	RDV 000662	08/19/1881
COOPER, DILLARD	RDV 000634	08/18/1881
CORDOVA, JOSE	RDV 001338	NO DATE
CORNER, EVIN	RDV 000130	11/21/1879
CORNER, EVIN	RDV 001339	NO DATE
CORONER, MARY, EVIN, EVAN	RDV 000851	10/28/1881
COURSEY, NANCY	RDV 000961	05/03/1882
COVINGTON, CHARLES	RDV 000715	08/20/1881
COX, JESSE	RDV 001202	12/24/1885
COX, SARAH, EUCLID M	RDV 000708	08/25/1881

Republic of Texas Donation Vouchers-Alphabetical Listing

Name	Voucher	Date
COY, ANTONIO	RDV 001340	NO DATE
COY, FELIPE	RDV 001341	REJECTED
COY, M J	RDV 000024	08/23/1879
COY, MARTHA J	RDV 001172	07/24/1885
CRADDOCK, JOHN R	RDV 000426	07/28/1881
CRAFT, JOHN C	RDV 001123	10/03/1884
CRAIN, JOEL B	RDV 000529	08/04/1881
CRANE, R T	RDV 000431	07/29/1881
CRAWFORD, ROBERT	RDV 000504	08/02/1881
CRAWFORD, W C	RDV 000256	07/15/1881
CRIBBS, HARRY	RDV 001342	NO DATE
CRIBS, HARRY	RDV 001043	04/24/1883
CRIER, RACHAEL, ANDREW	RDV 000954	04/28/1882
CRIST, DANIEL	RDV 000428	07/28/1881
CRISWELL, MARY E, WILLIAM	RDV 000339	07/22/1881
CRITTENDON, WILLIAM	RDV 000693	8/20/1881
CROCKETT, ROBERT P	RDV 000525	08/04/1881
CRONEA, CHARLES	RDV 001153	01/24/1885
CROPPER, PRISCILLA	RDV 001248	05/27/1886
CROUCH, JACKSON	RDV 000449	07/29/1881
CROWNOVER, LAVINIA, ARTER	RDV 000784	10/24/1881
CRUSE, PIETY, SQUIRE	RDV 001343	REJECTED
CRUZ, AROCHA, PENA, MARIA JESUSA	RDV 000061	09/11/1879
CUBIER, FERNANDO	RDV 000442	07/29/1881
CUNNINGHAM, JAMES	RDV 000613	08/17/1871
CUNNINGHAM, L C	RDV 000740	08/25/1881
CURBIER, FERNANDO	RDV 000118	11/14/1879
CURO, MARCELLUS	RDV 001344	REJECTED
CURRIER, MATIAS	RDV 000286	07/18/1881
CURVIER, MATIAS	RDV 000025	08/23/1879
DALE, E V	RDV 000222	07/14/1881
DALLAS, J L	RDV 000778	10/24/1881
DAMON, SAMUEL	RDV 000947	04/26/1882
DAMON, SAMUEL	RDV 001345	REJECTED
DANIEL, CYNTHIA	RDV 001115	09/25/1884
DANNETTELL, HENRY C	RDV 001346	REJECTED
DARDIN, STEPHEN H	RDV 000379	07/26/1881
DARSH, MARY ANN, EMERY	RDV 000710	08/25/1881
DAVEY, NANCY A	RDV 000677	08/19/1881
DAVIS, E A	RDV 000656	08/19/1881
DAVIS, ELIZA A	RDV 000059	09/11/1879
DAVIS, ELIZA A, E B	RDV 000579	08/08/1881
DAVIS, GEORGE W	RDV 000455	07/30/1881
DAVIS, JOHN	RDV 000173	05/14/1880
DAVIS, JOHN	RDV 000384	07/26/1881
DAVIS, SARAH, G W	RDV 001162	03/14/1885
DAWSON, BRITTON	RDV 000659	08/19/1881
DE CASSILLAS, GUADALUPE LUNA	RDV 001201	12/24/1885
DE FARIN, JOSEPHA SEPEDA	RDV 001252	06/05/1886

Name	Voucher	Date
DE FLORES, MELCHORA CORTES	RDV 001258	06/23/1886
DE GAYTAN, MICAELA LOSO A, AGAPITO	RDV 001141	01/20/1885
DE GOMEZ, CONCEPTION L	RDV 001093	05/08/1884
DE HENRIQUEZ, ACENCION M	RDV 000052	09/05/1879
DE LA GARZA, MARSELINO	RDV 000645	08/19/1881
DE MATA, JOSEPHA HERNANDEZ	RDV 001234	03/04/1886
DE RUBIO, PETRA VELA	RDV 001160	03/14/1885
DE RUIZ, CARMEN LONGORIA	RDV 001267	11/30/1886
DE SEAL, CASIMIRA C	RDV 001102	05/09/1884
DE XIMENES, TEADORA R	RDV 001195	11/21/1885
DEAN, CALOWAY	RDV 000572	08/08/1881
DEAN, WILLIAM B	RDV 001238	03/10/1886
DEBARD, E J	RDV 000477	08/02/1881
DEDMAN, W S	RDV 000254	07/15/1881
DEFFENBAUGH, ANTHONY	RDV 000288	07/18/1881
DELAPLAIN, A C	RDV 000462	08/02/1881
DEMORSE, CHARLES	RDV 000746	08/19/1881
DEMOSS, SUSAN, PETER	RDV 001348	NO DATE
DENMAN, JAMES	RDV 000207	02/28/1881
DENMAN, JAMES	RDV 000385	07/26/1881
DENMAN, JANE	RDV 000053	09/05/1879
DENMAN, JANE	RDV 001349	REJECTED
DENMAN, JANE, OBEDIAH	RDV 000930	04/20/1882
DENSON, MARY, C	RDV 000993	01/30/1883
DEVER, JAMES	RDV 000494	08/02/1881
DEVER, THOMAS	RDV 000418	07/28/1881
DEVORE, CORNELIUS	RDV 000417	07/28/1881
DEWEES, ANGELICA	RDV 001203	12/24/1885
DEWEES, ANGELINA, W B	RDV 001350	REJECTED
DEWITT, C C	RDV 000370	07/26/1881
DIAZ, CANUTO	RDV 001351	REJECTED
DIAZ, CANUTO	RDV 001353	NO DATE
DICKERSON, ELIZABETH, JAMES	RDV 001352	REJECTED
DIKES, LEWIS P	RDV 000849	10/28/1881
DIKES, M W	RDV 000818	10/28/1881
DINSMORE, AMANDA F	RDV 000139	12/01/1879
DINSMORE, SILAS, AMANDA	RDV 000841	10/28/1881
DODSON, A B	RDV 000897	11/28/1881
DOOM, R C	RDV 000557	08/08/1881
DORSETT, T M	RDV 000890	11/14/1881
DORSETT, T M	RDV 001354	NO DATE
DOUGLAS, DUGLASS, RICHARD	RDV 000472	08/02/1881
DOWESS, PHEBE, ISAAC	RDV 000500	08/02/1881
DOYLE, MATTHEW A	RDV 000204	10/30/1880
DOYLE, MATTHEW A	RDV 001034	04/07/1883
DRUMMOND, WESLEY	RDV 001116	09/25/1884
DUFFAN, FRANCIS T, MARY	RDV 000272	07/16/1881
DUGAT, JOSEPH L	RDV 001085	11/16/1883
DUNBAR, CAROLINE	RDV 000190	06/11/1880

Republic of Texas Donation Vouchers-Alphabetical Listing

DUNBAR, CAROLINE, WILLIAM	RDV 000770	10/21/1881
DUNBAUGH, L C, JACOB P	RDV 000495	08/02/1881
DUNCAN, C J, WILLIAM	RDV 000395	07/26/1881
DUNCAN, CHARLES	RDV 001005	02/01/1883
DUNCAN, CHARLES R	RDV 000521	08/02/1881
DUNCAN, REBECCA	RDV 000929	04/20/1882
DUNCAN, REBECCA, GREEN B	RDV 001355	NO DATE
DUNLAVY, ILIONE C, ALEXANDER	RDV 000836	10/28/1881
DUNMAN, ELIZABETH, MARTIN	RDV 001356	NO DATE
DUNMAN, JAMES T	RDV 000924	04/19/1882
DUNN, CHRISRINA MONTALVO, JAMES	RDV 000745	08/25/1881
DUNN, CHRISTIANA M	RDV 000123	11/15/1879
DUNN, LOUISA, MATTHEW	RDV 000846	10/28/1881
DUPLEX, JOHN B	RDV 001357	NO DATE
DUPUY, MATILDA, JOHN B	RDV 001138	01/20/1885
DUTY, WILLIAM	RDV 000001	08/12/1879
DUTY, WILLIAM	RDV 000983	11/17/1883
DUVAL, JOHN C	RDV 000187	05/26/1880
DUVAL, JOHN C	RDV 001025	03/14/1883
DYCHES, JOSIAH	RDV 000882	11/12/1881
DYKES, LEWIS P	RDV 000067	09/12/1879
EASTEP, ELIZA	RDV 001358	NO DATE
EASTEP, ELIZA, DANIEL	RDV 000699	08/20/1881
EASTLAND, N W	RDV 000351	07/23/1881
EATON, THOMAS H	RDV 000676	08/19/1881
EDENS, D H	RDV 000479	08/02/1881
EDEUS, SILAS	RDV 000738	08/25/1881
EDWARDS, AMANDA M E	RDV 000932	04/21/1882
EDWARDS, C O	RDV 000260	07/15/1881
EGGLESTON, JULIA	RDV 000176	05/18/1880
EGGLESTON, JULIA, A V R	RDV 000459	08/02/1881
ELEPHANE, HECK	RDV 001080	11/16/1883
ELIZARDO, TRINIDAD	RDV 001359	NO DATE
ELLEY, ELLY, GUSTAVE	RDV 000378	07/26/1881
ELLIOT, ANN, JAMES F	RDV 001139	01/20/1885
ELY, JOHN N	RDV 000620	08/17/1881
ENGLEDOW, ELVIRA, CREED S	RDV 000665	08/19/1881
ENGLETON, ELVIRA	RDV 001360	NO DATE
ENGLISH, LUCINDA	RDV 000179	05/17/1880
ENGLISH, LUCINDA, JAMES	RDV 001163	03/14/1885
ERATH, GEORGE B	RDV 000531	08/04/1881
ESPINOZA, YGNACIO	RDV 000050	09/04/1879
ESPINOZA, YGNACIO	RDV 001183	11/04/1885
ETHERIDGE, HOWARD	RDV 000831	10/28/1881
ETHRIDGE, HOWARD	RDV 000026	08/26/1879
EUBANKS, E N	RDV 001073	11/15/1883
EVANS, J, WILLIAM G	RDV 001060	07/07/1883
EVANS, WILLIAM T	RDV 000988	01/29/1883
EVETTS, SAMUEL G	RDV 000955	04/28/1882

Republic of Texas Donation Vouchers-Alphabetical Listing

Name	Voucher	Date
FAGAN, ELLEN, JOHN	RDV 000779	10/24/1881
FAIRES, W A	RDV 000347	07/23/1881
FARISH, OSCAR	RDV 000029	08/27/1879
FARISH, OSCAR	RDV 000226	07/14/1881
FARLEY, MASSILLON	RDV 001126	01/13/1885
FENNER, JOSEPH	RDV 000002	
FENNER, JOSEPH	RDV 000878	11/12/1881
FERGUSON, MARY, ALSTON	RDV 001061	07/07/1883
FERNANDEZ, ANTONIO	RDV 001194	11/21/1885
FERNANDEZ, ANTONIO	RDV 001362	NO DATE
FERRELL, JOHN P	RDV 000010	08/15/1879
FERRELL, JOHN P	RDV 000314	07/19/1881
FIELD, JOSEPH E	RDV 000967	05/08/1882
FIELDS, SARAH, ISAIAH S	RDV 000916	04/19/1882
FILE EMPTY	RDV 000695	
FILE EMPTY	RDV 000696	
FISHER, WILLMIRTH	RDV 000828	10/28/1881
FISK, GREENLEIF	RDV 000524	08/04/1881
FISK, SIMONA S, JAMES N	RDV 000499	08/02/1881
FLAVEL, MARY, LUKE M	RDV 001361	NO DATE
FLETCHER, ROBERT	RDV 000655	08/19/1881
FLORES, JUAN JOSE	RDV 001363	NO DATE
FLORES, ROQUE	RDV 001364	REJECTED
FORD, SIMON P	RDV 000056	09/09/1879
FORD, SIMON P	RDV 000337	07/22/1881
FORESTER, KIZZIE	RDV 001365	REJECTED
FOSTER, B F	RDV 000467	08/02/1881
FOSTER, JANE, JOHN	RDV 001366	NO DATE
FOSTER, JANE A	RDV 001236	03/10/1886
FRANCIS, MILLER	RDV 000538	08/05/1881
FREDERICKS, JOHN G	RDV 000994	01/30/1883
FREEMAN, THOMAS	RDV 001169	03/14/1885
FRIAR, ANN	RDV 000200	07/12/1880
FRIAR, ANNA, DANIEL B	RDV 000886	11/14/1881
FULLERTON, NANCY, HENRY	RDV 000914	04/19/1882
FULSHEAR, CHURCHILL	RDV 000904	01/14/1882
GAHAGAN, MARGARET, JAMES	RDV 001010	02/10/1883
GAHAGAN, MARGARET L, JAMES D	RDV 001367	REJECTED
GAINES, W B P	RDV 000357	07/25/1881
GALLARDO, REFUGIA	RDV 000048	09/04/1879
GALLATIN, ALBERT	RDV 000366	07/26/1881
GALLATIN, ALBERT	RDV 000172	05/14/1880
GALLIHAN, JOHN H	RDV 000169	05/14/1880
GAONA, PEDRO	RDV 000041	09/03/1879
GARCIA, GARZA, ORTIS, DELORES, CLEMENTE	RDV 000505	08/02/1881
GARCIA, ORTIZ, DOLORES	RDV 000084	09/24/1879
GARCIA, REMIGIO	RDV 001368	REJECTED
GARCIA, SIMON	RDV 000934	04/21/1882
GARNER, ISAAC	RDV 000535	08/04/1881

Name	Voucher	Date
GARNER, JACOB H	RDV 001154	01/24/1885
GARNER, JOHN	RDV 001016	02/21/1883
GARNER, MATILDA, DAVID	RDV 001035	04/07/1883
GARRETT, LAVISA, THOMAS B	RDV 000837	10/28/1881
GARRETT, LEVICY	RDV 000137	11/24/1879
GARVIN, MARY A, ROBERT	RDV 001369	REJECTED
GARZA, JOSE SIMON	RDV 001370	NO DATE
GARZA, QUIRINO	RDV 001371	NO DATE
GASHE, CHRISTINA, GOTTLEIB	RDV 001371.5	REJECTED
GASTANON, LUIS	RDV 000441	07/29/1881
GATES, AMOS	RDV 000753	10/19/1881
GATES, W N	RDV 001008	02/03/1883
GENTRY, F B	RDV 000729	08/25/1881
GEORGE, DAVID	RDV 000223	07/14/1881
GEORGE, DAVID	RDV 000036	08/29/1879
GIBSON, ABSOLOM	RDV 001099	05/08/1884
GIBSON, ARCHIBALD	RDV 001372	NO DATE
GIBSON, ARCHIBALD	RDV 000312	07/19/1881
GIBSON, ELIZABETH, JESSIE	RDV 000692	8/20/1881
GIBSON, MARY B	RDV 001204	12/24/1885
GIDDINGS, NAPOLEON B	RDV 001255	03/18/1886
GIDDINGS, NAPOLEON B	RDV 001373	REJECTED
GILBERT, MARTHA	RDV 000174	05/14/1880
GILBERT, MARTHA, JOHN F	RDV 000805	10/27/1881
GILLELAND, DIANNA, JAMES	RDV 000694	8/20/1881
GILLIAM, ELLEN, RICHARD G	RDV 000948	04/26/1882
GILLIAM, M A	RDV 001374	NO DATE
GILLIAM, MARGARET A, L W	RDV 000580	08/08/1881
GIMENES, TEODORA	RDV 000032	08/28/1879
GIMENES, TEODORA, JUAN	RDV 000227	07/14/1881
GLARY, REBECCA	RDV 001095	05/08/1884
GOLDEN, S A, PHILIP	RDV 000636	08/18/1881
GOMEZ, CONCEPCION	RDV 000049	09/04/1879
GOMEZ, JESUS	RDV 000035	08/28/1879
GOMEZ, JESUS	RDV 000319	07/19/1881
GOMEZ, LUIS	RDV 001375	NO DATE
GONZALES, DIEGO	RDV 001376	REJECTED
GONZALES, GRAVIEL	RDV 000090	09/30/1879
GONZALES, JUANA	RDV 001233	03/04/1886
GONZALES, RITA ALAMEDA, ANTONIO	RDV 001377	REJECTED
GOOD, JULIA A	RDV 000022	08/22/1879
GOOD, JULIA A, HANNIBAL	RDV 001026	03/22/1883
GOODMAN, J B	RDV 001380	REJECTED
GOODMAN, JOHN B	RDV 000687	08/20/1881
GOODMAN, STEPHEN	RDV 000157	05/11/1880
GOODMAN, STEPHEN	RDV 000686	08/20/1881
GOODRICH, SERENA, B B	RDV 000360	07/26/1881
GOODWIN, WILLIAM	RDV 000231	07/14/1881
GOODWIN, WILLIAM	RDV 001378	REJECTED

Republic of Texas Donation Vouchers-Alphabetical Listing

Name	Voucher	Date
GORHAM, LUCINDA, WILLIAM	RDV 000342	07/22/1881
GORMAN, J P	RDV 000078	09/22/1879
GORMAN, JAMES P	RDV 000850	10/28/1881
GORTARI, CASILLAS, ANTONIA	RDV 000062	09/11/1879
GOSSETT, A E	RDV 000716	08/25/1881
GOSSETT, J V D	RDV 000835	10/28/1881
GRAY, JAMES	RDV 000121	11/15/1879
GREEN, GEORGE	RDV 000329	07/20/1881
GREEN, JAMES	RDV 000425	07/28/1881
GREEN, MATILDA, DAVID G	RDV 000921	04/19/1882
GREEN, MICHAEL	RDV 001379	NO DATE
GREGG, CLARK	RDV 001159	03/13/1885
GREY, JAMES	RDV 000215	07/14/1881
GRIEGO, CLARA	RDV 001381	REJECTED
GRIFFIN, MARY ELIZABETH	RDV 001275	05/23/1887
GRIMES, RUFUS	RDV 000781	10/24/1881
GUERRA, ANTONIO	RDV 001382	NO DATE
GUERRERA, BRIGADO	RDV 001383	REJECTED
GUERRERO, JOSE MARIA	RDV 001384	NO DATE
GUERRERO, MARCOS	RDV 001385	NO DATE
GUEST, J J	RDV 000807	10/27/1881
GUEST, SARAH ANN	RDV 001170	03/14/1885
GUYMAN, JANE	RDV 000124	11/17/1879
GUYMAN, JANE, WILLIAM	RDV 000489	08/02/1881
HABERMACHER, STEPHEN	RDV 001221	02/20/1886
HABERMAKIN, STEPHEN	RDV 001386	REJECTED
HAGGARD, SQUIRE	RDV 000358	07/26/1881
HALEY, CHARLES	RDV 000806	10/27/1881
HALEY, CYRENIA, RICHARD	RDV 000953	04/26/1882
HALL, GEORGE H	RDV 000210	02/28/1881
HALL, GEORGE H	RDV 000282	07/18/1881
HALL, H H	RDV 000517	08/02/1881
HALL, JACKSON	RDV 000872	10/29/1881
HALL, L L , JOHN L	RDV 001390	NO DATE
HALL, L L, JOHN L	RDV 000942	04/21/1882
HALL, LUCINA L	RDV 000160	05/11/1880
HALL, R A, W A	RDV 001030	04/07/1883
HALL, ROBERT	RDV 000478	08/02/1881
HALL, WILLIAM	RDV 001391	REJECTED
HALL, WILLIAM G	RDV 001230	02/24/1886
HALLMARK, SARAH, A M	RDV 000671	08/19/1881
HALLMARK, WILLIAM C, ELIZABETH	RDV 001003	01/30/1883
HAM, MARY J, L B	RDV 000755	10/21/1881
HAMILTON, JAMES	RDV 000584	08/08/1881
HAMILTON, JAMES	RDV 001393	NO DATE
HAMILTON, NATHAN	RDV 000618	08/17/1881
HAMILTON, NATHAN	RDV 001394	NO DATE
HAMMEL, LUCINDA	RDV 001388	NO DATE
HANCOCK, GEORGE D, ELIZA L	RDV 000650	08/19/1881

Republic of Texas Donation Vouchers-Alphabetical Listing

Name	Voucher	Date
HANCOCK, J W	RDV 000570	08/08/1881
HANKS, W W	RDV 001396	NO DATE
HANKS, W W	RDV 000750	08/27/1881
HANNON, JREIMIAH, JOHN	RDV 001395	REJECTED
HANNUM, A B	RDV 001222	02/20/1886
HANSON, JOHN	RDV 001274	05/23/1887
HARBOUR, JAMES M	RDV 000902	01/07/1882
HARBOUR, JAMES M	RDV 000917	04/27/1882
HARDEMAN, OWEN B	RDV 001055	05/15/1883
HARDEN, MARTHA JANE	RDV 001223	02/20/1886
HARDESTY, GEORGE C	RDV 001387	NO DATE
HARDESTY, MARY F	RDV 000982	01/17/1882
HARDIMAN, E	RDV 001562	NO DATE
HARDIMAN, W P	RDV 000976	05/11/1882
HARDIMIN, JOHN M	RDV 001124	10/03/1884
HARDIN, CYNTHIA, FRANKLIN	RDV 000674	08/19/1881
HARDIN, MILTON A	RDV 000922	04/19/1882
HARDIN, W B	RDV 000131	11/21/1879
HARDIN, W B	RDV 000824	10/28/1881
HARDING, T B	RDV 000248	07/15/1881
HARMON, DAVID	RDV 001205	12/24/1885
HARMON, JOHN A	RDV 001132	01/17/1885
HARPER, EVALINA, JOHN	RDV 001157	01/24/1885
HARPER, N J, B J	RDV 001039	04/11/1883
HARRISON, ANN C, W D F	RDV 000931	04/21/1882
HARRISON, ANNA C, W D F	RDV 001389	NO DATE
HARVEY, JOHN	RDV 000700	08/22/1881
HARWOOD, JOHN	RDV 000823	10/28/1881
HASSELL, REBECCA S, JOHN W	RDV 000887	11/14/1881
HAWFORD, HENRY	RDV 001100	05/08/1884
HAWKINS, WILLIAM	RDV 001051	05/15/1883
HAWLEY, WILLIAM	RDV 000541	08/05/1881
HAY, ANDREW	RDV 001397	NO DATE
HEALER, JOHN W	RDV 001050	05/15/1883
HEARD, ESTHER F, W I F	RDV 000317	07/19/1881
HEARLEY, JULIAN	RDV 001131	01/15/1885
HEARN, THOMAS B	RDV 000754	10/20/1881
HECK, MARY E, R D	RDV 001398	NO DATE
HEFFLINGER, JAMES	RDV 001029	04/07/1883
HELEY, MARY	RDV 001105	05/08/1884
HENDERSON, JOHN	RDV 000561	08/08/1881
HENDERSON, JOHN	RDV 000153	05/11/1880
HENDRICKS, HENDRIX, E	RDV 001184	11/04/1885
HENDRICKS, LOUIISA S, THOMAS	RDV 000810	10/28/1881
HENDRY, JOHN	RDV 001090	01/17/1884
HENRIQUEZ, ASCENCION MARTINEZ, LUCIO	RDV 000247	07/15/1881
HENRY, ELIZABETH, ROBERT	RDV 000307	07/19/1881
HENRY, ISAAC R	RDV 000975	05/11/1882
HENRY, ISAAC R	RDV 001399	NO DATE

Republic of Texas Donation Vouchers-Alphabetical Listing

Name	Voucher	Date
HENSLEY, JOHN	RDV 000414	07/28/1881
HENSLEY, JOHN M	RDV 000211	03/02/1881
HENSLEY, JOHNSON	RDV 000016	08/21/1879
HENSLEY, JUANA, JACKSON	RDV 000830	10/28/1881
HENSLEY, SALLY	RDV 001125	10/03/1884
HENSON, POLLY	RDV 001278	06/06/1887
HERDER, GEORGE	RDV 000341	07/22/1881
HERNANDES, SANTIAGO	RDV 001402	NO DATE
HERNANDEZ, JESUS SR	RDV 001400	REJECTED
HERNANDEZ, MANUEL	RDV 001401	REJECTED
HERNANDEZ, MANUELA	RDV 000042	09/03/1879
HERNANDEZ, MANUELLA CANELAS, ANTONIO	RDV 000246	07/15/1881
HERREY, SAMUEL S	RDV 000421	07/28/1881
HERROW, J H	RDV 000591	08/11/1881
HESSKEW, WILLIAM A	RDV 000863	10/29/1881
HICKEY, EDWARD	RDV 001403	NO DATE
HIDALGO, PEDRO	RDV 001404	REJECTED
HIGHSMITH, B F	RDV 001405	NO DATE
HIGHSMITH, BENJAMIN F	RDV 000958	04/29/1882
HILL, A W	RDV 000592	08/11/1881
HILL, DAVID	RDV 000550	08/06/1881
HILL, ISAAC L	RDV 000605	08/17/1871
HILL, JAMES M	RDV 000336	07/22/1881
HILL, WILLIAM C J	RDV 001077	11/15/1883
HILLYER, WENTWORTH D	RDV 001243	05/20/1886
HILTON, EMILY	RDV 001406	NO DATE
HITCHCOCK, ANDREW J	RDV 000879	11/12/1881
HITCHCOCK, EMILY, L M	RDV 001408	NO DATE
HOBSON, ELIZA JANE, JOHN	RDV 000744	08/25/1881
HODGES, L J, JAMES	RDV 001161	03/14/1885
HODGES, SUSAN	RDV 000023	08/22/1879
HODGES, SUSAN, ROBERT	RDV 000393	07/26/1881
HOFFMAN, PHIBE	RDV 000859	10/29/1881
HOLDEMAN, DAVID	RDV 001392	REJECTED
HOLDERMAN, DAVID	RDV 001091	01/17/1884
HOLDERNESS, S M	RDV 000771	10/21/1881
HOLLIEN, HULDA, JOHN F	RDV 000765	10/21/1881
HOLLOWAY, SIMPSON	RDV 001045	05/08/1883
HOLSHOUSEN, C	RDV 000825	10/28/1881
HOOD, MARY A	RDV 001121	10/03/1884
HOOPER, A L, BENJAMIN FRANK	RDV 000811	10/28/1881
HOPE, RICHARD	RDV 000225	07/14/1881
HOPKINS, LUCY A	RDV 001409	REJECTED
HOPKINS, REBECCA, JAMES E	RDV 000617	08/17/1881
HOPSON, LUCIEN	RDV 000981	01/16/1882
HORBOUR, GEORGE W	RDV 000726	08/25/1881
HORNSBY, W W	RDV 000596	08/11/1881
HORTON, A	RDV 000251	07/15/1881
HORTON, ELIZA	RDV 000146	02/05/1880

Name	Voucher	Date
HOTCHKISS, RINALDO	RDV 000014	08/18/1879
HOTCHKISS, RINALDO	RDV 000786	10/24/1881
HOUSTON, E C, ANDREW	RDV 000575	08/08/1881
HOWARD, M F, GEORGE T	RDV 000228	07/14/1881
HOWARD, PHILIP	RDV 000276	07/16/1881
HOWTH, MARY E	RDV 000392	07/26/1881
HOWTH, WILLIAM EDWARD	RDV 000182	05/19/1880
HUBBLE, HUBBELL, ELIZA, JOHN	RDV 000463	08/02/1881
HUFF, WILLIAM	RDV 001246	05/26/1886
HUGHES, B F	RDV 001178	07/30/1885
HUGHES, BENJAMIN F	RDV 001410	REJECTED
HUISAR, SEFERINO	RDV 001407	NO DATE
HULME, W T	RDV 000876	11/12/1881
HUMPHRIES, B H	RDV 000402	07/26/1881
HUNT, WILLIAM	RDV 001411	DEAD AT TIME OF APPLICATION
HUNT, WILLIAM G	RDV 001206	12/24/1885
HUNTER, ROBERT H	RDV 000918	04/19/1882
HUNTER, WILLIAM L	RDV 000269	07/16/1881
HYLAND, JOSEPH	RDV 000869	10/29/1881
HYNES, JOHN	RDV 000666	08/19/1881
IDEN, NANCY A	RDV 001031	04/07/1883
IIAMS, JOHN	RDV 000076	09/18/1879
IIAMS, JOHN	RDV 000891	11/14/1881
INGRAM, JOHN	RDV 000470	08/02/1881
IRISH, EMILY, MILTON	RDV 000452	07/29/1881
IRVIN, NANCY	RDV 000092	10/01/1879
IRVIN, NANCY, J S	RDV 000444	07/29/1881
IRVINE, W D	RDV 000772	10/21/1881
ISAACKS, SARAH, WILLIAM	RDV 000501	08/02/1881
ISAACS, MARTHA, SAMUEL	RDV 000245	07/15/1881
ISAACS, MARTHA, SAMUEL	RDV 001412	REJECTED
ISAACS, SICIEY, A J	RDV 001047	05/15/1883
ISAACS, SICILY M	RDV 000080	09/24/1879
JACKSON, ANNA	RDV 001173	07/24/1885
JACKSON, JOSEPH	RDV 000586	08/09/1881
JACKSON, NARCISSA J, JOSEPH	RDV 001413	12/14/1885
JACOBS, M G	RDV 000564	08/08/1881
JAMES, JANE C, THOMAS	RDV 000244	07/15/1881
JAMES, MILBURN	RDV 001207	12/24/1885
JAMES, THOMAS	RDV 001414	NO DATE
JANUARY, JAMES B P	RDV 000536	08/04/1881
JEAN, JAMES M	RDV 001231	02/24/1886
JENKINS, J H	RDV 000959	04/29/1882
JETT, ABSOLOM	RDV 001416	REJECTED
JOHNES, M A, A H	RDV 001048	05/15/1883
JOHNSON, ELIZABETH, FRANCIS	RDV 000799	10/24/1881
JOHNSON, F W	RDV 000170	05/14/1880
JOHNSON, FRANK W	RDV 000271	07/16/1881

Republic of Texas Donation Vouchers-Alphabetical Listing

JOHNSON, JOHN	RDV 001101	05/08/1884
JOHNSON, JOHN R, BETHANY	RDV 000832	10/28/1881
JOHNSON, MARY	RDV 000122	11/15/1879
JOHNSON, MARY E, HEZIKIAH	RDV 000697	08/20/1881
JOHNSON, MATILDA	RDV 001224	02/20/1886
JOHNSON, SAMUEL	RDV 000399	07/26/1881
JOHNSON, WILLIAM	RDV 000438	07/29/1881
JOHNSON, WILLIAM	RDV 001037	04/07/1883
JOHNSTON, SOPHRONIA, SOLOMON	RDV 000630	08/18/1881
JONES, C M	RDV 000411	07/28/1881
JONES, D M	RDV 001415	NO DATE
JONES, DAVID M	RDV 000209	02/28/1881
JONES, GOERGE W	RDV 000537	08/04/1881
JONES, HETTIE	RDV 000194	06/06/1880
JONES, KEETON M	RDV 000856	10/29/1881
JONES, MARY, ANSON	RDV 000243	07/15/1881
JONES, NETTIE, J W	RDV 000242	07/15/1881
JORDAN, STACEY ANN	RDV 000844	10/28/1881
JORDEAN, MAHULDA, WILLIAM	RDV 001417	REJECTED
JOWELL, ELGIRA	RDV 001083	11/16/1883
KARNER, JOHN	RDV 000627	08/17/1881
KEAGHEY, WILLIAM S	RDV 000764	10/21/1881
KELLUM, EMILY, JAMES	RDV 000657	08/19/1881
KELLY, CONNELL O DONNELL	RDV 000162	05/12/1880
KELSO, ALFRED	RDV 000028	08/27/1879
KELSO, ALFRED	RDV 000707	08/25/1881
KEMP, CHARLOTTE	RDV 000101	10/28/1879
KENDALL, PETER	RDV 001017	02/21/1883
KENNARD, A D	RDV 001418	REJECTED
KENNARD, A D	RDV 001022	03/09/1883
KENNARD, M M	RDV 000359	07/26/1881
KENNARD, W E	RDV 000945	04/26/1882
KENT, DAVID B	RDV 000380	07/26/1881
KENT, DAVID B	RDV 001419	REJECTED
KERR, WILLIAM P	RDV 000340	07/22/1881
KIETH, JOHN HINTON	RDV 001185	11/04/1885
KIMBRO, NANCY	RDV 000100	10/28/1879
KIMBRO, NANCY, L K	RDV 000240	07/14/1881
KING, EMILY W, CHARLES F	RDV 000838	10/28/1881
KIRBEY, GEORGE	RDV 000308	07/19/1881
KIRBY, GEORGE	RDV 000089	09/30/1879
KIZER, P C, B P	RDV 000966	05/06/1882
KLEBURG, ROBERT	RDV 000522	08/02/1881
KOKERNOT, D L	RDV 000361	07/26/1881
KUYKENDALL, J H	RDV 000127	11/21/1879
KUYKENDALL, MARIA, ABNER	RDV 000984	01/12/1883
LACKEY, JERRISSA, JOHN J	RDV 000626	08/17/1881
LACY, W Y	RDV 000230	07/14/1881
LAMAR, HENRIETTA, M B	RDV 001040	04/11/1883

Name	Voucher	Date
LAMBERT, THOMASA G, WALTER	RDV 000933	04/21/1882
LANCASTER, EVA, JOSEPH	RDV 000749	08/27/1881
LANE, WALTEN	RDV 000077	09/18/1879
LANE, WALTER P	RDV 000238	07/14/1881
LATHAM, KING H	RDV 000900	12/24/1881
LATHAM, KING H	RDV 001420	NO DATE
LATIMER, H R	RDV 000375	07/26/1881
LATIMER, MARY, ALBERT H	RDV 000368	07/26/1881
LAWRENCE, G W	RDV 001208	12/24/1885
LAWRENCE, JOSEPH	RDV 000313	07/19/1881
LAWSON, MARY, ISAIAH D	RDV 000616	08/17/1881
LEE, THEODORE S	RDV 000192	06/09/1880
LEE, THEODORE S	RDV 000413	07/28/1881
LEEPER, HANNAH, SAMUEL	RDV 000986	01/29/1883
LEIPER, HANNAH	RDV 000017	08/21/1879
LEMON, JOHN	RDV 000829	10/28/1881
LESLIE, ANDREW JACKSON	RDV 001421	REJECTED
LEVEY, JOSEPH S	RDV 001422	REJECTED
LEWIS, ELIZA J, IRA R	RDV 000651	08/19/1881
LEWIS, G W	RDV 000068	09/13/1879
LEWIS, J E	RDV 000343	07/22/1881
LEWIS, JACOB	RDV 000154	05/11/1880
LEWIS, JOHN T	RDV 000091	10/01/1879
LEWIS, JOHN T	RDV 000419	07/28/1881
LEWIS, MARY, WILLIAM	RDV 001144	01/20/1885
LEWIS, MARY F	RDV 001209	12/24/1885
LEWIS, NANCY	RDV 001082	11/16/1883
LEWIS, NANCY, JAMES B	RDV 001423	NO DATE
LEWIS, WILLIAM MC T	RDV 000906	01/24/1882
LINDHEIMER, ELONORA	RDV 000212	03/02/1881
LINDHEIMER, F J	RDV 001424	NO DATE
LINDSEY, B F	RDV 000265	07/15/1881
LINDSEY, BENJAMIN F	RDV 000181	05/19/1880
LINDSEY, JAMES	RDV 000241	07/14/1881
LINDSEY, JAMES	RDV 001425	REJECTED
LINDSEY, P	RDV 001426	NO DATE
LINDSEY, PENNINGTON	RDV 000208	02/28/1881
LITTLE, HIRAM	RDV 001427	REJECTED
LITTLE, HIRAM	RDV 000808	10/27/1881
LOGAN, CAROLINE, GREENBERRY	RDV 000333	07/21/1881
LONG, ANDREW H	RDV 001428	NO DATE
LONGBOTHAM, R B	RDV 000989	01/29/1883
LONGLEY, CAMPBELL	RDV 000702	08/23/1881
LOPEZ, SERNA, MARIA FRANCISCO	RDV 001232	02/26/1886
LOPEZ, SIERNA, FRANCISCA	RDV 001429	NO DATE
LOPEZ, PETER	RDV 000985	01/12/1883
LORD, GEORGE	RDV 001430	REJECTED
LOVE, ELIZABETH M, WILLIAM	RDV 000615	08/17/1881
LOVE, G H	RDV 000371	07/26/1881

Republic of Texas Donation Vouchers-Alphabetical Listing

Name	Voucher	Date
LOVE, MARY A, DAVID H	RDV 000631	08/18/1881
LOW, M A	RDV 000147	03/12/1880
LOWE, M A	RDV 001094	05/08/1884
LUBBOCK, SARAH O	RDV 000148	05/07/1880
LUBBOCK, SARAH O, THOMAS S	RDV 000679	08/19/1881
LUCHENBACH, JAMES L	RDV 001133	01/20/1885
LUDLOW, L W	RDV 000549	08/08/1881
LUMPKINS, MARGARET	RDV 001265	11/30/1886
LUNA, DISEDARIO	RDV 001431	NO DATE
LYLE, JOHN K	RDV 001225	02/20/1886
LYNCH, PARTHENIA	RDV 001226	02/20/1886
LYON, H C	RDV 000305	07/19/1881
LYONS, DEWITT C	RDV 000316	07/19/1881
MACKEY, JOHN	RDV 000469	08/02/1881
MADDEN, LUCINDA	RDV 001210	12/24/1885
MADDIN, R W	RDV 001251	05/29/1886
MAGEE, NICINDA, RICHARD A	RDV 000465	08/02/1881
MAGILL, ELIZABETH A	RDV 000178	05/17/1880
MAGILL, ELIZABETH A, W H	RDV 000280	07/18/1881
MAHAN, EMMA H, P JENKS	RDV 000294	07/18/1881
MALDONALDO, MATIAS	RDV 001432	NO DATE
MANGEL, PROSPER	RDV 001027	03/23/1883
MANGUM, A S	RDV 000907	01/24/1882
MANTON, EDWARD	RDV 000338	07/20/1881
MARSHALL, JOHN	RDV 000513	08/02/1881
MARSHALL, JOSEPH T	RDV 000684	08/20/1881
MARSHALL, MARY E, THOMAS	RDV 001433	NO DATE
MARTIN, LISEY	RDV 001117	09/25/1884
MARTIN, MARY A	RDV 001081	11/16/1883
MARTIN, THOMAS	RDV 000701	08/22/1881
MARTINEZ, FERMAN	RDV 001435	REJECTED
MARTINEZ, MANUEL	RDV 001434	REJECTED
MASON, CHARLES	RDV 000412	07/28/1881
MASSIE, JANE, J W	RDV 000689	08/20/1881
MATA, ANDRES	RDV 001436	REJECTED
MATHEWS, LOUISA, THOMAS	RDV 000791	10/24/1881
MATTHEWS, DENISA	RDV 001218	01/09/1886
MATTHEWS, M W	RDV 000794	10/24/1881
MATTHEWS, R H	RDV 001021	03/09/1883
MATTHEWS, ROBERT H	RDV 001437	NO DATE
MAYS, ARIE, THOMAS H	RDV 000703	08/25/1881
MC ADAMS, JOHN	RDV 000629	08/18/1881
MC ANELLY, PLEASANT	RDV 000448	07/29/1881
MC ANNELLY, R D	RDV 000574	08/08/1881
MC CARTHY, EDWARD V	RDV 001438	NO DATE
MC CLAIN, RACHAEL A, HARRISON	RDV 001449	NO DATE
MC CLELAND, SARAH K, WILLIAM	RDV 001442	REJECTED
MC CLELLAND, SARAH, WILLIAM	RDV 000718	08/25/1881
MC CLURE, THOMAS	RDV 000577	08/08/1881

Republic of Texas Donation Vouchers-Alphabetical Listing

Name	Voucher	Date
MC CLURE, THOMAS	RDV 001443	NO DATE
MC CORCLE, E H, A T	RDV 001439	NO DATE
MC CORMICK, MICHAEL, EXELINE	RDV 000809	10/27/1881
MC COY, ELIZABETH	RDV 001440	NO DATE
MC COY, ELIZABETH	RDV 000141	12/04/1879
MC COY, GREEN	RDV 000956	04/28/1882
MC COY, MARTHA, WILLAIM	RDV 000804	10/27/1881
MC COY, PROSPECT	RDV 001441	REJECTED
MC CROCKLIN, JESSE L	RDV 000815	10/28/1881
MC CULLOCH, SAMUEL	RDV 000403	07/26/1881
MC CUTCHEON, WILLIAM	RDV 000453	07/29/1881
MC DANIEL, MARY M, GRANGER	RDV 001444	NO DATE
MC DONALD, DONALD	RDV 000723	08/25/1881
MC DONALD, DONALD	RDV 001445	NO DATE
MC DONOUGH, MARY, EDWARD	RDV 000439	07/29/1881
MC FADDEN, ELIZA	RDV 000066	09/12/1879
MC FADDIN, MC FADDEN, ELIZA, WILLIAM	RDV 000593	08/11/1881
MC FADDIN, MC FADIN, D H	RDV 000508	08/02/1881
MC FADDIN, WILLIAM	RDV 000663	08/19/1881
MC GAHEY, JAMES S	RDV 000970	05/11/1882
MC GAHEY, JAMES H	RDV 000011	08/15/1879
MC GEE, JOSEPH	RDV 000159	05/11/1880
MC GEE, JOSEPH	RDV 000383	07/26/1881
MC GEHEE, THOMAS G	RDV 000397	07/26/1881
MC GOWN, E J	RDV 001107	05/15/1884
MC GREW, JEFFERSON	RDV 001446	NO DATE
MC GREW, JEFFERSON	RDV 001186	11/04/1885
MC GUFFIN, J F	RDV 001447	NO DATE
MC GUFFIN, JOHN	RDV 000085	09/27/1879
MC HORSE, J W	RDV 000514	08/02/1881
MC INTIRE, ROBERT	RDV 000782	10/24/1881
MC KAY, DANIEL	RDV 000653	08/19/1881
MC KINNEY, ADALINE, DANIEL	RDV 001150	01/23/1885
MC KINNEY, SALLIE, ASHLEY	RDV 000607	08/17/1871
MC KINZIE, CLARISSA	RDV 001263	11/24/1886
MC KINZIE, CLARISSA, ALEXANDER	RDV 001448	REJECTED
MC KINZIE, WILLIAM S	RDV 000331	07/21/1881
MC KISICK, JOHN W	RDV 000854	10/28/1881
MC KNEELEY, SAM W	RDV 000644	08/19/1881
MC LAIN, RACHEL A, HARRISON	RDV 000775	10/21/1881
MC LAUGHLIN, STEPHEN	RDV 000330	07/20/1881
MC LEOD, DANIEL	RDV 001108	05/15/1884
MC MAHAN, ISAAC	RDV 000422	07/28/1881
MC MAHAN, JAMES B	RDV 000858	10/29/1881
MC MAHAN, SARAH	RDV 000445	07/29/1881
MC MAHAN, SARAH, JAMES	RDV 001451	NO DATE
MC MAHON, ISAAC	RDV 001450	REJECTED
MC MANNS, R O W	RDV 000597	08/11/1881
MC MASTERS, WILLIAM	RDV 000401	07/26/1881

Republic of Texas Donation Vouchers-Alphabetical Listing

Name	Voucher	Date
MC MILLAN, ANDREW	RDV 000608	08/17/1871
MC NEESE, PARROTT	RDV 000724	08/25/1881
MC TAYLOR, JOHN	RDV 001180	07/30/1885
MCLENNAN, JOHN	RDV 000937	04/21/1882
MELTON, HANNAH B, ETHAN	RDV 001452	NO DATE
MENCHACA, ANTONIO	RDV 000043	09/03/1879
MENCHACA, MIGUEL	RDV 001453	NO DATE
MENEFEE, GEORGE	RDV 000284	07/18/1881
MENEFEE, JOHN S	RDV 000566	08/08/1881
MERCHANT, BERRY	RDV 000381	07/26/1881
MERCHANT, S P, J D	RDV 000717	08/25/1881
MERCHANT, SARAH P, SARINDIA P	RDV 000199	07/12/1880
MEYERS, NANCY, JOHN	*See* MYERS, NANCY, JOHN	
MIDDLETON, ROBERT	RDV 000926	04/19/1882
MILES, EDWARD	RDV 000355	07/25/1881
MILES, EDWARD	RDV 000188	05/27/1880
MILLER, DANIEL	RDV 000641	08/19/1881
MILLER, ELIZABETH	RDV 000133	11/22/1879
MILLER, ELIZABETH, WILLIAM H	RDV 000534	08/04/1881
MILLER, ELIZABETH, WILLIAM P	RDV 000354	07/25/1881
MILLER, LEROY	RDV 000519	08/02/1881
MILLER, NANCY C, WILLIAM	RDV 001052	05/15/1883
MILLER, WILLIAM	RDV 001130	01/15/1885
MILLETT, C	RDV 001454	NO DATE
MILLETT, CLEMINTINA, SAMUEL	RDV 001024	03/19/1883
MILLICAN, WILLIS	RDV 001096	05/08/1884
MIRANDA, FRANCISCO	RDV 000074	09/17/1879
MIRANDO, FRANCISCO	RDV 000506	08/02/1881
MONEY, A M	RDV 001079	11/16/1883
MONTALBO, MANUEL	RDV 000233	07/14/1881
MONTEL, CHARLES SCHEIDE	RDV 001347	NO DATE
MONTGOMERY, JAMES	RDV 000166	05/13/1880
MONTGOMERY, JAMES	RDV 000257	07/15/1881
MONTGOMERY, MARY	RDV 000129	11/21/1879
MONTGOMERY, MARY, ANDREW	RDV 000497	08/02/1881
MONTGOMERY, MINERVA, MC GRADY	RDV 000408	07/28/1881
MONTOYA, JUAN	RDV 001455	REJECTED
MOORE, JAMES W	RDV 000007	08/13/1879
MOORE, JAMES W	RDV 000236	07/14/1881
MOORE, LOUIS	RDV 000530	08/04/1881
MOORE, NANCY ANN	RDV 001211	12/24/1885
MOORE, SALLY, SAMUEL F	RDV 000867	10/29/1881
MOORE, W H	RDV 000237	07/14/1881
MOORE, WILLIAM H	RDV 001456	NO DATE
MORGAN, JEMINA	RDV 000103	10/28/1879
MORGAN, JOHN D	RDV 001097	05/08/1884
MORGAN, HAMP	RDV 001212	12/24/1885
MORRIS, MINERVA, RISTON	RDV 001457	REJECTED
MORRIS, REBECCA ANN	RDV 001155	01/24/1885

Republic of Texas Donation Vouchers-Alphabetical Listing

MORRIS, SPENCER	RDV 000296	07/18/1881
MORRISON, ANN, GWYNN	RDV 000565	08/08/1881
MORRISON, MARY	RDV 001174	07/24/1885
MORRISS, MINERVA, RISTON	RDV 001069	07/28/1883
MORTIMER, MARY F	RDV 001458	NO DATE
MOSS, JANE, JAMES L	RDV 000567	08/08/1881
MOTT, GORDON N	RDV 001129	01/15/1885
MOTT, SAMUEL	RDV 001459	REJECTED
MUDD, F L	RDV 000709	08/25/1881
MUMFORD, JESSE	RDV 000698	08/22/1881
MURRAY, JOHN B	RDV 000903	01/09/1882
MYERS, NANCY, JOHN	RDV 000488	08/02/1881
MYERS, NANCY	RDV 000098	10/25/1879
MYRICK, HANAH ELLEN	RDV 001182	07/30/1885
NANCY, BALLARD	RDV 001286	REJECTED
NAVARRO, JESUSA	RDV 000040	09/03/1879
NAVARRO, JESUSA URON, NEPUMOCENO	RDV 000323	07/19/1881
NEILL, ANDREW	RDV 000250	07/15/1881
NEILL, GEORGE J	RDV 000599	08/12/1881
NELSON, W F	RDV 000614	08/17/1871
NETTLES, WILLIAM	RDV 000009	08/13/1879
NETTLES, WILLIAM	RDV 000430	07/29/1881
NEVILL, HARDIN	RDV 000909	04/18/1882
NEWMAN, WILIAM R	RDV 000466	08/02/1881
NEWMAN, WILLIAM R	RDV 000065	09/12/1879
NICHOLS, FANNIE, JOHN	RDV 001460	NO DATE
NORRIS, E	RDV 001461	REJECTED
NORRIS, E MRS	RDV 000938	04/21/1882
NUEVA, JUANA T V, CANDELANA V	RDV 001462	NO DATE
NUGENT, MARY	RDV 001187	11/04/1885
NUNLEY, ANDERSON	RDV 000516	08/02/1881
O CONNER, THOMAS	RDV 000667	08/19/1881
O HANLON, RICHARD	RDV 001464	NO DATE
OBANION, JENNINGS	RDV 000509	08/02/1881
OGSBURY, CHARLES A	RDV 000406	07/28/1881
O'HALEY, MARY	RDV 001463	NO DATE
OLIVA, ANTONIO	RDV 001465	NO DATE
OSBORN, JOHN L	RDV 000353	07/23/1881
OSBORN, THOMAS	RDV 000352	07/23/1881
OWENS, AMANDA	RDV 001213	12/24/1885
OWENS, M A	RDV 000920	04/19/1882
OWENS, RICHARD	RDV 001466	NO DATE
PACE, ELIZABETH, JAMES R	RDV 000654	08/19/1881
PACHECO, FRANCISCA F, BEURURLADO	RDV 001467	REJECTED
PACHECO, LUCIANO	RDV 001468	NO DATE
PALACIOS, JUAN	RDV 000161	05/11/1880
PALACIOS, JUAN JOSE	RDV 000562	08/08/188
PAMELL, SARAH A, HUGH G	RDV 000911	04/19/1882
PARKER, DANIEL	RDV 000410	07/28/1881

Republic of Texas Donation Vouchers-Alphabetical Listing

Name	Voucher	Date
PARKER, DRUCILLA	RDV 001272	05/05/1887
PARKER, ISAAC	RDV 000681	08/20/1881
PARKER, L E, JAMES W	RDV 000919	04/19/1882
PARKER, L J	RDV 001469	NO DATE
PARKER, LEVI J	RDV 000672	08/19/1881
PARKER, N A	RDV 001262	10/02/1886
PARR, SAMUEL	RDV 000637	08/19/1881
PASCHAL, BRIDGET	RDV 000175	05/17/1880
PASCHAL, BRIDGET, SAMUEL	RDV 000275	07/16/1881
PASCHAL, F L	RDV 000299	07/18/1881
PATE, JAME, WILLIAM	RDV 000588	08/11/1881
PATTERSON, EUGENIA	RDV 000020	08/09/1879
PATTERSON, EUGENIA, J S	RDV 000458	08/02/1881
PATTON, A B	RDV 000908	04/18/1882
PATTON, MOSES L	RDV 000553	08/08/1881
PATTRICK, GEORGE M	RDV 000877	11/12/1881
PAYNE, FLORINDA, THOMAS P	RDV 000901	01/03/1882
PAYNE, JOHN C	RDV 000423	07/28/1881
PEARMAN, M, GEORGE	RDV 000923	04/19/1882
PEBBLES, R R	RDV 000999	01/30/1883
PECK, BARTON, FRANCIS C	RDV 001074	11/15/1883
PERKINS, MARY S	RDV 000213	03/31/1881
PERKINS, MARY S	RDV 001088	01/14/1884
PERRY, ALBERT	RDV 000795	10/24/1881
PERRY, C R	RDV 000367	07/26/1881
PERRY, JANE H, DANIEL	RDV 000485	08/02/1881
PERRY, W M	RDV 000119	11/14/1879
PERRY, W M	RDV 000783	10/24/1881
PETERS, ELIZA	RDV 001242	05/20/1886
PETTERS, SARAH, JOHN F	RDV 000705	08/25/1881
PETTY, GEORGE W	RDV 000730	08/25/1881
PEVEHOUSE, DAVID	RDV 001470	REJECTED
PEVEHOUSE, DAVID	RDV 001276	06/06/1887
PEVYHOUSE, CYRENE, PEVEHOUSE, CYRINA	RDV 000191	06/11/1880
PHELPS, R A, JAMES A E	RDV 000415	07/28/1881
PHILLIPS, BENNETT	RDV 000812	10/28/1881
PHILLIPS, WILLIAM	RDV 000625	08/17/1881
PIER, J B	RDV 000543	08/05/1881
PIERCE, PHILIP R	RDV 000306	07/19/1881
PIERSON, JOHN HOGUE, NANCY	RDV 000774	10/21/1881
PILANT, G B	RDV 001188	11/04/1885
PITTMAN, E W	RDV 000450	07/29/1881
PITTS, JOHN	RDV 000224	07/14/1881
PLEASANTS, GEORGE W	RDV 000714	08/20/1881
PLUNKETT, JOHN	RDV 000301	07/18/1881
POINDEXTER, JOHN J	RDV 000544	08/05/1881
POLLAN, JOHN	RDV 000156	05/11/1880
POLLAN, JOHN	RDV 000446	07/29/1881
POOL, JONATHAN C	RDV 000839	10/28/1881

Republic of Texas Donation Vouchers-Alphabetical Listing

POST, CATHERINE, LEE R	RDV 000533	08/04/1881
POST, JOHN C	RDV 000532	08/04/1881
POWER, THOMASA, JAMES	RDV 000950	04/26/1882
PRESCOTT, CHARLES	RDV 000843	10/28/1881
PREWITT, ELISHA	RDV 000114	11/05/1879
PREWITT, ELISHA	RDV 000229	07/14/1881
PREWITT, HANNA, LEVI	RDV 000389	07/26/1881
PREWITT, SARAH H	RDV 001075	11/15/1883
PRICE, H W B	RDV 001471	REJECTED
PRICE, REESE D	RDV 000883	11/14/1881
PRICE, ROBERT	RDV 000507	08/02/1881
PRICE, ROBERT	RDV 001472	NO DATE
PRICE, SIBBA M	RDV 000097	10/22/1879
PRITTLE, WILLIAM J	RDV 001167	03/14/1885
PROCTOR, M D	RDV 001260	07/01/1886
PRUETT, REBECCA, BEASLEY	RDV 000688	08/20/1881
PUTMAN, MICHAEL	RDV 000751	09/15/1881
PUTMAN, MITCHELL	RDV 000044	09/03/1879
QUINN, PATRICK	RDV 001473	NO DATE
QUINN, PATRICK	RDV 000165	05/13/1880
QUINN, PATRICK	RDV 000492	08/02/1881
RABB, MARY, JOHN	RDV 001474	NO DATE
RAGLIN, H W	RDV 000407	07/28/1881
RAGSDALE, E A, PETER C	RDV 001475	NO DATE
RAGSDALE, E B	RDV 000971	05/11/1882
RAGSDALE, W J	RDV 000972	05/11/1882
RAINES, RHUDY S, JOHN D	RDV 000965	05/06/1882
RALPH, SOPHIA W, SAMUEL	RDV 001476	NO DATE
RAMIREZ, CARMEN	RDV 001235	03/04/1886
RAMSDALE, GEORGE	RDV 000434	07/29/1881
RAMSEY, MARGARET, MARTIN	RDV 001013	02/10/1883
RANDALL, OSBORNE W	RDV 000552	08/08/1881
RANKIN, ELIZABETH, FREDERICK H	RDV 001477	REJECTED
READ, THOMAS J	RDV 001004	02/01/1883
REAMES, S Y	RDV 000539	08/05/1881
REAVIS, RIVIS, FANNIE	RDV 001478	NO DATE
RECTOR, E G	RDV 000573	08/08/1881
RECTOR, NANCY H, CLAIBORNE	RDV 000889	11/14/1881
RECTOR, PENDELTON	RDV 000315	07/19/1881
REDFIELD, HENRY P	RDV 000345	07/22/1881
REED, E B	RDV 000661	08/19/1881
REED, ISAAC	RDV 000324	07/20/1881
REED, ISAAC	RDV 001479	NO DATE
REED, JEFFERSON	RDV 000264	07/15/1881
REED, MILES	RDV 001164	03/14/1885
REED, NATHANIEL	RDV 000545	08/05/1881
REED, WILLIAM	RDV 000258	07/15/1881
REISINHOOVEN, NAOMI, BENSON	RDV 001480	REJECTED
REIZENHOOVER, NAOMA	RDV 000081	09/24/1879

Republic of Texas Donation Vouchers-Alphabetical Listing

REYES, ANTONIA	RDV 001237	03/10/1886
REYES, DAMACIO	RDV 001481	NO DATE
REYES, JUAN	RDV 001482	NO DATE
REYNA, RAMON	RDV 001483	NO DATE
RHEA, ELEANOR, JOHN R	RDV 001484	NO DATE
RHEA, ELENOR	RDV 001189	11/04/1885
RICE, MARIA, WILLIAM	RDV 001486	NO DATE
RICHARDS, WILLIAM B	RDV 000790	10/24/1881
RICHARDSON, LUCINDA	RDV 000113	11/04/1879
RICHARDSON, WEST	RDV 001245	05/20/1886
RICKS, G W	RDV 000087	09/29/1879
RICKS, G W	RDV 000798	10/24/1881
RITCHEY, LOUISA C, JAMES M	RDV 001485	NO DATE
RITCHEY, JANE J	RDV 001261	07/06/1886
RITCHEY, LOUISA C	RDV 001214	12/24/1885
RIVAS, CAYETANO	RDV 001487	NO DATE
RIVAS, FELIPE	RDV 001488	REJECTED
ROARKE, LEO	RDV 001215	12/24/1885
ROBERTS, CHARLES	RDV 001128	01/14/1885
ROBERTS, MOSES F	RDV 000481	08/02/1881
ROBERTS, MOSES F	RDV 000071	09/13/1879
ROBERTSON, J B	RDV 000528	08/04/1881
ROBERTSON, MARY E, E STERLING C	RDV 000512	08/02/1881
ROBINSON, AMANDA ANN	RDV 001220	01/09/1886
ROBINSON, AMANDA ANN	RDV 001492	NO DATE
ROBINSON, FRANCIS	RDV 000892	11/15/1881
ROBINSON, GEORGE W	RDV 000685	08/20/1881
ROBINSON, JESSE	RDV 000046	09/04/1879
ROBINSON, JESSE	RDV 000756	10/21/1881
ROBINSON, JOEL W	RDV 000335	07/22/1881
ROBINSON, ZORASTER	RDV 000860	10/29/1881
ROBINSON, ZORASTER	RDV 001493	NO DATE
RODERIGUEZ, MARIA JUSUSA, AMBROSIO	RDV 000606	08/17/1871
RODRIGUEZ, JUAN	RDV 001489	NO DATE
RODRIGUEZ, JUSTO	RDV 001490	REJECTED
RODRIGUEZ, SATURNINO	RDV 001491	REJECTED
ROGERS, ELIZABETH, FRED	RDV 000712	08/25/1881
ROGERS, JOHN A	RDV 000253	07/15/1881
ROGERS, L M	RDV 001156	01/24/1885
ROGERS, SAMUEL C A	RDV 000283	07/18/1881
ROGERS, SARAH, JOHN K	RDV 000713	08/25/1881
ROGERS, SARAH, JOHN K	RDV 001494	NO DATE
ROLESTON, ELIZA	RDV 001118	09/25/1884
ROSS, RICHARD	RDV 001103	05/08/1884
ROUECHE, PETER	RDV 000582	08/08/1881
ROUTT, HENRY T	RDV 001495	REJECTED
ROWE, MYRA, JAMES	RDV 000898	11/28/1881
RUBIO, CASIMIRO, PETRA VELA	RDV 001496	REJECTED
RUBIO, PETRA VELA, CASIMIRO	RDV 001293	REJECTED

Republic of Texas Donation Vouchers-Alphabetical Listing

RUDDER, NATHANIEL	RDV 000865	10/29/1881
RUIZ, BERNADINO	RDV 001497	REJECTED
RUPLEY, WILLIAM	RDV 000899	12/06/1881
RUSK, ELIZABETH, DAVID	RDV 000474	08/02/1881
RUSSELL, ALEXANDER	RDV 001142	01/20/1885
RUSSELL, LAVINIA E	RDV 001247	05/26/1886
RUSSELL, SUSANNAH, SUSANA, ELI	RDV 000486	08/02/1881
RUSSELL, WILLIAM J	RDV 000027	08/26/1879
RUSSELL, WILLIAM O	RDV 000604	08/16/1881
RUTLEDGE, EMELINE	RDV 000186	05/25/1880
RUTLEDGE, EMELINE, RICHARD	RDV 000523	08/03/1881
RUYLE, SOLOMON	RDV 001179	07/30/1885
SADDLER, JOHN	RDV 000940	04/21/1882
SADLER, WILLIAM T	RDV 000612	08/17/1871
SALINAS, FRANCISCO	RDV 001257	06/19/1886
SALINAS, MARIA	RDV 000109	10/29/1879
SALINAS, MARIA S, MARGIL	RDV 000558	08/08/1881
SALINAS, PABLO	RDV 000075	09/17/1879
SALINAS, PABLO	RDV 000491	08/02/1881
SANCHES, CARMEL	RDV 001498	REJECTED
SANCHEZ, ANTONIO	RDV 000969	05/10/1882
SANDERS, JOHN	RDV 001175	07/24/1885
SANDERS, NANCY, WILLIAM B	RDV 000373	07/26/1881
SANDERS, RACHAEL	RDV 000202	09/24/1880
SAVERY, ASAHEL	RDV 000116	11/11/1879
SAVERY, ASAHEL	RDV 000595	08/11/1881
SCARBOROUGH, JANE C, LAWRENCE	RDV 000326	07/20/1881
SCARBOROUGH, JANE C, LAWRENCE	RDV 001499	REJECTED
SCATES, W B	RDV 000005	08/13/1879
SCATES, WILLIAM B	RDV 000255	07/15/1881
SCHLABORN, JOHN	RDV 000578	08/08/1881
SCHULTZ, JOHN	RDV 001503	REJECTED
SCHULTZ, JOHN	RDV 000289	07/18/1881
SCHURLOCK, WILLIAM	RDV 000787	10/24/1881
SCOTT, ELIZABETH	RDV 000195	06/06/1880
SCOTT, ELIZABETH, DAVID	RDV 000482	08/02/1881
SCOTT, GEORGE W	RDV 001500	NO DATE
SCOTT, LEVI P	RDV 000611	08/17/1871
SCOTT, M H, JAMES W	RDV 000704	08/25/1881
SCOTT, PHILIP B	RDV 000711	08/20/1881
SCURRY, EVANTHA	RDV 000198	07/10/1880
SCURRY, EVANTHA, RICHARDSON	RDV 000454	07/29/1881
SEATON, ELIZABETH	RDV 001190	11/04/1885
SEESOM, ELIZABETH	RDV 001106	05/14/1884
SELMAN, WESLEY	RDV 001104	05/08/1884
SELVERA, PILAR, ENRIQUE	RDV 001501	NO DATE
SEVIER, E G	RDV 001502	DEAD AT TIME OF CONSIDERATION
SEVIER, G W	RDV 000861	10/29/1881

Name	Voucher	Date
SHARP, MANERVA	RDV 000112	11/03/1879
SHARP, MINERVA, JOHN	RDV 000619	08/17/1881
SHAW, C A, JAMES	RDV 000833	10/28/1881
SHAW, G C	RDV 000813	10/28/1881
SHELTON, GEORGE W	RDV 000848	10/28/1881
SHERER, BERNARD	RDV 000827	10/28/1881
SHIVERS, CATHERINE O, L	RDV 000936	04/21/1882
SHORT, MARSHALL H	RDV 001112	05/23/1884
SIMPSON, M E, WILLIAM	RDV 001504	NO DATE
SIMPSON, NANCY, BARTLETT	RDV 001505	NO DATE
SIMPSON, PAMILIA, WILLIAM	RDV 000722	08/25/1881
SINCLAIR, CHRISTIANNA, RESIN	RDV 000675	08/19/1881
SINCLAIR, JOHN	RDV 001140	01/20/1885
SINGLETON, JOHN H	RDV 000866	10/29/1881
SKIDMORE, ANN M	RDV 001145	01/20/1885
SKILLERN, LUCY W, J C	RDV 000885	11/14/1881
SMATHERS, ISAAC	RDV 001506	NO DATE
SMATHERS, NANCY	RDV 001165	03/14/1885
SMITH, BETHEL	RDV 001014	02/10/1883
SMITH, BETHEL	RDV 001507	NO DATE
SMITH, ELIZABETH	RDV 000167	05/13/1880
SMITH, H M	RDV 000427	07/28/1881
SMITH, HENRY	RDV 000320	07/19/1881
SMITH, JACKSON	RDV 000875	11/12/1881
SMITH, JAMES	RDV 001508	REJECTED
SMITH, JOHN C	RDV 000643	08/19/1881
SMITH, JOYHN ROBERT	RDV 001512	REJECTED
SMITH, JULIA	RDV 000054	09/09/1879
SMITH, JULIA, WILEY	RDV 001020	03/09/1883
SMITH, LEMUEL	RDV 000639	08/19/1881
SMITH, LEMUEL	RDV 001510	REJECTED
SMITH, LYDIA ALMIRA, DANIEL D	RDV 000759	10/21/1881
SMITH, MAJOR	RDV 000206	02/26/1881
SMITH, MANAAN	RDV 001018	02/21/1883
SMITH, MARTHA ANN, LEROY H	RDV 001511	NO DATE
SMITH, NANNIE R	RDV 001216	12/24/1885
SMITH, THOMAS J	RDV 000140	12/03/1879
SMITH, THOMAS J	RDV 000502	08/02/1881
SMITH, WILLIAM	RDV 001065	07/07/1883
SMITH, WILLIAM J	RDV 001137	01/20/1885
SMYTH, EMELY, EMILY, ANDREW F	RDV 000551	08/08/1881
SMYTH, F M, GEORGE W	RDV 000583	08/08/1881
SNAILUM, THOMAS C	RDV 000747	08/25/1881
SOLAN, SAMUEL	RDV 000757	10/20/1881
SORSBY, W A	RDV 000719	08/25/1881
SOWELL, A J	RDV 000290	07/18/1881
SOWELL, ANDREW J	RDV 001513	REJECTED
SOWELL, RANSOM	RDV 000518	08/02/1881
SOWELL, RANSOM	RDV 001514	NO DATE

Republic of Texas Donation Vouchers-Alphabetical Listing

SPARKS, S F	RDV 000568	08/08/1881
SPARKS, W F	RDV 001067	07/28/1883
SPEER, JOHN	RDV 000150	05/11/1880
STANDIFER, J L	RDV 000602	08/16/1881
STANFIELD, W W O	RDV 000435	07/29/1881
STANLEY, MARY	RDV 001119	09/25/1884
STAPP, HUGH S	RDV 001266	11/30/1886
STEBBENS, ELIZABETH, CHARLES	RDV 000793	10/24/1881
STEBBINS, ELIZABETH	RDV 000142	01/02/1880
STEEL, MARY ANN	RDV 000944	04/21/1882
STEELE, ALFONZO	RDV 000647	08/19/1881
STEPHENSON, E B, J B	RDV 000600	08/12/1881
STEPHENSON, ELISHA	RDV 000870	10/29/1881
STEPHENSON, ELIZABETH B	RDV 000189	06/03/1880
STEPHENSON, ELIZABETH B	RDV 001515	NO DATE
STEPHENSON, HARRIET, IRA	RDV 001516	NO DATE
STEPHENSON, IRA	RDV 000894	11/15/1881
STEPHENSON, JAMES	RDV 000822	10/28/1881
STERN, ISAAC P	RDV 000332	07/21/1881
STEVENSON, JAMES P	RDV 000758	10/21/1881
STEVENSON, JAMES P	RDV 001517	NO DATE
STEWART, C B	RDV 000546	08/05/1881
STEWART, JOHN	RDV 000873	10/29/1881
STEWART, WILLIAM	RDV 000006	08/13/1879
STODDARD, JANE, J W	RDV 000852	10/28/1881
STOUT, B O	RDV 000642	08/19/1881
STOUT, HENRY	RDV 001249	05/27/1886
STOUT, HENRY	RDV 001518	NO DATE
STRAPP, R A, WILLIAM P	RDV 000762	10/21/1881
STROUT, JAMES S	RDV 001509	NO DATE
STUTEVILLE, JAMES C	RDV 000817	10/28/1881
SUANDERS, JOHN	RDV 000073	09/16/1879
SWEARENGEN, E	RDV 000309	07/19/1881
SWEENY, D F	RDV 001244	05/20/1886
SWEENY, JOHN	RDV 000682	08/20/1881
SWINGLE, LAURA E, ALFRED	RDV 000542	08/05/1881
SWISHER, JOHN M	RDV 000437	07/29/1881
SWOAP, MELVINA, B F	RDV 001519	NO DATE
SYPERT, W C	RDV 000949	04/26/1882
TANDY, SARAH A, ALBERT M	RDV 001146	01/20/1885
TANNER, CAROLINE, EDWARD	RDV 000720	08/25/1881
TANNER, CAROLINE E	RDV 000117	11/11/1879
TAYLOR, CAMPBELL	RDV 000443	07/29/1881
TAYLOR, CREED	RDV 001019	02/24/1883
TAYLOR, ELIZABETH, WILLIAM S	RDV 000416	07/28/1881
TEAL, ANNA	RDV 000816	10/28/1881
TEJADA, JOSE	RDV 001520	NO DATE
TEJADA, JUANA, GINIO	RDV 001521	NO DATE
TEJADA, PEDRO	RDV 001522	REJECTED

Name	Voucher	Date
TEJADA, REFUGIA	RDV 001523	REJECTED
TEJADA, SEBASTIAN	RDV 001524	NO DATE
TEVIS, JANE	RDV 000132	11/22/1879
TEVIS, JANE, GEORGE W	RDV 000957	04/28/1882
THOMAS, B	RDV 000300	07/18/1881
THOMAS, BEN	RDV 000095	10/01/1879
THOMAS, C A	RDV 000292	07/18/1881
THOMAS, CONSTANTIA A	RDV 001525	REJECTED
THOMAS, JAMES H	RDV 000943	04/21/1882
THOMAS, JULIA A, WILEY S	RDV 000862	10/29/1881
THOMAS, THEOPHILUS	RDV 001526	NO DATE
THOMASON, S E, WILLIAM C	RDV 001063	07/07/1883
THOMASON, W D	RDV 000278	07/18/1881
THOMPSON, JESSE	RDV 000476	08/02/1881
THOMPSON, M M, JESSE G	RDV 001032	04/07/1883
THOMPSON, SINGLETON	RDV 000105	10/28/1879
THOMPSON, SINGLETON, CLARINDA	RDV 000996	01/30/1883
THORN, JOHN	RDV 000632	08/18/1881
THORN, JOHN S	RDV 000197	07/07/1880
TIBBLES, FREDRICK A	RDV 000760	10/21/1881
TILTON, ANNIE, CHARLES	RDV 001527	NO DATE
TIMONEY, E H	RDV 000979	05/11/1882
TINDALL, WILLIAM P	RDV 000115	11/10/1879
TINDALL, WILLIAM P	RDV 000752	10/18/1881
TIPPETT, R J, WILLIAM	RDV 001528	NO DATE
TOBIN, MARTHA C	RDV 000664	08/19/1881
TODD, MARTHA ANN	RDV 001087	11/23/1883
TOLIVER, MARY, GEORGE W	RDV 001147	01/20/1885
TOM, JOHN F	RDV 000721	08/25/1881
TOMKINS, SUSAN	RDV 001196	11/21/1885
TOMPKINS, A N B	RDV 001529	NO DATE
TOOLE, MARTIN	RDV 000363	07/26/1881
TOWNSEND, L H, SPENCER	RDV 001007	02/03/1883
TOWNSEND, M	RDV 001149	01/20/1885
TOWNSEND, MARY ANN, MOSES	RDV 000853	10/28/1881
TOWNSEND, MATILDA	RDV 000138	11/28/1879
TRAVIESO, JUSTO	RDV 000086	09/29/1879
TREVINO, ANTONIO	RDV 000935	04/21/1882
TRIMBLE, R C	RDV 001191	11/04/1885
TUMLINSON, ELIZABETH, JOSEPH	RDV 000880	11/12/1881
TUMLINSON, PETER	RDV 000475	08/02/1881
TUMLINSON, PETER	RDV 001530	NO DATE
TURNER, JOHN	RDV 000484	08/02/1881
TURNER, WINSLOW	RDV 001531	DEAD AT TIME OF CONSIDERATION
TYLER, C C	RDV 000821	10/28/1881
UNDERHILL, DANIEL M	RDV 000792	10/24/1881
URON, ESTEVAN	RDV 001532	NO DATE
VALDEZ, FRANCISCA	RDV 000321	07/19/1881

Name	Voucher	Date
VALDEZ, FRANCISCO	RDV 000034	08/28/1879
VAN SICKLE, B A	RDV 000483	08/02/1881
VAN VECHTEN, D H	RDV 000274	07/16/1881
VAN VECHTEN, D H	RDV 001533	NO DATE
VANDERPOOL, EMILY, JAMES	RDV 000394	07/26/1881
VANSICKLE, MARY A, E S	RDV 001012	02/10/1883
VERNE, HENRY, ROSANNA	RDV 000910	04/19/1882
VOCHARY, MARY J, JOHN	RDV 001058	07/07/1883
VOCHERY, MARY J	RDV 000079	09/24/1879
VOTAW, E	RDV 000045	09/04/1879
VOTAW, ELIJAH	RDV 000293	07/18/1881
WADDELL, G W	RDV 001538	NO DATE
WADDLE, GEORGE W	RDV 000149	05/10/1880
WADE, JOHN M	RDV 000003	08/13/1859
WADE, NATHAN	RDV 000623	08/17/1881
WADE, RICHARD W	RDV 001253	06/05/1886
WAGONER, JANE, GEORGE	RDV 001540	NO DATE
WALDROP, WILEY, ELIZABETH	RDV 001534	REJECTED
WALKER, JOHN	RDV 000404	07/27/1881
WALKER, MARTIN	RDV 000741	08/25/1881
WALKER, PHILIP	RDV 000864	10/29/1881
WALKER, REBECCA	RDV 001229	02/20/1886
WALKER, SARAH	RDV 000102	10/28/1879
WALKER, SARAH A, JACOB	RDV 000589	08/11/1881
WALKER, SAUNDERS	RDV 000648	08/19/1881
WALKER, WILLIAM C	RDV 000737	08/25/1881
WALLING, ANN C, JESSIE	RDV 000268	07/16/1881
WALLING, M A	RDV 000214	07/14/1881
WALLING, MALINDA L, N D	RDV 001535	NO DATE
WALLING, MARTHA, JOHN C	RDV 001539	REJECTED
WALTENS, SARAH	RDV 001536	NO DATE
WALTERS, A C	RDV 000511	08/02/1881
WALTERS, JACOB	RDV 001072	11/15/1883
WALTERS, JACOB	RDV 001537	NO DATE
WALTERS, SARAH	RDV 001076	11/15/1883
WARD, AZUBA, RUSSELL	RDV 000801	10/25/1881
WARD, CAROLINE E	RDV 001250	05/27/1886
WARE, JOSEPH	RDV 001028	03/23/1883
WATSON, JOHN M	RDV 001254	06/07/1886
WATTS, HIRAM	RDV 000571	08/12/1881
WEATHERRED, MARY A, WILLIAM C	RDV 000761	10/21/1881
WEAVER, L G	RDV 000881	11/12/1881
WEAVER, L G	RDV 001541	REJECTED
WEBB, THOMAS R	RDV 000736	08/25/1881
WELCH, JEDEDIA	RDV 001227	02/20/1886
WELLS, HARRIETT, JOHN	RDV 000977	05/11/1882
WELLS, LEWIS	RDV 000277	07/18/1881
WELLS, M G, WAYMAN F	RDV 000997	01/12/1883
WELLS, M J	RDV 000420	07/28/1881

Republic of Texas Donation Vouchers-Alphabetical Listing

Name	Voucher	Date
WELLS, S G	RDV 000960	05/01/1882
WELLS, THEOPHILUS	RDV 000526	08/04/1881
WELLS, THEOPHILUS	RDV 001542	NO DATE
WEST, DELANY	RDV 001273	05/07/1887
WEST, FLORINDA, CLAIBORNE	RDV 000273	07/16/1881
WEST, JEFFERSON	RDV 001217	12/24/1885
WEST, SUSAN T, EDWARD	RDV 000365	07/26/1881
WHEAT, JOHN	RDV 000432	07/29/1881
WHEAT, R S	RDV 001042	04/24/1883
WHEAT, ROBERT S	RDV 001543	NO DATE
WHEELER, MARGARET, ELIGA	RDV 001548	NO DATE
WHEELER, PEGGY, ELIJAH	RDV 000767	10/21/1881
WHEELOCK, G R	RDV 000789	10/24/1881
WHEELOCK, MARY P, E L R	RDV 000788	10/24/1881
WHITAKER, BENJAMIN	RDV 000624	08/17/1881
WHITAKER, MADISON G	RDV 000464	08/02/1881
WHITE, CAREY	RDV 001239	03/10/1886
WHITE, ELIZABETH	RDV 001109	05/21/1884
WHITE, FRANCIS M	RDV 000302	07/18/1881
WHITE, JOHN C	RDV 000547	08/05/1881
WHITE, JOHN T	RDV 000171	05/14/1880
WHITE, K BINGHAM	RDV 001009	02/10/1883
WHITE, KATE, JOHN T	RDV 001546	REJECTED
WHITE, KERR B	RDV 001547	NO DATE
WHITE, LAVINIA K, JOHN M	RDV 000295	07/18/1881
WHITE, WILLIAM	RDV 000012	08/16/1879
WHITE, WILLIAM	RDV 000680	08/19/1881
WHITE, WILLIAM	RDV 001046	05/08/1883
WHITESIDES, J T	RDV 000973	05/11/1882
WHITING, LOUIS P	RDV 001545	REJECTED
WHITLEY, MARY, JOHN	RDV 000603	08/16/1881
WHITLOCK, ROBERT	RDV 000021	08/22/1879
WHITLOCK, ROBERT	RDV 000527	08/04/1881
WHITSTONE, ANDERSON	RDV 001544	NO DATE
WICKSON, CHARITY FRANCIS, DYRUM	RDV 001148	01/20/1885
WICKSON, CYRUS	RDV 000151	05/11/1880
WICKSON, CYRUS	RDV 001015	02/10/1883
WILBURN, RUTHA	RDV 001066	07/07/1883
WILCOX, PHILLIPENA, OZWIN	RDV 000310	07/19/1881
WILCOX, PHILOPENA	RDV 000013	08/18/1879
WILKINSON, MELVILLE	RDV 001240	03/16/1886
WILLIAM, STEPHEN	RDV 000015	08/19/1879
WILLIAMS, MITCHELL, NATHAN	RDV 000559	08/08/1881
WILLIAMS, AMANDA	RDV 000819	10/28/1881
WILLIAMS, EDWARD	RDV 001120	09/25/1884
WILLIAMS, H	RDV 000107	10/28/1879
WILLIAMS, HENRY	RDV 000768	10/21/1881
WILLIAMS, HENRY	RDV 001549	NO DATE
WILLIAMS, JAMES	RDV 000987	01/12/1883

WILLIAMS, JANE, L S	RDV 000888	11/14/1881
WILLIAMS, JANE, LEONARD	RDV 001550	NO DATE
WILLIAMS, MARY	RDV 001134	01/20/1885
WILLIAMS, REBECCA	RDV 000018	08/21/1879
WILLIAMS, REBECCA, RICHARD	RDV 001001	01/30/1883
WILLIAMS, SARAH J, JOSHUA	RDV 001551	NO DATE
WILLIAMS, SOPHIA, R M	RDV 000364	07/26/1881
WILLIAMS, STEPHEN	RDV 000554	08/08/1881
WILLIAMS, SUSANNA R, HENRY B	RDV 000739	08/25/1881
WILLIAMS, THOMAS J	RDV 000281	07/18/1881
WILLIAMS, THOMAS J	RDV 001552	NO DATE
WILLIAMS, WILLIAM	RDV 001092	05/08/1884
WILLIAMSON, ANN	RDV 000070	09/13/1879
WILLIAMSON, ANN, DAVID G	RDV 000287	07/18/1881
WILLIS, BRUCE	RDV 001310	NO DATE
WILSON, JAMES T D	RDV 000658	08/19/1881
WILSON, MAC, WILLIAM T	RDV 000382	07/26/1881
WILSON, MIMA, WALKER	RDV 000291	07/18/1881
WILSON, MINNA	RDV 000094	10/01/1879
WILSON, WILLIAM	RDV 001554	NO DATE
WINFIELD, ANN, E H	RDV 000346	07/23/1881
WINN, WALTER	RDV 001553	REJECTED
WINTERS, JAMES W	RDV 000769	10/21/1881
WINTERS, LARINIA, WILLIAM C	RDV 000587	08/11/1881
WINTERS, LAVINA	RDV 000104	10/28/1879
WOOD, ALFRED H	RDV 001555	NO DATE
WOOD, ALFRED HENRY	RDV 001228	02/20/1886
WOOD, JOHN H	RDV 000893	11/15/1881
WOOD, W R	RDV 000099	10/28/1879
WOOD, W R	RDV 000493	08/02/1881
WOODERSON, WILIAM	RDV 000298	07/18/1881
WOODLAND, HENRY	RDV 001269	02/05/1887
WOODS, ISABELLA, MONTRAVILLE, ISABELLA	RDV 000372	07/26/1881
WOODS, ISABELLE, MONTRAVILLE	RDV 001556	REJECTED
WOOTON, GREENVILLE T	RDV 001557	NO DATE
WRIGHT, AMANDA, G W	RDV 000520	08/02/1881
WYLY, JOSEPHINE L, ALFRED H	RDV 001053	05/15/1883
WYNNE, A J, R H	RDV 001006	02/01/1883
XIMINES, GIL	RDV 001558	NO DATE
YANCY, ELIZABETH	RDV 000152	05/11/1880
YANCY, ELIZABETH, JOHN	RDV 000560	08/08/1881
YARBOROUGH, P C, RANDOLPH	RDV 000905	01/14/1882
YEAMANS, JOSEPH	RDV 000004	08/13/1879
YEAMANS, JOSEPH	RDV 000490	08/02/1881
YOUNG, JAMES	RDV 000803	10/27/1881
YOUNG, JAMES	RDV 000991	01/30/1883
YOUNG, JAMES	RDV 001559	NO DATE
ZAPATA, SATURINO	RDV 001561	NO DATE
ZAPATA, GREGORIO	RDV 001560	REJECTED

Name	Voucher	Date
ZUBER, W P	RDV 000387	07/26/1881
ZUMWALT, ANDREW	RDV 000834	10/28/1881
ZUMWALT, T B	RDV 000978	05/11/1882
ZUNIGAS, MARINA, JOSE	RDV 000594	08/11/1881

Index to Rep. of Texas Donation Vouchers
Numerical Listing

File Number	Grantee's Name	Date/Description
RDV 000001	DUTY, WILLIAM	08/12/1879
RDV 000002	FENNER, JOSEPH	
RDV 000003	WADE, JOHN M	08/13/1879
RDV 000004	YEAMANS, JOSEPH	08/13/1879
RDV 000005	SCATES, W B	08/13/1879
RDV 000006	STEWART, WILLIAM	08/13/1879
RDV 000007	MOORE, JAMES W	08/13/1879
RDV 000008	BISHOP, W H	08/13/1879
RDV 000009	NETTLES, WILLIAM	08/13/1879
RDV 000010	FERRELL, JOHN P	08/15/1879
RDV 000011	MC GAHEY, JAMES H	08/15/1879
RDV 000012	WHITE, WILLIAM	08/16/1879
RDV 000013	WILCOX, PHILOPENA	08/18/1879
RDV 000014	HOTCHKISS, RINALDO	08/18/1879
RDV 000015	WILLIAM, STEPHEN	08/19/1879
RDV 000016	HENSLEY, JOHNSON	08/21/1879
RDV 000017	LEIPER, HANNAH	08/21/1879
RDV 000018	WILLIAMS, REBECCA	08/21/1879
RDV 000019	BENSON, ELLIS	08/21/1879
RDV 000020	PATTERSON, EUGENIA	08/09/1879
RDV 000021	WHITLOCK, ROBERT	08/22/1879
RDV 000022	GOOD, JULIA A	08/22/1879
RDV 000023	HODGES, SUSAN	08/22/1879
RDV 000024	COY, M J	08/23/1879
RDV 000025	CURVIER, MATIAS	08/23/1879
RDV 000026	ETHRIDGE, HOWARD	08/26/1879
RDV 000027	RUSSELL, WILLIAM J	08/26/1879
RDV 000028	KELSO, ALFRED	08/27/1879
RDV 000029	FARISH, OSCAR	08/27/1879
RDV 000030	BURKE, ANNA MARIA	08/27/1879
RDV 000031	ALSBURY, Y, RODRIGUEZ, MARIA	08/28/1879
RDV 000032	GIMENES, TEODORA	08/28/1879
RDV 000033	CHACON, ANTONIA	08/28/1879
RDV 000034	VALDEZ, FRANCISCO	08/28/1879
RDV 000035	GOMEZ, JESUS	08/28/1879
RDV 000036	GEORGE, DAVID	08/29/1879
RDV 000037	CASILLAS, MATEO	08/30/1879
RDV 000038	BUCKLEY, TYRE	08/30/1879
RDV 000039	CABASOS, ALBINO	09/13/1879
RDV 000040	NAVARRO, JESUSA	09/03/1879
RDV 000041	GAONA, PEDRO	09/03/1879
RDV 000042	HERNANDEZ, MANUELA	09/03/1879
RDV 000043	MENCHACA, ANTONIO	09/03/1879

Republic of Texas Donation Vouchers-Numerical Listing

RDV 000044	PUTMAN, MITCHELL	09/03/1879
RDV 000045	VOTAW, E	09/04/1879
RDV 000046	ROBINSON, JESSE	09/04/1879
RDV 000047	BROOKS, G W	09/04/1879
RDV 000048	GALLARDO, REFUGIA	09/04/1879
RDV 000049	GOMEZ, CONCEPCION	09/04/1879
RDV 000050	ESPINOZA, YGNACIO	09/04/1879
RDV 000051	ANDERSON, MARY J	09/05/1879
RDV 000052	DE HENRIQUEZ, ACENCION M	09/05/1879
RDV 000053	DENMAN, JANE	09/05/1879
RDV 000054	SMITH, JULIA	09/09/1879
RDV 000055	BARKER, ALITIA	09/09/1879
RDV 000056	FORD, SIMON P	09/09/1879
RDV 000057	COLLEY, MIRANDA	09/09/1879
RDV 000058	BURDITT, WILLIAM B	09/09/1879
RDV 000059	DAVIS, ELIZA A	09/11/1879
RDV 000060	BOX, LUCINDA	09/11/1879
RDV 000061	CRUZ, AROCHA, PENA, MARIA JESUSA	09/11/1879
RDV 000062	GORTARI, CASILLAS, ANTONIA	09/11/1879
RDV 000063	BUSTILLO, CLEMENTE	09/11/1879
RDV 000064	ALLEN, ELIJAH	09/12/1879
RDV 000065	NEWMAN, WILLIAM R	09/12/1879
RDV 000066	MC FADDEN, ELIZA	09/12/1879
RDV 000067	DYKES, LEWIS P	09/12/1879
RDV 000068	LEWIS, G W	09/13/1879
RDV 000069	ARMSTRONG, JAMES	09/13/1879
RDV 000070	WILLIAMSON, ANN	09/13/1879
RDV 000071	ROBERTS, MOSES F	09/13/1879
RDV 000072	CONTI, JULIAN	09/13/1879
RDV 000073	SUANDERS, JOHN	09/16/1879
RDV 000074	MIRANDA, FRANCISCO	09/17/1879
RDV 000075	SALINAS, PABLO	09/17/1879
RDV 000076	IIAMS, JOHN	09/18/1879
RDV 000077	LANE, WALTEN	09/18/1879
RDV 000078	GORMAN, J P	09/22/1879
RDV 000079	VOCHERY, MARY J	09/24/1879
RDV 000080	ISAACS, SICILY M	09/24/1879
RDV 000081	REIZENHOOVER, NAOMA	09/24/1879
RDV 000082	BROOKS, GILBERT	09/24/1879
RDV 000083	CARY, SETH	09/24/1879
RDV 000084	GARCIA, ORTIZ, DOLORES	09/24/1879
RDV 000085	MC GUFFIN, JOHN	09/27/1879
RDV 000086	TRAVIESO, JUSTO	09/29/1879
RDV 000087	RICKS, G W	09/29/1879
RDV 000088	CASTANON, LEWIS	09/29/1879
RDV 000089	KIRBY, GEORGE	09/30/1879
RDV 000090	GONZALES, GRAVIEL	09/30/1879
RDV 000091	LEWIS, JOHN T	10/01/1879
RDV 000092	IRVIN, NANCY	10/01/1879

Voucher	Name	Date
RDV 000093	BURLESON, JOSEPH	10/01/1879
RDV 000094	WILSON, MINNA	10/01/1879
RDV 000095	THOMAS, BEN	10/01/1879
RDV 000096	CARLETON, ELIZABETH M	10/04/1876
RDV 000097	PRICE, SIBBA M	10/22/1879
RDV 000098	MYERS, NANCY	10/25/1879
RDV 000099	WOOD, W R	10/28/1879
RDV 000100	KIMBRO, NANCY	10/28/1879
RDV 000101	KEMP, CHARLOTTE	10/28/1879
RDV 000102	WALKER, SARAH	10/28/1879
RDV 000103	MORGAN, JEMINA	10/28/1879
RDV 000104	WINTERS, LAVINA	10/28/1879
RDV 000105	THOMPSON, SINGLETON	10/28/1879
RDV 000106	BOWMAN, JAMES H	10/28/1879
RDV 000107	WILLIAMS, H	10/28/1879
RDV 000108	BYERLY, ADAMS	10/28/1879
RDV 000109	SALINAS, MARIA	10/29/1879
RDV 000110	BALLE, ANTONIO	11/03/1879
RDV 000111	BURNAM, CAROLINE	11/03/1879
RDV 000112	SHARP, MANERVA	11/03/1879
RDV 000113	RICHARDSON, LUCINDA	11/04/1879
RDV 000114	PREWITT, ELISHA	11/05/1879
RDV 000115	TINDALL, WILLIAM P	11/10/1879
RDV 000116	SAVERY, ASAHEL	11/11/1879
RDV 000117	TANNER, CAROLINE E	11/11/1879
RDV 000118	CURBIER, FERNANDO	11/14/1879
RDV 000119	PERRY, W M	11/14/1879
RDV 000120	BROWNING, H H	11/14/1879
RDV 000121	GRAY, JAMES	11/15/1879
RDV 000122	JOHNSON, MARY	11/15/1879
RDV 000123	DUNN, CHRISTIANA M	11/15/1879
RDV 000124	GUYMAN, JANE	11/17/1879
RDV 000125	ADAMS, REBECCA	11/18/1879
RDV 000126	COOK, MARY J	11/18/1879
RDV 000127	KUYKENDALL, J H	11/21/1879
RDV 000128	CHILDRESS, H M	11/21/1879
RDV 000129	MONTGOMERY, MARY	11/21/1879
RDV 000130	CORNER, EVIN	11/21/1879
RDV 000131	HARDIN, W B	11/21/1879
RDV 000132	TEVIS, JANE	11/22/1879
RDV 000133	MILLER, ELIZABETH	11/22/1879
RDV 000134	CALLIHAN, J J	11/22/1879
RDV 000135	BURNSTEAD, M W	11/24/1879
RDV 000136	BOSTICK, SION R	11/24/1879
RDV 000137	GARRETT, LEVICY	11/24/1879
RDV 000138	TOWNSEND, MATILDA	11/28/1879
RDV 000139	DINSMORE, AMANDA F	12/01/1879
RDV 000140	SMITH, THOMAS J	12/03/1879
RDV 000141	MC COY, ELIZABETH	12/04/1879

RDV 000142	STEBBINS, ELIZABETH	01/02/1880
RDV 000143	BURNS, JOSEPH	01/06/1880
RDV 000144	BREEDING, CHARLOTTE	01/22/1880
RDV 000145	CAIN, WILLIAM	01/24/1880
RDV 000146	HORTON, ELIZA	02/05/1880
RDV 000147	LOW, M A	03/12/1880
RDV 000148	LUBBOCK, SARAH O	05/07/1880
RDV 000149	WADDLE, GEORGE W	05/10/1880
RDV 000150	SPEER, JOHN	05/11/1880
RDV 000151	WICKSON, CYRUS	05/11/1880
RDV 000152	YANCY, ELIZABETH	05/11/1880
RDV 000153	HENDERSON, JOHN	05/11/1880
RDV 000154	LEWIS, JACOB	05/11/1880
RDV 000155	ARIOLA, GUADALUPE	05/11/1880
RDV 000156	POLLAN, JOHN	05/11/1880
RDV 000157	GOODMAN, STEPHEN	05/11/1880
RDV 000158	BREWSTER, H P	05/11/1880
RDV 000159	MC GEE, JOSEPH	05/11/1880
RDV 000160	HALL, LUCINA L	05/11/1880
RDV 000161	PALACIOS, JUAN	05/11/1880
RDV 000162	KELLY, CONNELL O DONNELL	05/12/1880
RDV 000163	ALLEN, WILLIAMS	05/13/1880
RDV 000164	BROWN, REUBEN R	05/13/1880
RDV 000165	QUINN, PATRICK	05/13/1880
RDV 000166	MONTGOMERY, JAMES	05/13/1880
RDV 000167	SMITH, ELIZABETH	05/13/1880
RDV 000168	BERRY, S	05/14/1880
RDV 000169	GALLIHAN, JOHN H	05/14/1880
RDV 000170	JOHNSON, F W	05/14/1880
RDV 000171	WHITE, JOHN T	05/14/1880
RDV 000172	GALLATIN, ALBERT	05/14/1880
RDV 000173	DAVIS, JOHN	05/14/1880
RDV 000174	GILBERT, MARTHA	05/14/1880
RDV 000175	PASCHAL, BRIDGET	05/17/1880
RDV 000176	EGGLESTON, JULIA	05/18/1880
RDV 000177	ALEXANDER, JANE G	05/17/1880
RDV 000178	MAGILL, ELIZABETH A	05/17/1880
RDV 000179	ENGLISH, LUCINDA	05/17/1880
RDV 000180	CADDEL, RHODA	05/19/1880
RDV 000181	LINDSEY, BENJAMIN F	05/19/1880
RDV 000182	HOWTH, WILLIAM EDWARD	05/19/1880
RDV 000183	ALSBURY, JUANA N	05/19/1880
RDV 000184	ALAMEDA, JOSE	05/22/1880
RDV 000185	ATKINSON, MARGARET	05/22/1880
RDV 000186	RUTLEDGE, EMELINE	05/25/1880
RDV 000187	DUVAL, JOHN C	05/26/1880
RDV 000188	MILES, EDWARD	05/27/1880
RDV 000189	STEPHENSON, ELIZABETH B	06/03/1880
RDV 000190	DUNBAR, CAROLINE	06/11/1880

RDV 000191 .... PEVYHOUSE, CYRENE, PEVEHOUSE, CYRINA 06/11/1880
RDV 000192 .... LEE, THEODORE S.. 06/09/1880
RDV 000193 .... AROCHA, MACEDONIO 06/26/1880
RDV 000194 .... JONES, HETTIE... 06/06/1880
RDV 000195 .... SCOTT, ELIZABETH 06/06/1880
RDV 000196 .... BUNDICK, CLEMENTINE 06/06/1880
RDV 000197 .... THORN, JOHN S 07/07/1880
RDV 000198 .... SCURRY, EVANTHA 07/10/1880
RDV 000199 .... MERCHANT, SARAH P, SARINDIA P 07/12/1880
RDV 000200 .... FRIAR, ANN 07/12/1880
RDV 000201 .... CHOATE, MARY 07/12/1880
RDV 000202 .... SANDERS, RACHAEL.. 09/24/1880
RDV 000203 .... BERRY, A J.. 10/20/1880
RDV 000204 .... DOYLE, MATTHEW A 10/30/1880
RDV 000205 .... BROOKS, GEORGE W 02/26/1881
RDV 000206 .... SMITH, MAJOR... 02/26/1881
RDV 000207 .... DENMAN, JAMES 02/28/1881
RDV 000208 .... LINDSEY, PENNINGTON... 02/28/1881
RDV 000209 .... JONES, DAVID M 02/28/1881
RDV 000210 .... HALL, GEORGE H 02/28/1881
RDV 000211 .... HENSLEY, JOHN M.. 03/02/1881
RDV 000212 .... LINDHEIMER, ELONORA 03/02/1881
RDV 000213 .... PERKINS, MARY S... 03/31/1881
RDV 000214 .... WALLING, M A 07/14/1881
RDV 000215 .... GREY, JAMES 07/14/1881
RDV 000216 .... BRILL, SOLOMAN W... 07/14/1881
RDV 000217 .... CONLEE, M E, CONLEE, PRESTON 07/14/1881
RDV 000218 .... CONNELL, SARAH JANE, CONNELL, DAVID C 07/14/1881
RDV 000219 .... AUSTIN, ELIZABETH A, WILLIAM T........................... 07/14/1881
RDV 000220 .... CLEVELAND, ELIZA J, J A H 07/14/1881
RDV 000221 .... BOSTICK, S R.. 07/14/1881
RDV 000222 .... DALE, E V.. 07/14/1881
RDV 000223 .... GEORGE, DAVID.. 07/14/1881
RDV 000224 .... PITTS, JOHN 07/14/1881
RDV 000225 .... HOPE, RICHARD 07/14/1881
RDV 000226 .... FARISH, OSCAR... 07/14/1881
RDV 000227 .... GIMENES, TEODORA, JUAN.. 07/14/1881
RDV 000228 .... HOWARD, M F, GEORGE T 07/14/1881
RDV 000229 .... PREWITT, ELISHA 07/14/1881
RDV 000230 .... LACY, W Y 07/14/1881
RDV 000231 .... GOODWIN, WILLIAM 07/14/1881
RDV 000232 .... CHILDRESS, H M 07/14/1881
RDV 000233 .... MONTALBO, MANUEL... 07/14/1881
RDV 000234 .... ABLES, MARY ANN, HARRISON..................................... 07/14/1881
RDV 000235 .... COOK, JOSEPH THOMAS 07/14/1881
RDV 000236 .... MOORE, JAMES W 07/14/1881
RDV 000237 .... MOORE, W H.. 07/14/1881
RDV 000238 .... LANE, WALTER P.. 07/14/1881
RDV 000239 .... CONNELL, WILLIAM 07/14/1881

Republic of Texas Donation Vouchers-Numerical Listing

RDV 000240	KIMBRO, NANCY, L K	07/14/1881
RDV 000241	LINDSEY, JAMES	07/14/1881
RDV 000242	JONES, NETTIE, J W	07/15/1881
RDV 000243	JONES, MARY, ANSON	07/15/1881
RDV 000244	JAMES, JANE C, THOMAS	07/15/1881
RDV 000245	ISAACS, MARTHA, SAMUEL	07/15/1881
RDV 000246	HERNANDEZ, MANUELLA CANELAS, ANTONIO	07/15/1881
RDV 000247	HENRIQUEZ, ASCENCION MARTINEZ, LUCIO	07/15/1881
RDV 000248	HARDING, T B	07/15/1881
RDV 000249	BUNTON, HERMINE, JOHN W	07/15/1881
RDV 000250	NEILL, ANDREW	07/15/1881
RDV 000251	HORTON, A	07/15/1881
RDV 000252	BLOUNT, S W	07/15/1881
RDV 000253	ROGERS, JOHN A	07/15/1881
RDV 000254	DEDMAN, W S	07/15/1881
RDV 000255	SCATES, WILLIAM B	07/15/1881
RDV 000256	CRAWFORD, W C	07/15/1881
RDV 000257	MONTGOMERY, JAMES	07/15/1881
RDV 000258	REED, WILLIAM	07/15/1881
RDV 000259	ARRIOLA, ARIOLA, GUADALUPE	07/15/1881
RDV 000260	EDWARDS, C O	07/15/1881
RDV 000261	BISHOP, W H	07/15/1881
RDV 000262	CHILDRESS, ROBERT	07/15/1881
RDV 000263	CAYCE, SHADRACH	07/15/1881
RDV 000264	REED, JEFFERSON	07/15/1881
RDV 000265	LINDSEY, B F	07/15/1881
RDV 000266	CARTWRIGHT, MATTHEW W	07/16/1881
RDV 000267	CHATHAM, THOMAS	07/16/1881
RDV 000268	WALLING, ANN C, JESSIE	07/16/1881
RDV 000269	HUNTER, WILLIAM L	07/16/1881
RDV 000270	BAMHART, JOSEPH	07/16/1881
RDV 000271	JOHNSON, FRANK W	07/16/1881
RDV 000272	DUFFAN, FRANCIS T, MARY	07/16/1881
RDV 000273	WEST, FLORINDA, CLAIBORNE	07/16/1881
RDV 000274	VAN VECHTEN, D H	07/16/1881
RDV 000275	PASCHAL, BRIDGET, SAMUEL	07/16/1881
RDV 000276	HOWARD, PHILIP	07/16/1881
RDV 000277	WELLS, LEWIS	07/18/1881
RDV 000278	THOMASON, W D	07/18/1881
RDV 000279	BRUMMETT, HARRISON	07/18/1881
RDV 000280	MAGILL, ELIZABETH A, W H	07/18/1881
RDV 000281	WILLIAMS, THOMAS J	07/18/1881
RDV 000282	HALL, GEORGE H	07/18/1881
RDV 000283	ROGERS, SAMUEL C A	07/18/1881
RDV 000284	MENEFEE, GEORGE	07/18/1881
RDV 000285	BRUTON, ELISHA	07/18/1881
RDV 000286	CURRIER, MATIAS	07/18/1881
RDV 000287	WILLIAMSON, ANN, DAVID G	07/18/1881
RDV 000288	DEFFENBAUGH, ANTHONY	07/18/1881

Republic of Texas Donation Vouchers-Numerical Listing

RDV 000289	SCHULTZ, JOHN	07/18/1881
RDV 000290	SOWELL, A J	07/18/1881
RDV 000291	WILSON, MIMA, WALKER	07/18/1881
RDV 000292	THOMAS, C A	07/18/1881
RDV 000293	VOTAW, ELIJAH	07/18/1881
RDV 000294	MAHAN, EMMA H, P JENKS	07/18/1881
RDV 000295	WHITE, LAVINIA K, JOHN M	07/18/1881
RDV 000296	MORRIS, SPENCER	07/18/1881
RDV 000297	BRISCOE, MARY J, ANDREW	07/18/1881
RDV 000298	WOODERSON, WILIAM	07/18/1881
RDV 000299	PASCHAL, F L	07/18/1881
RDV 000300	THOMAS, B	07/18/1881
RDV 000301	PLUNKETT, JOHN	07/18/1881
RDV 000302	WHITE, FRANCIS M	07/18/1881
RDV 000303	BRUCE, WILLIS	07/18/1881
RDV 000304	BURKE, ANNA, DAVID N	07/18/1881
RDV 000305	LYON, H C	07/19/1881
RDV 000306	PIERCE, PHILIP R	07/19/1881
RDV 000307	HENRY, ELIZABETH, ROBERT	07/19/1881
RDV 000308	KIRBEY, GEORGE	07/19/1881
RDV 000309	SWEARENGEN, E	07/19/1881
RDV 000310	WILCOX, PHILLIPENA, OZWIN	07/19/1881
RDV 000311	ARCHER, ROSA, JOHN A	07/19/1881
RDV 000312	GIBSON, ARCHIBALD	07/19/1881
RDV 000313	LAWRENCE, JOSEPH	07/19/1881
RDV 000314	FERRELL, JOHN P	07/19/1881
RDV 000315	RECTOR, PENDELTON	07/19/1881
RDV 000316	LYONS, DEWITT C	07/19/1881
RDV 000317	HEARD, ESTHER F, W I F	07/19/1881
RDV 000318	BROOKS, G W	07/19/1881
RDV 000319	GOMEZ, JESUS	07/19/1881
RDV 000320	SMITH, HENRY	07/19/1881
RDV 000321	VALDEZ, FRANCISCA	07/19/1881
RDV 000322	CONTI, JULIAN	07/19/1881
RDV 000323	NAVARRO, JESUSA URON, NEPUMOCENO	07/19/1881
RDV 000324	REED, ISAAC	07/20/1881
RDV 000325	BROWN, R R	07/20/1881
RDV 000326	SCARBOROUGH, JANE C, LAWRENCE	07/20/1881
RDV 000327	CHACON, ANTONIO RODRIGUEZ, CARLOS	07/20/1881
RDV 000328	ANDERSON, HOLLAND	07/20/1881
RDV 000329	GREEN, GEORGE	07/20/1881
RDV 000330	MC LAUGHLIN, STEPHEN	07/20/1881
RDV 000331	MC KINZIE, WILLIAM S	07/21/1881
RDV 000332	STERN, ISAAC P	07/21/1881
RDV 000333	LOGAN, CAROLINE, GREENBERRY	07/21/1881
RDV 000334	CLARK, CAROLINE E, JAMES	07/21/1881
RDV 000335	ROBINSON, JOEL W	07/22/1881
RDV 000336	HILL, JAMES M	07/22/1881
RDV 000337	FORD, SIMON P	07/22/1881

Voucher	Name	Date
RDV 000338	MANTON, EDWARD	07/20/1881
RDV 000339	CRISWELL, MARY E, WILLIAM	07/22/1881
RDV 000340	KERR, WILLIAM P	07/22/1881
RDV 000341	HERDER, GEORGE	07/22/1881
RDV 000342	GORHAM, LUCINDA, WILLIAM	07/22/1881
RDV 000343	LEWIS, J E	07/22/1881
RDV 000344	BREEDING, LOUISA, JOHN	07/22/1881
RDV 000345	REDFIELD, HENRY P	07/22/1881
RDV 000346	WINFIELD, ANN, E H	07/23/1881
RDV 000347	FAIRES, W A	07/23/1881
RDV 000348	COOK, TEMPERENCE, HAMILTON	07/23/1881
RDV 000349	CARLETON, ELIZABETH, WILLIAM	07/23/1881
RDV 000350	BALLE, ANTONIO	07/23/1881
RDV 000351	EASTLAND, N W	07/23/1881
RDV 000352	OSBORN, THOMAS	07/23/1881
RDV 000353	OSBORN, JOHN L	07/23/1881
RDV 000354	MILLER, ELIZABETH, WILLIAM P	07/25/1881
RDV 000355	MILES, EDWARD	07/25/1881
RDV 000356	BREWSTER, H P	07/25/1881
RDV 000357	GAINES, W B P	07/25/1881
RDV 000358	HAGGARD, SQUIRE	07/26/1881
RDV 000359	KENNARD, M M	07/26/1881
RDV 000360	GOODRICH, SERENA, B B	07/26/1881
RDV 000361	KOKERNOT, D L	07/26/1881
RDV 000362	BUFFINGTON, A	07/26/1881
RDV 000363	TOOLE, MARTIN	07/26/1881
RDV 000364	WILLIAMS, SOPHIA, R M	07/26/1881
RDV 000365	WEST, SUSAN T, EDWARD	07/26/1881
RDV 000366	GALLATIN, ALBERT	07/26/1881
RDV 000367	PERRY, C R	07/26/1881
RDV 000368	LATIMER, MARY, ALBERT H	07/26/1881
RDV 000369	BOWMAN, JAMES H	07/26/1881
RDV 000370	DEWITT, C C	07/26/1881
RDV 000371	LOVE, G H	07/26/1881
RDV 000372	WOODS, ISABELLA, MONTRAVILLE, ISABELLA	07/26/1881
RDV 000373	SANDERS, NANCY, WILLIAM B	07/26/1881
RDV 000374	BLAND, JOHN	07/26/1881
RDV 000375	LATIMER, H R	07/26/1881
RDV 000376	BAKER, JOHN B	07/26/1881
RDV 000377	ALLEN, GEORGE	07/26/1881
RDV 000378	ELLEY, ELLY, GUSTAVE	07/26/1881
RDV 000379	DARDIN, STEPHEN H	07/26/1881
RDV 000380	KENT, DAVID B	07/26/1881
RDV 000381	MERCHANT, BERRY	07/26/1881
RDV 000382	WILSON, MAC, WILLIAM T	07/26/1881
RDV 000383	MC GEE, JOSEPH	07/26/1881
RDV 000384	DAVIS, JOHN	07/26/1881
RDV 000385	DENMAN, JAMES	07/26/1881
RDV 000386	BROWN, HIRAM	07/26/1881

RDV 000387 .... ZUBER, W P 07/26/1881
RDV 000388 .... ANDERSON, HUGH 07/26/1881
RDV 000389 .... PREWITT, HANNA, LEVI 07/26/1881
RDV 000390 .... BRYAN, ELIZABETH, CHRISTOPHER 07/26/1881
RDV 000391 .... CANNON, WILLIAM J 07/26/1881
RDV 000392 .... HOWTH, MARY E 07/26/1881
RDV 000393 .... HODGES, SUSAN, ROBERT 07/26/1881
RDV 000394 .... VANDERPOOL, EMILY, JAMES 07/26/1881
RDV 000395 .... DUNCAN, C J, WILLIAM 07/26/1881
RDV 000396 .... BROWN, EDWARD 07/26/1881
RDV 000397 .... MC GEHEE, THOMAS G 07/26/1881
RDV 000398 .... AUSTIN, N 07/26/1881
RDV 000399 .... JOHNSON, SAMUEL 07/26/1881
RDV 000400 .... CASILLAS, MATEO 07/26/1881
RDV 000401 .... MC MASTERS, WILLIAM 07/26/1881
RDV 000402 .... HUMPHRIES, B H 07/26/1881
RDV 000403 .... MC CULLOCH, SAMUEL 07/26/1881
RDV 000404 .... WALKER, JOHN 07/27/1881
RDV 000405 .... AVERY, WILLIS 07/28/1881
RDV 000406 .... OGSBURY, CHARLES A 07/28/1881
RDV 000407 .... RAGLIN, H W 07/28/1881
RDV 000408 .... MONTGOMERY, MINERVA, MC GRADY 07/28/1881
RDV 000409 .... COCHRAN, BETSY, THOMAS 07/28/1881
RDV 000410 .... PARKER, DANIEL 07/28/1881
RDV 000411 .... JONES, C M 07/28/1881
RDV 000412 .... MASON, CHARLES 07/28/1881
RDV 000413 .... LEE, THEODORE S 07/28/1881
RDV 000414 .... HENSLEY, JOHN 07/28/1881
RDV 000415 .... PHELPS, R A, JAMES A E 07/28/1881
RDV 000416 .... TAYLOR, ELIZABETH, WILLIAM S 07/28/1881
RDV 000417 .... DEVORE, CORNELIUS 07/28/1881
RDV 000418 .... DEVER, THOMAS 07/28/1881
RDV 000419 .... LEWIS, JOHN T 07/28/1881
RDV 000420 .... WELLS, M J 07/28/1881
RDV 000421 .... HERREY, SAMUEL S 07/28/1881
RDV 000422 .... MC MAHAN, ISAAC 07/28/1881
RDV 000423 .... PAYNE, JOHN C 07/28/1881
RDV 000424 .... BUCKLY, TYRE 07/28/1881
RDV 000425 .... GREEN, JAMES 07/28/1881
RDV 000426 .... CRADDOCK, JOHN R 07/28/1881
RDV 000427 .... SMITH, H M 07/28/1881
RDV 000428 .... CRIST, DANIEL 07/28/1881
RDV 000429 .... BENSON, ELLIS 07/29/1881
RDV 000430 .... NETTLES, WILLIAM 07/29/1881
RDV 000431 .... CRANE, R T 07/29/1881
RDV 000432 .... WHEAT, JOHN 07/29/1881
RDV 000433 .... CHOATE, MARY, DAVID 07/29/1881
RDV 000434 .... RAMSDALE, GEORGE 07/29/1881
RDV 000435 .... STANFIELD, W W O 07/29/1881

RDV 000436	BLEDSOE, GEORGE L	07/29/1881
RDV 000437	SWISHER, JOHN M	07/29/1881
RDV 000438	JOHNSON, WILLIAM	07/29/1881
RDV 000439	MC DONOUGH, MARY, EDWARD	07/29/1881
RDV 000440	CAMPBELL, ANGERINA, JOSEPH	07/29/1881
RDV 000441	GASTANON, LUIS	07/29/1881
RDV 000442	CUBIER, FERNANDO	07/29/1881
RDV 000443	TAYLOR, CAMPBELL	07/29/1881
RDV 000444	IRVIN, NANCY, J S	07/29/1881
RDV 000445	MC MAHAN, SARAH	07/29/1881
RDV 000446	POLLAN, JOHN	07/29/1881
RDV 000447	BREEDING, CHARLOTTE, W B	07/29/1881
RDV 000448	MC ANELLY, PLEASANT	07/29/1881
RDV 000449	CROUCH, JACKSON	07/29/1881
RDV 000450	PITTMAN, E W	07/29/1881
RDV 000451	BURNS, JOSEPH	07/29/1881
RDV 000452	IRISH, EMILY, MILTON	07/29/1881
RDV 000453	MC CUTCHEON, WILLIAM	07/29/1881
RDV 000454	SCURRY, EVANTHA, RICHARDSON	07/29/1881
RDV 000455	DAVIS, GEORGE W	07/30/1881
RDV 000456	BURLESON, JOSEPH	08/01/1881
RDV 000457	BUSTILLO, CLEMENTE	08/01/1881
RDV 000458	PATTERSON, EUGENIA, J S	08/02/1881
RDV 000459	EGGLESTON, JULIA, A V R	08/02/1881
RDV 000460	BURNAM, CAROLINE, WILLIAM O	08/02/1881
RDV 000461	BARKER, ALITIA, WILLIAM	08/02/1881
RDV 000462	DELAPLAIN, A C	08/02/1881
RDV 000463	HUBBLE, HUBBELL, ELIZA, JOHN	08/02/1881
RDV 000464	WHITAKER, MADISON G	08/02/1881
RDV 000465	MAGEE, NICINDA, RICHARD A	08/02/1881
RDV 000466	NEWMAN, WILIAM R	08/02/1881
RDV 000467	FOSTER, B F	08/02/1881
RDV 000468	CARUTHERS, MARY, JOHN	08/02/1881
RDV 000469	MACKEY, JOHN	08/02/1881
RDV 000470	INGRAM, JOHN	08/02/1881
RDV 000471	BLUNDELL, WILLIAM	08/02/1881
RDV 000472	DOUGLAS, DUGLASS, RICHARD	08/02/1881
RDV 000473	BRYAN, ANNA M, JOHN	08/02/1881
RDV 000474	RUSK, ELIZABETH, DAVID	08/02/1881
RDV 000475	TUMLINSON, PETER	08/02/1881
RDV 000476	THOMPSON, JESSE	08/02/1881
RDV 000477	DEBARD, E J	08/02/1881
RDV 000478	HALL, ROBERT	08/02/1881
RDV 000479	EDENS, D H	08/02/1881
RDV 000480	CALDEN, R J	08/02/1881
RDV 000481	ROBERTS, MOSES F	08/02/1881
RDV 000482	SCOTT, ELIZABETH, DAVID	08/02/1881
RDV 000483	VAN SICKLE, B A	08/02/1881
RDV 000484	TURNER, JOHN	08/02/1881

RDV 000485 .... PERRY, JANE H, DANIEL 08/02/1881
RDV 000486 .... RUSSELL, SUSANNAH, SUSANA, ELI 08/02/1881
RDV 000487 .... ALLEN, ELIJAH 08/02/1881
RDV 000488 .... MYERS, MEYERS, NANCY, JOHN 08/02/1881
RDV 000489 .... GUYMAN, JANE, WILLIAM 08/02/1881
RDV 000490 .... YEAMANS, JOSEPH 08/02/1881
RDV 000491 .... SALINAS, PABLO 08/02/1881
RDV 000492 .... QUINN, PATRICK 08/02/1881
RDV 000493 .... WOOD, W R 08/02/1881
RDV 000494 .... DEVER, JAMES 08/02/1881
RDV 000495 .... DUNBAUGH, L C, JACOB P 08/02/1881
RDV 000496 .... 08/02/1881
RDV 000497 .... MONTGOMERY, MARY, ANDREW 08/02/1881
RDV 000498 .... BOYCE, ROBERT P 08/02/1881
RDV 000499 .... FISK, SIMONA S, JAMES N 08/02/1881
RDV 000500 .... DOWESS, PHEBE, ISAAC 08/02/1881
RDV 000501 .... ISAACKS, SARAH, WILLIAM 08/02/1881
RDV 000502 .... SMITH, THOMAS J 08/02/1881
RDV 000503 .... BROOKS, GILBERT 08/02/1881
RDV 000504 .... CRAWFORD, ROBERT 08/02/1881
RDV 000505 .... GARCIA, GARZA, ORTIS, DELORES, CLEMENTE 08/02/1881
RDV 000506 .... MIRANDO, FRANCISCO 08/02/1881
RDV 000507 .... PRICE, ROBERT 08/02/1881
RDV 000508 .... MC FADDIN, MC FADIN, D H 08/02/1881
RDV 000509 .... OBANION, JENNINGS 08/02/1881
RDV 000510 .... BRYAN, MOSES AUSTIN 08/02/1881
RDV 000511 .... WALTERS, A C 08/02/1881
RDV 000512 .... ROBERTSON, MARY E, E STERLING C 08/02/1881
RDV 000513 .... MARSHALL, JOHN 08/02/1881
RDV 000514 .... MC HORSE, J W 08/02/1881
RDV 000515 .... BURLESON, AARON 08/02/1881
RDV 000516 .... NUNLEY, ANDERSON 08/02/1881
RDV 000517 .... HALL, H H 08/02/1881
RDV 000518 .... SOWELL, RANSOM 08/02/1881
RDV 000519 .... MILLER, LEROY 08/02/1881
RDV 000520 .... WRIGHT, AMANDA, G W 08/02/1881
RDV 000521 .... DUNCAN, CHARLES R 08/02/1881
RDV 000522 .... KLEBURG, ROBERT 08/02/1881
RDV 000523 .... RUTLEDGE, EMELINE, RICHARD 08/03/1881
RDV 000524 .... FISK, GREENLEIF 08/04/1881
RDV 000525 .... CROCKETT, ROBERT P 08/04/1881
RDV 000526 .... WELLS, THEOPHILUS 08/04/1881
RDV 000527 .... WHITLOCK, ROBERT 08/04/1881
RDV 000528 .... ROBERTSON, J B 08/04/1881
RDV 000529 .... CRAIN, JOEL B 08/04/1881
RDV 000530 .... MOORE, LOUIS 08/04/1881
RDV 000531 .... ERATH, GEORGE B 08/04/1881
RDV 000532 .... POST, JOHN C 08/04/1881
RDV 000533 .... POST, CATHERINE, LEE R 08/04/1881

Republic of Texas Donation Vouchers-Numerical Listing

RDV 000534 .... MILLER, ELIZABETH, WILLIAM H 08/04/1881
RDV 000535 .... GARNER, ISAAC 08/04/1881
RDV 000536 .... JANUARY, JAMES B P 08/04/1881
RDV 000537 .... JONES, GOERGE W 08/04/1881
RDV 000538 .... FRANCIS, MILLER 08/05/1881
RDV 000539 .... REAMES, S Y 08/05/1881
RDV 000540 .... CAMPBELL, CAROLINE M K D, RUFUS 08/05/1881
RDV 000541 .... HAWLEY, WILLIAM 08/05/1881
RDV 000542 .... SWINGLE, LAURA E, ALFRED 08/05/1881
RDV 000543 .... PIER, J B 08/05/1881
RDV 000544 .... POINDEXTER, JOHN J 08/05/1881
RDV 000545 .... REED, NATHANIEL 08/05/1881
RDV 000546 .... STEWART, C B 08/05/1881
RDV 000547 .... WHITE, JOHN C 08/05/1881
RDV 000548 .... ARMSTRONG, CORDELIA, JAMES 08/06/1881
RDV 000549 .... LUDLOW, L W 08/08/1881
RDV 000550 .... HILL, DAVID 08/06/1881
RDV 000551 .... SMYTH, EMELY, EMILY, ANDREW F 08/08/1881
RDV 000552 .... RANDALL, OSBORNE W 08/08/1881
RDV 000553 .... PATTON, MOSES L 08/08/1881
RDV 000554 .... WILLIAMS, STEPHEN 08/08/1881
RDV 000555 .... BYERLY, WILLIAM 08/08/1881
RDV 000556 .... BYERLY, ADAM 08/08/1881
RDV 000557 .... DOOM, R C 08/08/1881
RDV 000558 .... SALINAS, MARIA S, MARGIL 08/08/1881
RDV 000559 .... WILLIAMS, MITCHELL, NATHAN 08/08/1881
RDV 000560 .... YANCY, ELIZABETH, JOHN 08/08/1881
RDV 000561 .... HENDERSON, JOHN 08/08/1881
RDV 000562 .... PALACIOS, JUAN JOSE 08/08/1881
RDV 000563 .... BERRY, JOHN B 08/08/1881
RDV 000564 .... JACOBS, M G 08/08/1881
RDV 000565 .... MORRISON, ANN, GWYNN 08/04/1881
RDV 000566 .... MENEFEE, JOHN S 08/08/1881
RDV 000567 .... MOSS, JANE, JAMES L 08/08/1881
RDV 000568 .... SPARKS, S F 08/08/1881
RDV 000569 .... CAMPBELL, JOHN 08/08/1881
RDV 000570 .... HANCOCK, J W 08/08/1881
RDV 000571 .... WATTS, HIRAM 08/12/1881
RDV 000572 .... DEAN, CALOWAY 08/08/1881
RDV 000573 .... RECTOR, E G 08/08/1881
RDV 000574 .... MC ANNELLY, R D 08/08/1881
RDV 000575 .... HOUSTON, E C, ANDREW 08/08/1881
RDV 000576 .... CLOUD, REBECCA J, J W 08/08/1881
RDV 000577 .... MC CLURE, THOMAS 08/08/1881
RDV 000578 .... SCHLABORN, JOHN 08/08/1881
RDV 000579 .... DAVIS, ELIZA A, E B 08/08/1881
RDV 000580 .... GILLIAM, MARGARET A, L W 08/08/1881
RDV 000581 .... BENNETT, JAMES 08/08/1881
RDV 000582 .... ROUECHE, PETER 08/08/1881

RDV 000583 .... SMYTH, F M, GEORGE W 08/08/1881
RDV 000584 .... HAMILTON, JAMES 08/08/1881
RDV 000585 .... BLAIR, L J, JOHN 08/09/1881
RDV 000586 .... JACKSON, JOSEPH 08/09/1881
RDV 000587 .... WINTERS, LARINIA, WILLIAM C 08/11/1881
RDV 000588 .... PATE, JAME, WILLIAM 08/11/1881
RDV 000589 .... WALKER, SARAH A, JACOB 08/11/1881
RDV 000590 .... BILLINGSLEY, ELIZ A, JESSIE 08/11/1881
RDV 000591 .... HERROW, J H 08/11/1881
RDV 000592 .... HILL, A W 08/11/1881
RDV 000593 .... MC FADDIN, MC FADDEN, ELIZA, WILLIAM 08/11/1881
RDV 000594 .... ZUNIGAS, MARINA, JOSE 08/11/1881
RDV 000595 .... SAVERY, ASAHEL 08/11/1881
RDV 000596 .... HORNSBY, W W 08/11/1881
RDV 000597 .... MC MANNS, R O W 08/11/1881
RDV 000598 .... ARMSTRONG, JAMES C 08/11/1881
RDV 000599 .... NEILL, GEORGE J 08/12/1881
RDV 000600 .... STEPHENSON, E B, J B 08/12/1881
RDV 000601 .... BRUNER, G C 08/12/1881
RDV 000602 .... STANDIFER, J L 08/16/1881
RDV 000603 .... WHITLEY, MARY, JOHN 08/16/1881
RDV 000604 .... RUSSELL, WILLIAM O 08/16/1881
RDV 000605 .... HILL, ISAAC L 08/17/1871
RDV 000606 .... RODERIGUEZ, MARIA JUSUSA, AMBROSIO 08/17/1871
RDV 000607 .... MC KINNEY, SALLIE, ASHLEY 08/17/1871
RDV 000608 .... MC MILLAN, ANDREW 08/17/1871
RDV 000609 .... COLE, SIDNEY L, DAVID 08/17/1871
RDV 000610 .... BUNDICK, CLEMENTINE, THOMAS W 08/17/1871
RDV 000611 .... SCOTT, LEVI P 08/17/1871
RDV 000612 .... SADLER, WILLIAM T 08/17/1871
RDV 000613 .... CUNNINGHAM, JAMES 08/17/1871
RDV 000614 .... NELSON, W F 08/17/1871
RDV 000615 .... LOVE, ELIZABETH M, WILLIAM 08/17/1881
RDV 000616 .... LAWSON, MARY, ISAIAH D 08/17/1881
RDV 000617 .... HOPKINS, REBECCA, JAMES E 08/17/1881
RDV 000618 .... HAMILTON, NATHAN 08/17/1881
RDV 000619 .... SHARP, MINERVA, JOHN 08/17/1881
RDV 000620 .... ELY, JOHN N 08/17/1881
RDV 000621 .... ABLES, J S 08/17/1881
RDV 000622 .... COLLEY, MARINDA, C C 08/17/1881
RDV 000623 .... WADE, NATHAN 08/17/1881
RDV 000624 .... WHITAKER, BENJAMIN 08/17/1881
RDV 000625 .... PHILLIPS, WILLIAM 08/17/1881
RDV 000626 .... LACKEY, JERRISSA, JOHN J 08/17/1881
RDV 000627 .... KARNER, JOHN 08/17/1881
RDV 000628 .... CAMPBELL, A M, D W 08/17/1881
RDV 000629 .... MC ADAMS, JOHN 08/18/1881
RDV 000630 .... JOHNSTON, SOPHRONIA, SOLOMON 08/18/1881
RDV 000631 .... LOVE, MARY A, DAVID H 08/18/1881

RDV	Name	Date
RDV 000632	THORN, JOHN	08/18/1881
RDV 000633	BURLESON, MARILDA, AARON	08/18/1881
RDV 000634	COOPER, DILLARD	08/18/1881
RDV 000635	CASTLEMAN, SOPHRONIA, JACOB	08/18/1881
RDV 000636	GOLDEN, S A, PHILIP	08/18/1881
RDV 000637	PARR, SAMUEL	08/19/1881
RDV 000638	BROYLES, JOSEPH	08/19/1881
RDV 000639	SMITH, LEMUEL	08/19/1881
RDV 000640	ALLBRIGHT, A F	08/19/1881
RDV 000641	MILLER, DANIEL	08/19/1881
RDV 000642	STOUT, B O	08/19/1881
RDV 000643	SMITH, JOHN C	08/19/1881
RDV 000644	MC KNEELEY, SAM W	08/19/1881
RDV 000645	DE LA GARZA, MARSELINO	08/19/1881
RDV 000646	COLLARD, L M	08/19/1881
RDV 000647	STEELE, ALFONZO	08/19/1881
RDV 000648	WALKER, SAUNDERS	08/19/1881
RDV 000649	COLLINSWORTH, S R, G M	08/19/1881
RDV 000650	HANCOCK, GEORGE D, ELIZA L	08/19/1881
RDV 000651	LEWIS, ELIZA J, IRA R	08/19/1881
RDV 000652	CAREY, SETH	08/19/1881
RDV 000653	MC KAY, DANIEL	08/19/1881
RDV 000654	PACE, ELIZABETH, JAMES R	08/19/1881
RDV 000655	FLETCHER, ROBERT	08/19/1881
RDV 000656	DAVIS, E A	08/19/1881
RDV 000657	KELLUM, EMILY, JAMES	08/19/1881
RDV 000658	WILSON, JAMES T D	08/19/1881
RDV 000659	DAWSON, BRITTON	08/19/1881
RDV 000660	COLLARD, J S	08/19/1881
RDV 000661	REED, E B	08/19/1881
RDV 000662	COOKE, COOK, F L	08/19/1881
RDV 000663	MC FADDIN, WILLIAM	08/19/1881
RDV 000664	TOBIN, MARTHA C	08/19/1881
RDV 000665	ENGLEDOW, ELVIRA, CREED S	08/19/1881
RDV 000666	HYNES, JOHN	08/19/1881
RDV 000667	O CONNER, THOMAS	08/19/1881
RDV 000668	CAYCE, MARY F, HENRY P	08/19/1881
RDV 000669	BURCH, JAMES	08/19/1881
RDV 000670	BIRD, DANIEL	08/19/1881
RDV 000671	HALLMARK, SARAH, A M	08/19/1881
RDV 000672	PARKER, LEVI J	08/19/1881
RDV 000673	CHAPMAN, CAROLINE, GEORGE W	08/19/1881
RDV 000674	HARDIN, CYNTHIA, FRANKLIN	08/19/1881
RDV 000675	SINCLAIR, CHRISTIANNA, RESIN	08/19/1881
RDV 000676	EATON, THOMAS H	08/19/1881
RDV 000677	DAVEY, NANCY A	08/19/1881
RDV 000678	CAIN, WILLIAM	08/19/1881
RDV 000679	LUBBOCK, SARAH O, THOMAS S	08/19/1881
RDV 000680	WHITE, WILLIAM	08/19/1881

RDV 000681	PARKER, ISAAC	08/20/1881
RDV 000682	SWEENY, JOHN	08/20/1881
RDV 000683	ADDISON, NATHANIEL	08/20/1881
RDV 000684	MARSHALL, JOSEPH T	08/20/1881
RDV 000685	ROBINSON, GEORGE W	08/20/1881
RDV 000686	GOODMAN, STEPHEN	08/20/1881
RDV 000687	GOODMAN, JOHN B	08/20/1881
RDV 000688	PRUETT, REBECCA, BEASLEY	08/20/1881
RDV 000689	MASSIE, JANE, J W	08/20/1881
RDV 000690	BORDEN, JOHN P	08/20/1881
RDV 000691	ANDERSON, WASHINGTON	08/19/1881
RDV 000692	GIBSON, ELIZABETH, JESSIE	8/20/1881
RDV 000693	CRITTENDON, WILLIAM	8/20/1881
RDV 000694	GILLELAND, DIANNA, JAMES	8/20/1881
RDV 000695	FILE EMPTY	
RDV 000696	FILE EMPTY	
RDV 000697	JOHNSON, MARY E, HEZIKIAH	08/20/1881
RDV 000698	MUMFORD, JESSE	08/22/1881
RDV 000699	EASTEP, ELIZA, DANIEL	08/20/1881
RDV 000700	HARVEY, JOHN	08/22/1881
RDV 000701	MARTIN, THOMAS	08/22/1881
RDV 000702	LONGLEY, CAMPBELL	08/23/1881
RDV 000703	MAYS, ARIE, THOMAS H	08/25/1881
RDV 000704	SCOTT, M H, JAMES W	08/25/1881
RDV 000705	PETTERS, SARAH, JOHN F	08/25/1881
RDV 000706	BEESON, JESSE	08/25/1881
RDV 000707	KELSO, ALFRED	08/25/1881
RDV 000708	COX, SARAH, EUCLID M	08/25/1881
RDV 000709	MUDD, F L	08/25/1881
RDV 000710	DARSH, MARY ANN, EMERY	08/25/1881
RDV 000711	SCOTT, PHILIP B	08/20/1881
RDV 000712	ROGERS, ELIZABETH, FRED	08/25/1881
RDV 000713	ROGERS, SARAH, JOHN K	08/25/1881
RDV 000714	PLEASANTS, GEORGE W	08/20/1881
RDV 000715	COVINGTON, CHARLES	08/20/1881
RDV 000716	GOSSETT, A E	08/25/1881
RDV 000717	MERCHANT, S P, J D	08/25/1881
RDV 000718	MC CLELLAND, SARAH, WILLIAM	08/25/1881
RDV 000719	SORSBY, W A	08/25/1881
RDV 000720	TANNER, CAROLINE, EDWARD	08/25/1881
RDV 000721	TOM, JOHN F	08/25/1881
RDV 000722	SIMPSON, PAMILIA, WILLIAM	08/25/1881
RDV 000723	MC DONALD, DONALD	08/25/1881
RDV 000724	MC NEESE, PARROTT	08/25/1881
RDV 000725	ALLCORN, LYDIA, JAMES	08/20/1881
RDV 000726	HORBOUR, GEORGE W	08/25/1881
RDV 000727	CHAMBERLAIN, WILLARD	08/25/1881
RDV 000728	CLEMONS, LEWIS C	08/25/1881
RDV 000729	GENTRY, F B	08/25/1881

Republic of Texas Donation Vouchers-Numerical Listing

RDV 000730 .... PETTY, GEORGE W 08/25/1881
RDV 000731 .... ANDERSON, E P, JOHN D 08/25/1881
RDV 000732 .... BALCH, JOHN 08/25/1881
RDV 000733 .... BROOKS, GEORGE W 08/25/1881
RDV 000734 .... BLAND, PRESTON 08/25/1881
RDV 000735 .... BRINGHURST, GEORGE H 08/25/1881
RDV 000736 .... WEBB, THOMAS R 08/25/1881
RDV 000737 .... WALKER, WILLIAM C 08/25/1881
RDV 000738 .... EDEUS, SILAS 08/25/1881
RDV 000739 .... WILLIAMS, SUSANNA R, HENRY B 08/25/1881
RDV 000740 .... CUNNINGHAM, L C 08/25/1881
RDV 000741 .... WALKER, MARTIN 08/25/1881
RDV 000742 .... ANDERSON, MARY J, JOHN 08/25/1881
RDV 000743 .... ALAMEDA, ALEMEDA, JOSE 08/25/1881
RDV 000744 .... HOBSON, ELIZA JANE, JOHN 08/25/1881
RDV 000745 .... DUNN, CHRISRINA MONTALVO, JAMES 08/25/1881
RDV 000746 .... DEMORSE, CHARLES 08/19/1881
RDV 000747 .... SNAILUM, THOMAS C 08/25/1881
RDV 000748 .... BLUNDELL, SOLOMON 08/25/1881
RDV 000749 .... LANCASTER, EVA, JOSEPH 08/27/1881
RDV 000750 .... HANKS, W W 08/27/1881
RDV 000751 .... PUTMAN, MICHAEL 09/15/1881
RDV 000752 .... TINDALL, WILLIAM P 10/18/1881
RDV 000753 .... GATES, AMOS 10/19/1881
RDV 000754 .... HEARN, THOMAS B 10/20/1881
RDV 000755 .... HAM, MARY J, L B 10/21/1881
RDV 000756 .... ROBINSON, JESSE 10/21/1881
RDV 000757 .... SOLAN, SAMUEL 10/20/1881
RDV 000758 .... STEVENSON, JAMES P 10/21/1881
RDV 000759 .... SMITH, LYDIA ALMIRA, DANIEL D 10/21/1881
RDV 000760 .... TIBBLES, FREDRICK A 10/21/1881
RDV 000761 .... WEATHERRED, MARY A, WILLIAM C 10/21/1881
RDV 000762 .... STRAPP, R A, WILLIAM P 10/21/1881
RDV 000763 .... BROWNING, H H, GEORGE W 10/21/1881
RDV 000764 .... KEAGHEY, WILLIAM S 10/21/1881
RDV 000765 .... HOLLIEN, HULDA, JOHN F 10/21/1881
RDV 000766 .... ALLAN, CATHARINE, JAMES C 10/21/1881
RDV 000767 .... WHEELER, PEGGY, ELIJAH 10/21/1881
RDV 000768 .... WILLIAMS, HENRY 10/21/1881
RDV 000769 .... WINTERS, JAMES W 10/21/1881
RDV 000770 .... DUNBAR, CAROLINE, WILLIAM 10/21/1881
RDV 000771 .... HOLDERNESS, S M 10/21/1881
RDV 000772 .... IRVINE, W D 10/21/1881
RDV 000773 .... BURCH, VALENTINE 10/21/1881
RDV 000774 .... PIERSON, JOHN HOGUE, NANCY 10/21/1881
RDV 000775 .... MC LAIN, RACHEL A, HARRISON 10/21/1881
RDV 000776 .... BARROW, REUBEN 10/21/1881
RDV 000777 .... ALLCORN, JULIA 10/24/1881
RDV 000778 .... DALLAS, J L 10/24/1881

Voucher	Name	Date
RDV 000779	FAGAN, ELLEN, JOHN	10/24/1881
RDV 000780	BOWMAN, JOHN J	10/24/1881
RDV 000781	GRIMES, RUFUS	10/24/1881
RDV 000782	MC INTIRE, ROBERT	10/24/1881
RDV 000783	PERRY, W M	10/24/1881
RDV 000784	CROWNOVER, LAVINIA, ARTER	10/24/1881
RDV 000785	BELCHER, BARSHEBA, ISAM G	10/24/1881
RDV 000786	HOTCHKISS, RINALDO	10/24/1881
RDV 000787	SCHURLOCK, WILLIAM	10/24/1881
RDV 000788	WHEELOCK, MARY P, E L R	10/24/1881
RDV 000789	WHEELOCK, G R	10/24/1881
RDV 000790	RICHARDS, WILLIAM B	10/24/1881
RDV 000791	MATHEWS, LOUISA, THOMAS	10/24/1881
RDV 000792	UNDERHILL, DANIEL M	10/24/1881
RDV 000793	STEBBENS, ELIZABETH, CHARLES	10/24/1881
RDV 000794	MATTHEWS, M W	10/24/1881
RDV 000795	PERRY, ALBERT	10/24/1881
RDV 000796	COLLINS, BELA	10/24/1881
RDV 000797	BURKE, SUSAN, BENJAMIN	10/24/1881
RDV 000798	RICKS, G W	10/24/1881
RDV 000799	JOHNSON, ELIZABETH, FRANCIS	10/24/1881
RDV 000800	BUMSTEAD, M W	10/24/1881
RDV 000801	WARD, AZUBA, RUSSELL	10/25/1881
RDV 000802	COLLARD, J H	10/30/1881
RDV 000803	YOUNG, JAMES	10/27/1881
RDV 000804	MC COY, MARTHA, WILLAIM	10/27/1881
RDV 000805	GILBERT, MARTHA, JOHN F	10/27/1881
RDV 000806	HALEY, CHARLES	10/27/1881
RDV 000807	GUEST, J J	10/27/1881
RDV 000808	LITTLE, HIRAM	10/27/1881
RDV 000809	MC CORMICK, MICHAEL, EXELINE	10/27/1881
RDV 000810	HENDRICKS, LOUIISA S, THOMAS	10/28/1881
RDV 000811	HOOPER, A L, BENJAMIN FRANK	10/28/1881
RDV 000812	PHILLIPS, BENNETT	10/28/1881
RDV 000813	SHAW, G C	10/28/1881
RDV 000815	MC CROCKLIN, JESSE L	10/28/1881
RDV 000816	TEAL, ANNA	10/28/1881
RDV 000817	STUTEVILLE, JAMES C	10/28/1881
RDV 000818	DIKES, M W	10/28/1881
RDV 000819	WILLIAMS, AMANDA	10/28/1881
RDV 000820	BYFIELD, LUCINDA, HOLMES	10/28/1881
RDV 000821	TYLER, C C	10/28/1881
RDV 000822	STEPHENSON, JAMES	10/28/1881
RDV 000823	HARWOOD, JOHN	10/28/1881
RDV 000824	HARDIN, W B	10/28/1881
RDV 000825	HOLSHOUSEN, C	10/28/1881
RDV 000826	BURDITT, W B	10/28/1881
RDV 000827	SHERER, BERNARD	10/28/1881
RDV 000828	FISHER, WILLMIRTH	10/28/1881

Republic of Texas Donation Vouchers-Numerical Listing

RDV 000829	LEMON, JOHN	10/28/1881
RDV 000830	HENSLEY, JUANA, JACKSON	10/28/1881
RDV 000831	ETHERIDGE, HOWARD	10/28/1881
RDV 000832	JOHNSON, JOHN R, BETHANY	10/28/1881
RDV 000833	SHAW, C A, JAMES	10/28/1881
RDV 000834	ZUMWALT, ANDREW	10/28/1881
RDV 000835	GOSSETT, J V D	10/28/1881
RDV 000836	DUNLAVY, ILIONE C, ALEXANDER	10/28/1881
RDV 000837	GARRETT, LAVISA, THOMAS B	10/28/1881
RDV 000838	KING, EMILY W, CHARLES F	10/28/1881
RDV 000839	POOL, JONATHAN C	10/28/1881
RDV 000840	CALLIHAN, JOHANNA F, THOMAS J	10/28/1881
RDV 000841	DINSMORE, SILAS, AMANDA	10/28/1881
RDV 000842	ALEXANDER, JANE G, LYMAN W	10/28/1881
RDV 000843	PRESCOTT, CHARLES	10/28/1881
RDV 000844	JORDAN, STACEY ANN	10/28/1881
RDV 000845	AMSLER, MARY, CHARLES	10/28/1881
RDV 000846	DUNN, LOUISA, MATTHEW	10/28/1881
RDV 000847	BARTLETT, JOSEPH C	10/28/1881
RDV 000848	SHELTON, GEORGE W	10/28/1881
RDV 000849	DIKES, LEWIS P	10/28/1881
RDV 000850	GORMAN, JAMES P	10/28/1881
RDV 000851	CORONER, MARY, EVIN, EVAN	10/28/1881
RDV 000852	STODDARD, JANE, J W	10/28/1881
RDV 000853	TOWNSEND, MARY ANN, MOSES	10/28/1881
RDV 000854	MC KISICK, JOHN W	10/28/1881
RDV 000855	BENNETT, MILES	10/28/1881
RDV 000856	JONES, KEETON M	10/29/1881
RDV 000857	BASS, ARCHIBALD	10/29/1881
RDV 000858	MC MAHAN, JAMES B	10/29/1881
RDV 000859	HOFFMAN, PHIBE	10/29/1881
RDV 000860	ROBINSON, ZORASTER	10/29/1881
RDV 000861	SEVIER, G W	10/29/1881
RDV 000862	THOMAS, JULIA A, WILEY S	10/29/1881
RDV 000863	HESSKEW, WILLIAM A	10/29/1881
RDV 000864	WALKER, PHILIP	10/29/1881
RDV 000865	RUDDER, NATHANIEL	10/29/1881
RDV 000866	SINGLETON, JOHN H	10/29/1881
RDV 000867	MOORE, SALLY, SAMUEL F	10/29/1881
RDV 000868	CHISUM, JOHN	10/29/1881
RDV 000869	HYLAND, JOSEPH	10/29/1881
RDV 000870	STEPHENSON, ELISHA	10/29/1881
RDV 000871	COOK, MARY J	10/29/1881
RDV 000872	HALL, JACKSON	10/29/1881
RDV 000873	STEWART, JOHN	10/29/1881
RDV 000874	BERRY, ANDREW J	11/12/1881
RDV 000875	SMITH, JACKSON	11/12/1881
RDV 000876	HULME, W T	11/12/1881
RDV 000877	PATTRICK, GEORGE M	11/12/1881

RDV 000878	FENNER, JOSEPH	11/12/1881
RDV 000879	HITCHCOCK, ANDREW J	11/12/1881
RDV 000880	TUMLINSON, ELIZABETH, JOSEPH	11/12/1881
RDV 000881	WEAVER, L G	11/12/1881
RDV 000882	DYCHES, JOSIAH	11/12/1881
RDV 000883	PRICE, REESE D	11/14/1881
RDV 000884	BLUNDELL, FRANCIS	11/14/1881
RDV 000885	SKILLERN, LUCY W, J C	11/14/1881
RDV 000886	FRIAR, ANNA, DANIEL B	11/14/1881
RDV 000887	HASSELL, REBECCA S, JOHN W	11/14/1881
RDV 000888	WILLIAMS, JANE, L S	11/14/1881
RDV 000889	RECTOR, NANCY H, CLAIBORNE	11/14/1881
RDV 000890	DORSETT, T M	11/14/1881
RDV 000891	IIAMS, JOHN	11/14/1881
RDV 000892	ROBINSON, FRANCIS	11/15/1881
RDV 000893	WOOD, JOHN H	11/15/1881
RDV 000894	STEPHENSON, IRA	11/15/1881
RDV 000895	CERVANTES, AGAJITO	11/17/1881
RDV 000896	BOONE, NANCY, GARRETT E	11/19/1881
RDV 000897	DODSON, A B	11/28/1881
RDV 000898	ROWE, MYRA, JAMES	11/28/1881
RDV 000899	RUPLEY, WILLIAM	12/06/1881
RDV 000900	LATHAM, KING H	12/24/1881
RDV 000901	PAYNE, FLORINDA, THOMAS P	01/03/1882
RDV 000902	HARBOUR, JAMES M	01/07/1882
RDV 000903	MURRAY, JOHN B	01/09/1882
RDV 000904	FULSHEAR, CHURCHILL	01/14/1882
RDV 000905	YARBOROUGH, P C, RANDOLPH	01/14/1882
RDV 000906	LEWIS, WILLIAM MC T	01/24/1882
RDV 000907	MANGUM, A S	01/24/1882
RDV 000908	PATTON, A B	04/18/1882
RDV 000909	NEVILL, HARDIN	04/18/1882
RDV 000910	VERNE, HENRY, ROSANNA	04/19/1882
RDV 000911	PAMELL, SARAH A, HUGH G	04/19/1882
RDV 000912	ASHWORTH, MARY, AARON	04/19/1882
RDV 000913	CHERRY, JOHN	04/19/1882
RDV 000914	FULLERTON, NANCY, HENRY	04/19/1882
RDV 000915	CHERRY, ELAN, WILLIAM	04/19/1882
RDV 000916	FIELDS, SARAH, ISAIAH S	04/19/1882
RDV 000917	HARBOUR, JAMES M	04/27/1882
RDV 000918	HUNTER, ROBERT H	04/19/1882
RDV 000919	PARKER, L E, JAMES W	04/19/1882
RDV 000920	OWENS, M A	04/19/1882
RDV 000921	GREEN, MATILDA, DAVID G	04/19/1882
RDV 000922	HARDIN, MILTON A	04/19/1882
RDV 000923	PEARMAN, M, GEORGE	04/19/1882
RDV 000924	DUNMAN, JAMES T	04/19/1882
RDV 000925	BURLESON, NANCY B, JONATHAN	04/19/1882
RDV 000926	MIDDLETON, ROBERT	04/19/1882

Republic of Texas Donation Vouchers-Numerical Listing

RDV 000927 .... ALLEN, BENJAMIN 04/20/1882
RDV 000928 .... BEATY, RACHAEL, JOHN B 04/20/1882
RDV 000929 .... DUNCAN, REBECCA 04/20/1882
RDV 000930 .... DENMAN, JANE, OBEDIAH 04/20/1882
RDV 000931 .... HARRISON, ANN C, W D F 04/21/1882
RDV 000932 .... EDWARDS, AMANDA M E 04/21/1882
RDV 000933 .... LAMBERT, THOMASA G, WALTER 04/21/1882
RDV 000934 .... GARCIA, SIMON 04/21/1882
RDV 000935 .... TREVINO, ANTONIO 04/21/1882
RDV 000936 .... SHIVERS, CATHERINE O, L 04/21/1882
RDV 000937 .... MCLENNAN, JOHN 04/21/1882
RDV 000938 .... NORRIS, E MRS 04/21/1882
RDV 000939 .... CLAPP, ELI 04/21/1882
RDV 000940 .... SADDLER, JOHN 04/21/1882
RDV 000941 .... BATES, SILAS H 04/21/1882
RDV 000942 .... HALL, L L, JOHN L 04/21/1882
RDV 000943 .... THOMAS, JAMES H 04/21/1882
RDV 000944 .... STEEL, MARY ANN 04/21/1882
RDV 000945 .... KENNARD, W E 04/26/1882
RDV 000946 .... BRYAN, WILLIAM J 04/26/1882
RDV 000947 .... DAMON, SAMUEL 04/26/1882
RDV 000948 .... GILLIAM, ELLEN, RICHARD G 04/26/1882
RDV 000949 .... SYPERT, W C 04/26/1882
RDV 000950 .... POWER, THOMASA, JAMES 04/26/1882
RDV 000951 .... AROCHA, MACEDONIO 04/26/1882
RDV 000952 .... CASIAS, GRAVIEL 04/26/1882
RDV 000953 .... HALEY, CYRENIA, RICHARD 04/26/1882
RDV 000954 .... CRIER, RACHAEL, ANDREW 04/28/1882
RDV 000955 .... EVETTS, SAMUEL G 04/28/1882
RDV 000956 .... MC COY, GREEN 04/28/1882
RDV 000957 .... TEVIS, JANE, GEORGE W 04/28/1882
RDV 000958 .... HIGHSMITH, BENJAMIN F 04/29/1882
RDV 000959 .... JENKINS, J H 04/29/1882
RDV 000960 .... WELLS, S G 05/01/1882
RDV 000961 .... COURSEY, NANCY 05/03/1882
RDV 000962 .... BUQUOR, P L 05/05/1882
RDV 000963 .... BOONE, J W 05/06/1882
RDV 000964 .... BARTON, ELDER B 05/06/1882
RDV 000965 .... RAINES, RHUDY S, JOHN D 05/06/1882
RDV 000966 .... KIZER, P C, B P 05/06/1882
RDV 000967 .... FIELD, JOSEPH E 05/08/1882
RDV 000968 .... CARUTHERS, WILLIAM 05/08/1882
RDV 000969 .... SANCHEZ, ANTONIO 05/10/1882
RDV 000970 .... MC GAHEY, JAMES S 05/11/1882
RDV 000971 .... RAGSDALE, E B 05/11/1882
RDV 000972 .... RAGSDALE, W J 05/11/1882
RDV 000973 .... WHITESIDES, J T 05/11/1882
RDV 000974 .... CONE, SOPHRENIA E, HENRY H 05/11/1882
RDV 000975 .... HENRY, ISAAC R 05/11/1882

Republic of Texas Donation Vouchers-Numerical Listing

RDV 000976 .... HARDIMAN, W P 05/11/1882
RDV 000977 .... WELLS, HARRIETT, JOHN 05/11/1882
RDV 000978 .... ZUMWALT, T B 05/11/1882
RDV 000979 .... TIMONEY, E H 05/11/1882
RDV 000980 .... BANKS, REASON 01/15/1883
RDV 000981 .... HOPSON, LUCIEN 01/16/1882
RDV 000982 .... HARDESTY, MARY F 01/17/1882
RDV 000983 .... DUTY, WILLIAM 11/17/1883
RDV 000984 .... KUYKENDALL, MARIA, ABNER 01/12/1883
RDV 000985 .... LOPEZ, PETER 01/12/1883
RDV 000986 .... LEEPER, HANNAH, SAMUEL 01/29/1883
RDV 000987 .... WILLIAMS, JAMES 01/12/1883
RDV 000988 .... EVANS, WILLIAM T 01/29/1883
RDV 000989 .... LONGBOTHAM, R B 01/29/1883
RDV 000990 .... ALLEN, ELISHA 01/29/1883
RDV 000991 .... YOUNG, JAMES... 01/30/1883
RDV 000992 .... BOX, LUCINDA, JOHN 01/30/1883
RDV 000993 .... DENSON, MARY, C 01/30/1883
RDV 000994 .... FREDERICKS, JOHN G 01/30/1883
RDV 000995 .... BARCLAY, ANDERSON 01/30/1883
RDV 000996 .... THOMPSON, SINGLETON, CLARINDA 01/30/1883
RDV 000997 .... WELLS, M G, WAYMAN F 01/12/1883
RDV 000998 .... BUTLER, H M H 01/30/1883
RDV 000999 .... PEBBLES, R R 01/30/1883
RDV 001000
RDV 001001 .... WILLIAMS, REBECCA, RICHARD 01/30/1883
RDV 001002 .... ANDERSON, JOHN W 01/30/1883
RDV 001003 .... HALLMARK, WILLIAM C, ELIZABETH 01/30/1883
RDV 001004 .... READ, THOMAS J 02/01/1883
RDV 001005 .... DUNCAN, CHARLES 02/01/1883
RDV 001006 .... WYNNE, A J, R H 02/01/1883
RDV 001007 .... TOWNSEND, L H, SPENCER 02/03/1883
RDV 001008 .... GATES, W N 02/03/1883
RDV 001009 .... WHITE, K BINGHAM 02/10/1883
RDV 001010 .... GAHAGAN, MARGARET, JAMES 02/10/1883
RDV 001011 .... BROWN, RICHARD 02/10/1883
RDV 001012 .... VANSICKLE, MARY A, E S 02/10/1883
RDV 001013 .... RAMSEY, MARGARET, MARTIN 02/10/1883
RDV 001014 .... SMITH, BETHEL 02/10/1883
RDV 001015 .... WICKSON, CYRUS 02/10/1883
RDV 001016 .... GARNER, JOHN 02/21/1883
RDV 001017 .... KENDALL, PETER 02/21/1883
RDV 001018 .... SMITH, MANAAN 02/21/1883
RDV 001019 .... TAYLOR, CREED 02/24/1883
RDV 001020 .... SMITH, JULIA, WILEY 03/09/1883
RDV 001021 .... MATTHEWS, R H 03/09/1883
RDV 001022 .... KENNARD, A D 03/09/1883
RDV 001023 .... CALLAHAN, JOHN H 03/09/1883
RDV 001024 .... MILLETT, CLEMINTINA, SAMUEL 03/19/1883

RDV 001025	DUVAL, JOHN C	03/14/1883
RDV 001026	GOOD, JULIA A, HANNIBAL	03/22/1883
RDV 001027	MANGEL, PROSPER	03/23/1883
RDV 001028	WARE, JOSEPH	03/23/1883
RDV 001029	HEFFLINGER, JAMES	04/07/1883
RDV 001030	HALL, R A, W A	04/07/1883
RDV 001031	IDEN, NANCY A	04/07/1883
RDV 001032	THOMPSON, M M, JESSE G	04/07/1883
RDV 001033	ANGLIN, MARY L, ABRAM	04/07/1883
RDV 001034	DOYLE, MATTHEW A	04/07/1883
RDV 001035	GARNER, MATILDA, DAVID	04/07/1883
RDV 001036	ANTHONY, RODNEY	04/07/1883
RDV 001037	JOHNSON, WILLIAM	04/07/1883
RDV 001038	CABASES, ALBENO	04/11/1883
RDV 001039	HARPER, N J, B J	04/11/1883
RDV 001040	LAMAR, HENRIETTA, M B	04/11/1883
RDV 001041	BARROW, BENJAMIN	04/24/1883
RDV 001042	WHEAT, R S	04/24/1883
RDV 001043	CRIBS, HARRY	04/24/1883
RDV 001044	CHERRY, LAURA, AARON	04/24/1883
RDV 001045	HOLLOWAY, SIMPSON	05/08/1883
RDV 001046	WHITE, WILLIAM	05/08/1883
RDV 001047	ISAACS, SICIEY, A J	05/15/1883
RDV 001048	JOHNES, M A, A H	05/15/1883
RDV 001049	BLOODGOOD, LEVICY, WILLIAM	05/15/1883
RDV 001050	HEALER, JOHN W	05/15/1883
RDV 001051	HAWKINS, WILLIAM	05/15/1883
RDV 001052	MILLER, NANCY C, WILLIAM	05/15/1883
RDV 001053	WYLY, JOSEPHINE L, ALFRED H	05/15/1883
RDV 001054	CHISOLM, MARY A, ENOCH P	05/15/1883
RDV 001055	HARDEMAN, OWEN B	05/15/1883
RDV 001056	BELL, NANCY M, THOMAS B	07/07/1883
RDV 001057	CLEMONS, AUSTIN	07/07/1883
RDV 001058	VOCHARY, MARY J, JOHN	07/07/1883
RDV 001059	COLEB, HOLLOWAY	07/07/1883
RDV 001060	EVANS, J, WILLIAM G	07/07/1883
RDV 001061	FERGUSON, MARY, ALSTON	07/07/1883
RDV 001062	BRAY, JOHN L	07/07/1883
RDV 001063	THOMASON, S E, WILLIAM C	07/07/1883
RDV 001064	CLARK, ABI, JOHN	07/07/1883
RDV 001065	SMITH, WILLIAM	07/07/1883
RDV 001066	WILBURN, RUTHA	07/07/1883
RDV 001067	SPARKS, W F	07/28/1883
RDV 001068	BOWMAN, N, JOSEPH	07/28/1883
RDV 001069	MORRISS, MINERVA, RISTON	07/28/1883
RDV 001070	ALLEN, NANCY	07/28/1883
RDV 001071	BREWTON, DAVID	11/15/1883
RDV 001072	WALTERS, JACOB	11/15/1883
RDV 001073	EUBANKS, E N	11/15/1883

RDV 001074	PECK, BARTON, FRANCIS C	11/15/1883
RDV 001075	PREWITT, SARAH H	11/15/1883
RDV 001076	WALTERS, SARAH	11/15/1883
RDV 001077	HILL, WILLIAM C J	11/15/1883
RDV 001078	ALLEN, JOHN	11/15/1883
RDV 001079	MONEY, A M	11/16/1883
RDV 001080	ELEPHANE, HECK	11/16/1883
RDV 001081	MARTIN, MARY A	11/16/1883
RDV 001082	LEWIS, NANCY	11/16/1883
RDV 001083	JOWELL, ELGIRA	11/16/1883
RDV 001084	BRINGHAM, MARGARET	11/16/1883
RDV 001085	DUGAT, JOSEPH L	11/16/1883
RDV 001086	CLANTON, PATIENCE	11/16/1883
RDV 001087	TODD, MARTHA ANN	11/23/1883
RDV 001088	PERKINS, MARY S	01/14/1884
RDV 001089	BOON, N	01/17/1884
RDV 001090	HENDRY, JOHN	01/17/1884
RDV 001091	HOLDERMAN, DAVID	01/17/1884
RDV 001092	WILLIAMS, WILLIAM	05/08/1884
RDV 001093	DE GOMEZ, CONCEPTION L	05/08/1884
RDV 001094	LOWE, M A	05/08/1884
RDV 001095	GLARY, REBECCA	05/08/1884
RDV 001096	MILLICAN, WILLIS	05/08/1884
RDV 001097	MORGAN, JOHN D	05/08/1884
RDV 001098	CHARLES, ELIZABETH J	05/08/1884
RDV 001099	GIBSON, ABSOLOM	05/08/1884
RDV 001100	HAWFORD, HENRY	05/08/1884
RDV 001101	JOHNSON, JOHN	05/08/1884
RDV 001102	DE SEAL, CASIMIRA C	05/09/1884
RDV 001103	ROSS, RICHARD	05/08/1884
RDV 001104	SELMAN, WESLEY	05/08/1884
RDV 001105	HELEY, MARY	05/08/1884
RDV 001106	SEESOM, ELIZABETH	05/14/1884
RDV 001107	MC GOWN, E J	05/15/1884
RDV 001108	MC LEOD, DANIEL	05/15/1884
RDV 001109	WHITE, ELIZABETH	05/21/1884
RDV 001110	ASHWORTH, DELAIDE	05/21/1884
RDV 001111	BERRY, HENRIETTA	05/21/1884
RDV 001112	SHORT, MARSHALL H	05/23/1884
RDV 001113	COLLINS, D J	08/02/1884
RDV 001114	ALLEY, NANCY	09/25/1884
RDV 001115	DANIEL, CYNTHIA	09/25/1884
RDV 001116	DRUMMOND, WESLEY	09/25/1884
RDV 001117	MARTIN, LISEY	09/25/1884
RDV 001118	ROLESTON, ELIZA	09/25/1884
RDV 001119	STANLEY, MARY	09/25/1884
RDV 001120	WILLIAMS, EDWARD	09/25/1884
RDV 001121	HOOD, MARY A	10/03/1884
RDV 001122	BLAND, SUSANNA	10/03/1884

Republic of Texas Donation Vouchers-Numerical Listing

RDV 001123	CRAFT, JOHN C	10/03/1884
RDV 001124	HARDIMIN, JOHN M	10/03/1884
RDV 001125	HENSLEY, SALLY	10/03/1884
RDV 001126	FARLEY, MASSILLON	01/13/1885
RDV 001127	ALEXANDER, AREA	01/14/1885
RDV 001128	ROBERTS, CHARLES	01/14/1885
RDV 001129	MOTT, GORDON N	01/15/1885
RDV 001130	MILLER, WILLIAM	01/15/1885
RDV 001131	HEARLEY, JULIAN	01/15/1885
RDV 001132	HARMON, JOHN A	01/17/1885
RDV 001133	LUCHENBACH, JAMES L	01/20/1885
RDV 001134	WILLIAMS, MARY	01/20/1885
RDV 001135	BECKNELL, MELINDA	01/20/1885
RDV 001136	BOX, M E, STILWELL	01/20/1885
RDV 001137	SMITH, WILLIAM J	01/20/1885
RDV 001138	DUPUY, MATILDA, JOHN B	01/20/1885
RDV 001139	ELLIOT, ANN, JAMES F	01/20/1885
RDV 001140	SINCLAIR, JOHN	01/20/1885
RDV 001141	DE GAYTAN, MICAELA LOSO A, AGAPITO	01/20/1885
RDV 001142	RUSSELL, ALEXANDER	01/20/1885
RDV 001143	BROWN, WILLIAM S	01/20/1885
RDV 001144	LEWIS, MARY, WILLIAM	01/20/1885
RDV 001145	SKIDMORE, ANN M	01/20/1885
RDV 001146	TANDY, SARAH A, ALBERT M	01/20/1885
RDV 001147	TOLIVER, MARY, GEORGE W	01/20/1885
RDV 001148	WICKSON, CHARITY FRANCIS, DYRUM	01/20/1885
RDV 001149	TOWNSEND, M	01/20/1885
RDV 001150	MC KINNEY, ADALINE, DANIEL	01/23/1885
RDV 001151	ATKINSON, MARGARET, JESSE B	01/23/1885
RDV 001152	CAMPBELL, MILLIE	01/24/1885
RDV 001153	CRONEA, CHARLES	01/24/1885
RDV 001154	GARNER, JACOB H	01/24/1885
RDV 001155	MORRIS, REBECCA ANN	01/24/1885
RDV 001156	ROGERS, L M	01/24/1885
RDV 001157	HARPER, EVALINA, JOHN	01/24/1885
RDV 001158	CHERRY, CATHERINE	01/24/1885
RDV 001159	GREGG, CLARK	03/13/1885
RDV 001160	DE RUBIO, PETRA VELA	03/14/1885
RDV 001161	HODGES, L J, JAMES	03/14/1885
RDV 001162	DAVIS, SARAH, G W	03/14/1885
RDV 001163	ENGLISH, LUCINDA, JAMES	03/14/1885
RDV 001164	REED, MILES	03/14/1885
RDV 001165	SMATHERS, NANCY	03/14/1885
RDV 001166	BLANTON, JACOB	03/14/1885
RDV 001167	PRITTLE, WILLIAM J	03/14/1885
RDV 001168	BEST, LUCINDA	03/14/1885
RDV 001169	FREEMAN, THOMAS	03/14/1885
RDV 001170	GUEST, SARAH ANN	03/14/1885
RDV 001171	COCKRELL, SIMON	07/25/1885

Voucher	Name	Date
RDV 001172	COY, MARTHA J	07/24/1885
RDV 001173	JACKSON, ANNA	07/24/1885
RDV 001174	MORRISON, MARY	07/24/1885
RDV 001175	SANDERS, JOHN	07/24/1885
RDV 001176	BECKNELL, JOHN	07/30/1885
RDV 001177	CAYCE, JOHN M	07/30/1885
RDV 001178	HUGHES, B F	07/30/1885
RDV 001179	RUYLE, SOLOMON	07/30/1885
RDV 001180	MC TAYLOR, JOHN	07/30/1885
RDV 001181	CLARK, ELIZABETH	07/30/1885
RDV 001182	MYRICK, HANAH ELLEN	07/30/1885
RDV 001183	ESPINOZA, YGNACIO	11/04/1885
RDV 001184	HENDRICKS, HENDRIX, E	11/04/1885
RDV 001185	KIETH, JOHN HINTON	11/04/1885
RDV 001186	MC GREW, JEFFERSON	11/04/1885
RDV 001187	NUGENT, MARY	11/04/1885
RDV 001188	PILANT, G B	11/04/1885
RDV 001189	RHEA, ELENOR	11/04/1885
RDV 001190	SEATON, ELIZABETH	11/04/1885
RDV 001191	TRIMBLE, R C	11/04/1885
RDV 001192	ALLCORN, T J	11/04/1885
RDV 001193	BEATTY, VIRGINIA	11/05/1885
RDV 001194	FERNANDEZ, ANTONIO	11/21/1885
RDV 001195	DE XIMENES, TEADORA R	11/21/1885
RDV 001196	TOMKINS, SUSAN	11/21/1885
RDV 001197	BUCKLEY, CATHERINE	12/21/1885
RDV 001198	ALLEN, WILLIAM	12/24/1885
RDV 001199	BELL, PETER	12/24/1885
RDV 001200	BELL, SAM	12/24/1885
RDV 001201	DE CASSILLAS, GUADALUPE LUNA	12/24/1885
RDV 001202	COX, JESSE	12/24/1885
RDV 001203	DEWEES, ANGELICA	12/24/1885
RDV 001204	GIBSON, MARY B	12/24/1885
RDV 001205	HARMON, DAVID	12/24/1885
RDV 001206	HUNT, WILLIAM G	12/24/1885
RDV 001207	JAMES, MILBURN	12/24/1885
RDV 001208	LAWRENCE, G W	12/24/1885
RDV 001209	LEWIS, MARY F	12/24/1885
RDV 001210	MADDEN, LUCINDA	12/24/1885
RDV 001211	MOORE, NANCY ANN	12/24/1885
RDV 001212	MORGAN, HAMP	12/24/1885
RDV 001213	OWENS, AMANDA	12/24/1885
RDV 001214	RITCHEY, LOUISA C	12/24/1885
RDV 001215	ROARKE, LEO	12/24/1885
RDV 001216	SMITH, NANNIE R	12/24/1885
RDV 001217	WEST, JEFFERSON	12/24/1885
RDV 001218	MATTHEWS, DENISA	01/09/1886
RDV 001219	CARRO, MARCELIOUS	01/09/1886
RDV 001220	ROBINSON, AMANDA ANN	01/09/1886

RDV 001221	HABERMACHER, STEPHEN	02/20/1886
RDV 001222	HANNUM, A B	02/20/1886
RDV 001223	HARDEN, MARTHA JANE	02/20/1886
RDV 001224	JOHNSON, MATILDA	02/20/1886
RDV 001225	LYLE, JOHN K	02/20/1886
RDV 001226	LYNCH, PARTHENIA	02/20/1886
RDV 001227	WELCH, JEDEDIA	02/20/1886
RDV 001228	WOOD, ALFRED HENRY	02/20/1886
RDV 001229	WALKER, REBECCA	02/20/1886
RDV 001230	HALL, WILLIAM G	02/24/1886
RDV 001231	JEAN, JAMES M	02/24/1886
RDV 001232	LOPEZ, SERNA, MARIA FRANCISCO	02/26/1886
RDV 001233	GONZALES, JUANA	03/04/1886
RDV 001234	DE MATA, JOSEPHA HERNANDEZ	03/04/1886
RDV 001235	RAMIREZ, CARMEN	03/04/1886
RDV 001236	FOSTER, JANE A	03/10/1886
RDV 001237	REYES, ANTONIA	03/10/1886
RDV 001238	DEAN, WILLIAM B	03/10/1886
RDV 001239	WHITE, CAREY	03/10/1886
RDV 001240	WILKINSON, MELVILLE	03/16/1886
RDV 001241	BORDER, C E	05/20/1886
RDV 001242	PETERS, ELIZA	05/20/1886
RDV 001243	HILLYER, WENTWORTH D	05/20/1886
RDV 001244	SWEENY, D F	05/20/1886
RDV 001245	RICHARDSON, WEST	05/20/1886
RDV 001246	HUFF, WILLIAM	05/26/1886
RDV 001247	RUSSELL, LAVINIA E	05/26/1886
RDV 001248	CROPPER, PRISCILLA	05/27/1886
RDV 001249	STOUT, HENRY	05/27/1886
RDV 001250	WARD, CAROLINE E	05/27/1886
RDV 001251	MADDIN, R W	05/29/1886
RDV 001252	DE FARIN, JOSEPHA SEPEDA	06/05/1886
RDV 001253	WADE, RICHARD W	06/05/1886
RDV 001254	WATSON, JOHN M	06/07/1886
RDV 001255	GIDDINGS, NAPOLEON B	03/18/1886
RDV 001256	CANTUN, AGAPITO	06/17/1886
RDV 001257	SALINAS, FRANCISCO	06/19/1886
RDV 001258	DE FLORES, MELCHORA CORTES	06/23/1886
RDV 001259	CLARK, SUSAN	07/01/1886
RDV 001260	PROCTOR, M D	07/01/1886
RDV 001261	RITCHEY, JANE J	07/06/1886
RDV 001262	PARKER, N A	10/02/1886
RDV 001263	MC KINZIE, CLARISSA	11/24/1886
RDV 001264	ANDREWS, MARTHA E	11/30/1886
RDV 001265	LUMPKINS, MARGARET	11/30/1886
RDV 001266	STAPP, HUGH S	11/30/1886
RDV 001267	DE RUIZ, CARMEN LONGORIA	11/30/1886
RDV 001268	BRITTRANG, THOMAS	12/23/1886
RDV 001269	WOODLAND, HENRY	02/05/1887

RDV 001270	BERRY, N A	02/16/1887
RDV 001271	AMASON, SARAH A	05/05/1887
RDV 001272	PARKER, DRUCILLA	05/05/1887
RDV 001273	WEST, DELANY	05/07/1887
RDV 001274	HANSON, JOHN	05/23/1887
RDV 001275	GRIFFIN, MARY ELIZABETH	05/23/1887
RDV 001276	PEVEHOUSE, DAVID	06/06/1887
RDV 001277	BECK, JOHN	06/06/1887
RDV 001278	HENSON, POLLY	06/06/1887
RDV 001279	ARCHER, ROSA	06/06/1887
RDV 001280	AROCHA, MACEDONIO	REJECTED
RDV 001281	ASHWORTH, DELAIDE, WILLIAM	REJECTED
RDV 001282	ABBOTTS, LANCELOT	REJECTED
RDV 001283	ANDERSON, HUGH	REJECTED
RDV 001284	ALMANAC, BRUNO	REJECTED
RDV 001285	ABLES, MARY ANN	REJECTED
RDV 001286	NANCY, BALLARD	REJECTED
RDV 001287	BARKLEY, CATHREN, RICHARD A	REJECTED
RDV 001288	BARNETT, MARY, THOMAS	REJECTED
RDV 001289	BARROW, REUBIN	REJECTED
RDV 001290	BASQUEZ, ANTONIO	07/15/1881
RDV 001291	BECKNELL, MELINDA L, WILLIAM A	REJECTED
RDV 001292	BEGLY, JOHN	REJECTED
RDV 001293	RUBIO, PETRA VELA, CASIMIRO	REJECTED
RDV 001294	BELDIN, ELIZABETH, S C	REJECTED
RDV 001295	BERRY, SEABORN	REJECTED
RDV 001296	BERRY, SEABORN	REJECTED
RDV 001297	BIRDWELL, GEORGE	WITHDRAWN
RDV 001298	BEVINS, SEABORN	REJECTED
RDV 001299	BLANTON, JACOB	REJECTED
RDV 001300	BLUNDELL, FRANCIS	NO DATE
RDV 001301	BLUNDELL, WILLIAM	NO DATE
RDV 001302	BOONE, J W	NO DATE
RDV 001303	BORDERS, STEPHEN A	REJECTED
RDV 001304	BASQUEZ, ANTOLINO	NO DATE
RDV 001305	BRATTON, WILLIAM	REJECTED
RDV 001306	BROOKS, G W	NO DATE
RDV 001307	BROWN, EDWARD	NO DATE
RDV 001308	BROWN, HIRAM	NO DATE
RDV 001309	BROWN, RICHARD	NO DATE
RDV 001310	WILLIS, BRUCE	NO DATE
RDV 001311	BRUMMETT, HARRISON	NO DATE
RDV 001312	BRUNTON, DAVID D	NO DATE
RDV 001313	BYARS, N T	NO DATE
RDV 001314	BUTLER, H W W	REJECTED
RDV 001315	BURTON, STEPHEN H	REJECTED
RDV 001316	BURNAM, JESSE	NO DATE
RDV 001317	BURK, SUSAN, BENJAMIN	NO DATE
RDV 001318	BRUTON, ELISHA	NO DATE

Republic of Texas Donation Vouchers-Numerical Listing

RDV 001319	CHAMBLISS, S L	NO DATE
RDV 001320	CABARUBIO, JULIAN	REJECTED
RDV 001321	CADENHEAD, JAMES G	REJECTED
RDV 001322	CANTU, AGAPITO	NO DATE
RDV 001323	CARRELLO, MATIAS	NO DATE
RDV 001324	CASANOVA, REMEJIO	NO DATE
RDV 001325	CASTILLO, CAYETANO	NO DATE
RDV 001326	CASTILLO, FRANCIS	REJECTED
RDV 001327	CHAVES, LEANDRO	NO DATE
RDV 001328	CHERRY, CATHERINE, SMITH R	REJECTED
RDV 001329	CHERRY, JOHN	NO DATE
RDV 001330	CHILDRESS, JOHN	REJECTED
RDV 001331	CLARK, SUSAN, HENRY	REJECTED
RDV 001332	CLARK, CAROLINE E, JAMES	NO DATE
RDV 001333	CLARK, L H	REJECTED
RDV 001334	CLEVELAND, ELIZA, J A H	NO DATE
RDV 001335	CLAYTON, JAMES	NO DATE
RDV 001336	COCKRELL, SIMON	NO DATE
RDV 001337	COOK, JOSEPH THOMAS	NO DATE
RDV 001338	CORDOVA, JOSE	NO DATE
RDV 001339	CORNER, EVIN	NO DATE
RDV 001340	COY, ANTONIO	NO DATE
RDV 001341	COY, FELIPE	REJECTED
RDV 001342	CRIBBS, HARRY	NO DATE
RDV 001343	CRUSE, PIETY, SQUIRE	REJECTED
RDV 001344	CURO, MARCELLUS	REJECTED
RDV 001345	DAMON, SAMUEL	REJECTED
RDV 001346	DANNETTELL, HENRY C	REJECTED
RDV 001347	MONTEL, CHARLES SCHEIDE	NO DATE
RDV 001348	DEMOSS, SUSAN, PETER	NO DATE
RDV 001349	DENMAN, JANE	REJECTED
RDV 001350	DEWEES, ANGELINA, W B	REJECTED
RDV 001351	DIAZ, CANUTO	REJECTED
RDV 001352	DICKERSON, ELIZABETH, JAMES	REJECTED
RDV 001353	DIAZ, CANUTO	NO DATE
RDV 001354	DORSETT, T M	NO DATE
RDV 001355	DUNCAN, REBECCA, GREEN B	NO DATE
RDV 001356	DUNMAN, ELIZABETH, MARTIN	NO DATE
RDV 001357	DUPLEX, JOHN B	NO DATE
RDV 001358	EASTEP, ELIZA	NO DATE
RDV 001359	ELIZARDO, TRINIDAD	NO DATE
RDV 001360	ENGLETON, ELVIRA	NO DATE
RDV 001361	FLAVEL, MARY, LUKE M	NO DATE
RDV 001362	FERNANDEZ, ANTONIO	NO DATE
RDV 001363	FLORES, JUAN JOSE	NO DATE
RDV 001364	FLORES, ROQUE	REJECTED
RDV 001365	FORESTER, KIZZIE	REJECTED
RDV 001366	FOSTER, JANE, JOHN	NO DATE
RDV 001367	GAHAGAN, MARGARET L, JAMES D	REJECTED

Republic of Texas Donation Vouchers-Numerical Listing

RDV 001368	GARCIA, REMIGIO	REJECTED
RDV 001369	GARVIN, MARY A, ROBERT	REJECTED
RDV 001370	GARZA, JOSE SIMON	NO DATE
RDV 001371	GARZA, QUIRINO	NO DATE
RDV 001371.5	GASHE, CHRISTINA, GOTTLEIB	REJECTED
RDV 001372	GIBSON, ARCHIBALD	NO DATE
RDV 001373	GIDDINGS, NAPOLEON B	REJECTED
RDV 001374	GILLIAM, M A	NO DATE
RDV 001375	GOMEZ, LUIS	NO DATE
RDV 001376	GONZALES, DIEGO	REJECTED
RDV 001377	GONZALES, RITA ALAMEDA, ANTONIO	REJECTED
RDV 001378	GOODWIN, WILLIAM	REJECTED
RDV 001379	GREEN, MICHAEL	NO DATE
RDV 001380	GOODMAN, J B	REJECTED
RDV 001381	GRIEGO, CLARA	REJECTED
RDV 001382	GUERRA, ANTONIO	NO DATE
RDV 001383	GUERRERA, BRIGADO	REJECTED
RDV 001384	GUERRERO, JOSE MARIA	NO DATE
RDV 001385	GUERRERO, MARCOS	NO DATE
RDV 001386	HABERMAKIN, STEPHEN	REJECTED
RDV 001387	HARDESTY, GEORGE C	NO DATE
RDV 001388	HAMMEL, LUCINDA	NO DATE
RDV 001389	HARRISON, ANNA C, W D F	NO DATE
RDV 001390	HALL, L L, JOHN L	NO DATE
RDV 001391	HALL, WILLIAM	REJECTED
RDV 001392	HOLDEMAN, DAVID	REJECTED
RDV 001393	HAMILTON, JAMES	NO DATE
RDV 001394	HAMILTON, NATHAN	NO DATE
RDV 001395	HANNON, JREIMIAH, JOHN	REJECTED
RDV 001396	HANKS, W W	NO DATE
RDV 001397	HAY, ANDREW	NO DATE
RDV 001398	HECK, MARY E, R D	NO DATE
RDV 001399	HENRY, ISAAC R	NO DATE
RDV 001400	HERNANDEZ, JESUS SR	REJECTED
RDV 001401	HERNANDEZ, MANUEL	REJECTED
RDV 001402	HERNANDES, SANTIAGO	NO DATE
RDV 001403	HICKEY, EDWARD	NO DATE
RDV 001404	HIDALGO, PEDRO	REJECTED
RDV 001405	HIGHSMITH, B F	NO DATE
RDV 001406	HILTON, EMILY	NO DATE
RDV 001407	HUISAR, SEFERINO	NO DATE
RDV 001408	HITCHCOCK, EMILY, L M	NO DATE
RDV 001409	HOPKINS, LUCY A	REJECTED
RDV 001410	HUGHES, BENJAMIN F	REJECTED
RDV 001411	HUNT, WILLIAM	DEAD AT TIME OF APPLICATION
RDV 001412	ISAACS, MARTHA, SAMUEL	REJECTED
RDV 001413	JACKSON, NARCISSA J, JOSEPH	12/14/1885
RDV 001414	JAMES, THOMAS	NO DATE

Republic of Texas Donation Vouchers-Numerical Listing

RDV 001415	JONES, D M	NO DATE
RDV 001416	JETT, ABSOLOM	REJECTED
RDV 001417	JORDEAN, MAHULDA, WILLIAM	REJECTED
RDV 001418	KENNARD, A D	REJECTED
RDV 001419	KENT, DAVID B	REJECTED
RDV 001420	LATHAM, KING H	NO DATE
RDV 001421	LESLIE, ANDREW JACKSON	REJECTED
RDV 001422	LEVEY, JOSEPH S	REJECTED
RDV 001423	LEWIS, NANCY, JAMES B	NO DATE
RDV 001424	LINDHEIMER, F J	NO DATE
RDV 001425	LINDSEY, JAMES	REJECTED
RDV 001426	LINDSEY, P	NO DATE
RDV 001427	LITTLE, HIRAM	REJECTED
RDV 001428	LONG, ANDREW H	NO DATE
RDV 001429	LOPEZ, SIERNA, FRANCISCA	NO DATE
RDV 001430	LORD, GEORGE	REJECTED
RDV 001431	LUNA, DISEDARIO	NO DATE
RDV 001432	MALDONALDO, MATIAS	NO DATE
RDV 001433	MARSHALL, MARY E, THOMAS	NO DATE
RDV 001434	MARTINEZ, MANUEL	REJECTED
RDV 001435	MARTINEZ, FERMAN	REJECTED
RDV 001436	MATA, ANDRES	REJECTED
RDV 001437	MATTHEWS, ROBERT H	NO DATE
RDV 001438	MC CARTHY, EDWARD V	NO DATE
RDV 001439	MC CORCLE, E H, A T	NO DATE
RDV 001440	MC COY, ELIZABETH	NO DATE
RDV 001441	MC COY, PROSPECT	REJECTED
RDV 001442	MC CLELAND, SARAH K, WILLIAM	REJECTED
RDV 001443	MC CLURE, THOMAS	NO DATE
RDV 001444	MC DANIEL, MARY M, GRANGER	NO DATE
RDV 001445	MC DONALD, DONALD	NO DATE
RDV 001446	MC GREW, JEFFERSON	NO DATE
RDV 001447	MC GUFFIN, J F	NO DATE
RDV 001448	MC KINZIE, CLARISSA, ALEXANDER	REJECTED
RDV 001449	MC CLAIN, RACHAEL A, HARRISON	NO DATE
RDV 001450	MC MAHON, ISAAC	REJECTED
RDV 001451	MC MAHAN, SARAH, JAMES	NO DATE
RDV 001452	MELTON, HANNAH B, ETHAN	NO DATE
RDV 001453	MENCHACA, MIGUEL	NO DATE
RDV 001454	MILLETT, C	NO DATE
RDV 001455	MONTOYA, JUAN	REJECTED
RDV 001456	MOORE, WILLIAM H	NO DATE
RDV 001457	MORRIS, MINERVA, RISTON	REJECTED
RDV 001458	MORTIMER, MARY F	NO DATE
RDV 001459	MOTT, SAMUEL	REJECTED
RDV 001460	NICHOLS, FANNIE, JOHN	NO DATE
RDV 001461	NORRIS, E	REJECTED
RDV 001462	NUEVA, JUANA T V, CANDELANA V	NO DATE
RDV 001463	O'HALEY, MARY	NO DATE

Republic of Texas Donation Vouchers-Numerical Listing

RDV 001464	O HANLON, RICHARD	NO DATE
RDV 001465	OLIVA, ANTONIO	NO DATE
RDV 001466	OWENS, RICHARD	NO DATE
RDV 001467	PACHECO, FRANCISCA F, BEURURLADO	REJECTED
RDV 001468	PACHECO, LUCIANO	NO DATE
RDV 001469	PARKER, L J	NO DATE
RDV 001470	PEVEHOUSE, DAVID	REJECTED
RDV 001471	PRICE, H W B	REJECTED
RDV 001472	PRICE, ROBERT	NO DATE
RDV 001473	QUINN, PATRICK	NO DATE
RDV 001474	RABB, MARY, JOHN	NO DATE
RDV 001475	RAGSDALE, E A, PETER C	NO DATE
RDV 001476	RALPH, SOPHIA W, SAMUEL	NO DATE
RDV 001477	RANKIN, ELIZABETH, FREDERICK H	REJECTED
RDV 001478	REAVIS, RIVIS, FANNIE	NO DATE
RDV 001479	REED, ISAAC	NO DATE
RDV 001480	REISINHOOVEN, NAOMI, BENSON	REJECTED
RDV 001481	REYES, DAMACIO	NO DATE
RDV 001482	REYES, JUAN	NO DATE
RDV 001483	REYNA, RAMON	NO DATE
RDV 001484	RHEA, ELEANOR, JOHN R	NO DATE
RDV 001485	RITCHEY, LOUISA C, JAMES M	NO DATE
RDV 001486	RICE, MARIA, WILLIAM	NO DATE
RDV 001487	RIVAS, CAYETANO	NO DATE
RDV 001488	RIVAS, FELIPE	REJECTED
RDV 001489	RODRIGUEZ, JUAN	NO DATE
RDV 001490	RODRIGUEZ, JUSTO	REJECTED
RDV 001491	RODRIGUEZ, SATURNINO	REJECTED
RDV 001492	ROBINSON, AMANDA ANN	NO DATE
RDV 001493	ROBINSON, ZORASTER	NO DATE
RDV 001494	ROGERS, SARAH, JOHN K	NO DATE
RDV 001495	ROUTT, HENRY T	REJECTED
RDV 001496	RUBIO, CASIMIRO, PETRA VELA	REJECTED
RDV 001497	RUIZ, BERNADINO	REJECTED
RDV 001498	SANCHES, CARMEL	REJECTED
RDV 001499	SCARBOROUGH, JANE C, LAWRENCE	REJECTED
RDV 001500	SCOTT, GEORGE W	NO DATE
RDV 001501	SELVERA, PILAR, ENRIQUE	NO DATE
RDV 001502	SEVIER, E G	DEAD AT TIME OF CONSIDERATION
RDV 001503	SCHULTZ, JOHN	REJECTED
RDV 001504	SIMPSON, M E, WILLIAM	NO DATE
RDV 001505	SIMPSON, NANCY, BARTLETT	NO DATE
RDV 001506	SMATHERS, ISAAC	NO DATE
RDV 001507	SMITH, BETHEL	NO DATE
RDV 001508	SMITH, JAMES	REJECTED
RDV 001509	STROUT, JAMES S	NO DATE
RDV 001510	SMITH, LEMUEL	REJECTED
RDV 001511	SMITH, MARTHA ANN, LEROY H	NO DATE

RDV 001512	SMITH, JOYHN ROBERT	REJECTED
RDV 001513	SOWELL, ANDREW J	REJECTED
RDV 001514	SOWELL, RANSOM	NO DATE
RDV 001515	STEPHENSON, ELIZABETH B	NO DATE
RDV 001516	STEPHENSON, HARRIET, IRA	NO DATE
RDV 001517	STEVENSON, JAMES P	NO DATE
RDV 001518	STOUT, HENRY	NO DATE
RDV 001519	SWOAP, MELVINA, B F	NO DATE
RDV 001520	TEJADA, JOSE	NO DATE
RDV 001521	TEJADA, JUANA, GINIO	NO DATE
RDV 001522	TEJADA, PEDRO	REJECTED
RDV 001523	TEJADA, REFUGIA	REJECTED
RDV 001524	TEJADA, SEBASTIAN	NO DATE
RDV 001525	THOMAS, CONSTANTIA A	REJECTED
RDV 001526	THOMAS, THEOPHILUS	NO DATE
RDV 001527	TILTON, ANNIE, CHARLES	NO DATE
RDV 001528	TIPPETT, R J, WILLIAM	NO DATE
RDV 001529	TOMPKINS, A N B	NO DATE
RDV 001530	TUMLINSON, PETER	NO DATE
RDV 001531	TURNER, WINSLOW	DEAD AT TIME OF CONSIDERATION
RDV 001532	URON, ESTEVAN	NO DATE
RDV 001533	VAN VECHTEN, D H	NO DATE
RDV 001534	WALDROP, WILEY, ELIZABETH	REJECTED
RDV 001535	WALLING, MALINDA L, N D	NO DATE
RDV 001536	WALTENS, SARAH	NO DATE
RDV 001537	WALTERS, JACOB	NO DATE
RDV 001538	WADDELL, G W	NO DATE
RDV 001539	WALLING, MARTHA, JOHN C	REJECTED
RDV 001540	WAGONER, JANE, GEORGE	NO DATE
RDV 001541	WEAVER, L G	REJECTED
RDV 001542	WELLS, THEOPHILUS	NO DATE
RDV 001543	WHEAT, ROBERT S	NO DATE
RDV 001544	WHITSTONE, ANDERSON	NO DATE
RDV 001545	WHITING, LOUIS P	REJECTED
RDV 001546	WHITE, KATE, JOHN T	REJECTED
RDV 001547	WHITE, KERR B	NO DATE
RDV 001548	WHEELER, MARGARET, ELIGA	NO DATE
RDV 001549	WILLIAMS, HENRY	NO DATE
RDV 001550	WILLIAMS, JANE, LEONARD	NO DATE
RDV 001551	WILLIAMS, SARAH J, JOSHUA	NO DATE
RDV 001552	WILLIAMS, THOMAS J	NO DATE
RDV 001553	WINN, WALTER	REJECTED
RDV 001554	WILSON, WILLIAM	NO DATE
RDV 001555	WOOD, ALFRED H	NO DATE
RDV 001556	WOODS, ISABELLE, MONTRAVILLE	REJECTED
RDV 001557	WOOTON, GREENVILLE T	NO DATE
RDV 001558	XIMINES, GIL	NO DATE
RDV 001559	YOUNG, JAMES	NO DATE

Republic of Texas Donation Vouchers-Numerical Listing

RDV 001560 .... ZAPATA, GREGORIO .... REJECTED
RDV 001561 .... ZAPATA, SATURINO .... NO DATE
RDV 001562 .... HARDIMAN, E .... NO DATE

The Confederate Scrip Voucher Files, 1881–1883

❧ Concordance to Claims ❦

❧ Alphabetical Surname Index ❦

❧ Numerical Listing ❦

Guide to the Confederate Scrip Vouchers

The original documents are stored in the archives of the Texas General Land Office, the oldest national/state agency in Texas as it was founded in 1835. Microfilm of the originals is available at either the Texas General Land Office reading room in Austin or at Clayton Library in Houston. The concordance below gives the storage box number. All of the originals are now stored in mylar sleeves. Except for cases when the microfilm is not legible, copies made from the microfilm will only be available.

Correct complete citation for documents in the Confederate Scrip Vouchers

[document], [date of document], [Name of Claimant], File No. [file number], Box G [number], Texas General Land Office, *Confederate Scrip Voucher Files, 1881–1883* (microfilm edition; Austin, Tex.: Clayton Library Friends, 2003), roll [number].

Concordance
Box.......... File Numbers

Box	File Numbers	Box	File Numbers	Box	File Numbers
G 59	1 through 62	G 68	649 through 729	G 77	1420 through 1499
G 60	63 through 128	G 69	730 through 819	G 78	1500 through 1582
G 61	129 through 199	G 70	820 through 905	G 79	1583 through 1665
G 62	200 through 268	G 71	906 through 999	G 80	1666 through 1755
G 63	269 through 339	G 72	1000 through 1077	G 81	1756 through 1837
G 64	350 through 401	G 73	1078 through 1159	G 82	1838 through 1927
G 65	402 through 480	G 74	1160 through 1238	G 83	1928 through 1999
G 66	481 through 565	G 75	1239 through 1329	G 84	2000 through 2069
G 67	566 through 648	G 76	1330 through 1419		

Index to Confederate Scrip Vouchers Alphabetical Listing

Grantee's Name	**File Number**	**Description**
ABSHEAR, WILLIAM	CSV 001262	11/23/1881
ACKER, AMOS	CSV 001566	09/12/1881
ACKER, W H	CSV 001270	11/23/1881
ADAM, ANTON	CSV 000857	09/15/1881
ADAM, E R	CSV 000219	07/01/1881
ADAMS, A M	CSV 001719	02/18/1882
ADAMS, T F	CSV 000307	08/08/1881
ADARE, WILLIAM	CSV 001591	11/14/1881
ADEMS, AMMAZILLA	CSV 000022	ADEMS, BENJAMIN, 07/01/1881
ADER, GORDON	CSV 000306	GORDON, L C, 08/08/1881
AGUILAR, NEPOMUCENO	CSV 001395	11/29/1881
AIKIN, J M	CSV 001832	07/12/1881
AILLS, THOMAS	CSV 001920	08/09/1881
AINSWORTH, DAVID H	CSV 001290	11/23/1881
ALDEREHE, JOSE	CSV 001888	01/16/1882
ALEXANDER, H	CSV 000832	09/17/1881
ALEXANDER, J S	CSV 001401	11/30/1881
ALLAN, CHARLES	CSV 001645	02/14/1882
ALLDAY, M A	CSV 000982	ALLDAY, J F, 09/20/1881
ALLEN, ADAMIRAM	CSV 001077	07/11/1881
ALLEN, B F	CSV 000242	07/18/1881
ALLEN, CATHERIN	CSV 001076	ALLEN, BERRY, 07/11/1881
ALLEN, E T	CSV 002052	12/11/1882
ALLEN, GEORGE	CSV 000044	07/11/1881
ALLEN, J E	CSV 002053	12/11/1882
ALLEN, JOHN W	CSV 000222	08/06/1881
ALLEN, MARTHA A	CSV 000270	ALLEN, THOMAS J, 08/08/1881
ALLEN, P M	CSV 000566	08/18/1881
ALLEN, SARAH	CSV 000590	ALLEN, D Y, 08/23/1881
ALLEN, W W	CSV 001576	12/17/1881
ALLISON, RACHAEL	CSV 000390	ALLISON, W M, 07/13/1881
ALLISON, S P	CSV 002055	11/14/1882
ALSOP, MARY	CSV 001357	ALSOP, ARTHUR, 11/16/1881
ALSTON, JAMES NOAH	CSV 001738	03/08/1882
ALSTON, W W	CSV 000004	07/07/1881
ALVERY, D S	CSV 001253	11/14/1881
AMOX, SARAH A	CSV 000214	AMOX, CORNELIUS, 07/18/1881
ANDERSON, A D	CSV 000796	08/08/1881
ANDERSON, CATHERINE	CSV 000899	ANDERSON, WILLIAM P, 09/13/1881

Confederate Scrip Vouchers-Alphabetical Listing

Name	Voucher	Date
ANDERSON, J M	CSV 001907	05/12/1882
ANDERSON, JAMES	CSV 000810	07/25/1881
ANDERSON, M B	CSV 000719	08/08/1881
ANDERSON, T T C	CSV 001879	04/29/1882
ANDERSON, W V	CSV 000427	08/08/1881
ANDREWS, A C	CSV 001670	ANDREWS, HARRY, 02/13/1882
ANDREWS, E B	CSV 001550	11/14/1881
ANDREWS, G A	CSV 001027	10/11/1881
ANDREWS, MARTHA	CSV 001674	02/21/1882
ANGAN, THOMAS	CSV 000180	08/01/1881
ANISWORTH, D G	CSV 001921	05/16/1882
ANNBOYLE, MARY	CSV 001480	12/12/1881
ANSILEU, CLARISSA	CSV 000506	08/20/1881
ARLEDGE, WILLIAM M	CSV 000342	08/08/1881
ARMSTRONG, G H	CSV 000073	07/13/1881
ARMSTRONG, J M	CSV 000557	07/11/1881
ARNOLD, ELI	CSV 001858	04/17/1882
ASHLEY, E P	CSV 001710	02/28/1882
ASHLEY, ROBERT A	CSV 000629	08/08/1881
ASHMORE, M J	CSV 000540	07/14/1881
ASHWORTH, MONROE	CSV 000294	08/08/1881
ATCHLEY, MARTHA	CSV 000077	07/18/1881
ATKINS, W A	CSV 001312	11/14/1881
ATKINSON, LOUIS	CSV 000731	08/11/1881
ATTAWAY, DAVID	CSV 000271	08/08/1881
ATTAWAY, JOSEPH	CSV 001646	02/15/1882
ATWELL, JAMES	CSV 001776	03/28/1882
ATWOOD, C M	CSV 001176	11/17/1881
ATWOOD, MARY	CSV 000020	ATWOOD, THOMAS, 07/02/1881
AUSLEY, J T	CSV 001929	05/18/1882
AUSTIN, J L	CSV 000452	07/01/1881
AUTREY, E A	CSV 001237	11/21/1881
AYER, DAVID	CSV 001644	11/15/1881
AYRES, NANCY	CSV 000602	AYRES, WILLIAM A, 08/23/1881
BABAR, THOS A	CSV 000014	07/07/1881.
BADER, CHRISTINA	CSV 001496	11/16/1881
BAGLEY, T G	CSV 001007	10/01/1881
BAILEY, A E	CSV 000104	07/16/1881
BAILEY, S P	CSV 001506	11/26/1881
BAILEY, SALLY	CSV 001037	BAILEY, AUTHOR NILE, 10/13/1881
BAILEY, TABITHA	CSV 001685	02/25/1882
BAILEY, W G	CSV 002012	09/27/1882
BAINES, J M	CSV 000088	07/19/1881
BAKER, E A	CSV 000589	BAKER, JOSEPH, 07/07/1881
BAKER, FRANKLIN	CSV 001892	03/13/1882

Confederate Scrip Vouchers-Alphabetical Listing

BAKER, G C	CSV 001448	12/06/1881
BAKER, J H	CSV 000075	07/18/1881
BAKER, J W S	CSV 001138	11/08/1881
BAKER, SORILDA	CSV 000024	BAKER, THOMAS, 07/05/1881
BALDEREE, JANE	CSV 000722	BALDREE, STERLING, 08/08/1881
BALDWIN, B J	CSV 000142	07/07/1881
BALL, KENEDY W	CSV 001611	01/23/1882
BALLARD, FRANCIS	CSV 001396	BALLARD, MATT, 11/30/1881
BALLARD, SARAH A	CSV 000554	08/08/1881
BAMPLIN, W A	CSV 000278	07/22/1881
BANDY, PIKE	CSV 001003	10/03/1881
BANKSTON, MARY J	CSV 001754	03/14/1882
BARBEE, A E	CSV 000660	BARBEE, J P, 08/08/1881
BARBEE, JON	CSV 001503	11/16/1881
BARBER, NANCY	CSV 000129	BARBER, GEORGE, 07/18/1881
BARGAINER, VINA	CSV 000450	BARGAINER, JAMES, 08/09/1881
BARKER, HENRY	CSV 000950	09/27/1881
BARKER, S A	CSV 000021	BARKER, A J, 07/01/1881
BARNES, ELIZABETH	CSV 000715	BARNES, ROBERT, 08/26/1881
BARNES, FRANK	CSV 001482	12/13/1881
BARNES, JOSEPH	CSV 000250	07/02/1881
BARNETT, R G	CSV 001049	10/15/1881
BARNETT, W F G	CSV 000539	08/10/1881
BARNWELL, SAMUEL M	CSV 000103	07/06/1881
BARRICK, BYRD M	CSV 000033	BARRICK, S K, 07/02/1881
BARRON, JASPER	CSV 001292	11/23/1881
BARRON, M	CSV 000685	, J J, 08/08/1881
BARRON, MILDRED	CSV 000358	08/09/1881
BARTLETT, L	CSV 002048	06/12/1882
BARTON, ELIZA C	CSV 001569	BARTON, WILSON P, 01/06/1882
BARTON, JOHN M	CSV 000647	07/01/1881
BARTON, LEM	CSV 000326	08/08/1881
BARTON, N A	CSV 001957	02/15/1882
BASHAM, W R	CSV 000787	08/20/1881
BASS, JAMES	CSV 001910	05/15/1882
BASS, JAMES H	CSV 001680	10/01/1881
BASSETT, NOAH	CSV 001167	11/17/1881
BATES, WILLIAM	CSV 002044	11/14/1882
BAUER, ANDERSON	CSV 000861	09/21/1881
BAUTA, WILLIAM	CSV 000434	08/11/1881
BAUTWELL, A R	CSV 000007	07/07/1881
BAXLEY, A E	CSV 000585	BAXLEY, R W, 08/08/1881
BAXTER, S H	CSV 001571	BAXTER, J, 12/31/1881
BAZINETT, S W	CSV 001066	BAZINETT, WILLIAM, 10/11/1881

Confederate Scrip Vouchers-Alphabetical Listing

BEAL, D R	CSV 000223	07/09/1881
BEAN, E M	CSV 000085	07/18/1881
BEARD, JULIA	CSV 000123	BEARD, WILLIAM, 07/11/1881
BEASLEY, F	CSV 001620	01/28/1882
BEAVERS, R H	CSV 000122	07/25/1881
BECKHAM, R E	CSV 001615	01/23/1882
BELCHER, ROBERT	CSV 000687	08/24/1881
BELL, GEORGE P	CSV 000619	08/21/1881
BELL, JACKSON	CSV 000463	08/13/1881
BELLAMY, J F	CSV 000900	09/08/1881
BENKILBACH, GEORGE	CSV 001568	01/06/1882
BENNATT, BEN M	CSV 000852	09/12/1881
BENNETT, R O	CSV 001585	01/10/1882
BENSON, J W	CSV 001153	11/16/1881
BERNAL, LEONARDO	CSV 001668	02/15/1882
BERRY, MILES	CSV 001375	10/22/1881
BERRYMAN, FREDERICK	CSV 001084	08/08/1881
BERRYMAN, H W	CSV 000976	09/26/1881
BEUL, JOHN, BOIL, HONAS	CSV 000846	09/12/1881
BIDWELL, E B	CSV 001739	02/17/1882
BILLS, J W	CSV 000188	07/26/1881
BIRDWELL, B F	CSV 001903	05/04/1882
BIRDWELL, NANCY	CSV 000030	BIRDWELL, J R, 07/11/1881
BIRDWELL, S L	CSV 000423	08/15/1881
BIRMINGHAM, E J	CSV 000079	07/19/1881
BIRMION, W A	CSV 000067	07/11/1881
BISHOP, J B	CSV 001736	02/17/1882
BISHOP, J R	CSV 001173	11/14/1881
BISHOP, M	CSV 001578	07/13/1881
BITTICK, MARY ANN	CSV 001836	BITTICK, GEORGE C, 04/17/1882
BLACK, E M	CSV 000918	09/23/1881
BLACK, SIMEON	CSV 001791	08/09/1881
BLACKWELL, MARY L	CSV 000927	09/24/1881
BLACKWELL, SARAH P	CSV 000259	BLACKWELL, H F, 08/09/1881
BLAIR, CHARLES W	CSV 001392	11/29/1881
BLAIR, J D	CSV 000544	08/22/1881
BLAIR, J J	CSV 001264	11/17/1881
BLAKE, A M	CSV 000184	07/28/1881
BLAKE, JAMES C	CSV 000428	08/15/1881
BLAKELY, S T	CSV 001637	12/31/1881
BLAKWAY, W T	CSV 001123	08/12/1881
BLANKENSHIP, F M	CSV 000990	08/08/1881
BLANTON, W W	CSV 001426	12/03/1881
BLAUD, B F	CSV 000533	08/20/1881
BLEDSOE, E W	CSV 000009	BLEDSOE, JOHN, 07/07/1881
BLESSINGTON, J P	CSV 001630	02/13/1882
BLOODSWORTH, J N	CSV 001400	11/30/1881
BLOUNT, B F	CSV 000601	08/09/1881

Confederate Scrip Vouchers-Alphabetical Listing

BLUE, JNO W	CSV 000297	08/11/1881
BLUNDELL, J A	CSV 000944	09/03/1881
BLUNDELL, MILES F	CSV 000435	08/09/1881
BOASE, W J	CSV 000015	07/07/1881.
BOATWRIGHT, R	CSV 000462	BOATWRIGHT, D T, 08/08/1881
BODINE, SARAH A	CSV 001711	02/17/1882
BOESE, CHARLES	CSV 001210	11/19/1881
BOHAMON, NANCY	CSV 000575	08/22/1881
BOLTON, E W	CSV 001387	11/29/1881
BOOTHE, MARY	CSV 001881	03/14/1882
BOOZMAN, AMANDA	CSV 001091	BOOZMAN, EZEKIEL, 10/17/1881
BORDEN, GEORGE	CSV 001575	11/14/1881
BOREN, FRANCIS	CSV 000119	BOREN, PERRY, 07/05/1881
BOWDEN, W R	CSV 001362	11/26/1881
BOWLES, TOM	CSV 001145	09/20/1881
BOWMAN, W H	CSV 001865	04/20/1882
BOYAKIN, L R	CSV 001878	04/29/1882
BOYD, OLLIVER	CSV 000819	09/05/1881
BOYLE, W H	CSV 000607	08/08/1881
BRACE, JAMES	CSV 001606	12/21/1881
BRACK, HENDERSON	CSV 000843	08/09/1881
BRACKEN, T E	CSV 000408	08/15/1881
BRADFIELD, JOHN W	CSV 000107	07/22/1881
BRADFORD, POWELL	CSV 002013	11/15/1881
BRAGG. W T	CSV 001582	01/10/1882
BRANMONT, JACOB	CSV 000586	08/19/1881
BRANSOM, JAMES W	CSV 000168	07/12/1881
BRANTLY, R A	CSV 001330	11/25/1881
BRASWELL, W N	CSV 000820	09/15/1881
BREWER, ELISHA K	CSV 000924	09/23/1881
BREWER, T E	CSV 001590	07/10/1881
BREWER, WILLIAM M	CSV 001086	10/15/1881
BREWSTER, A M	CSV 000682	BREWSTER, B F S, 08/14/1881
BRIGAND, A L	CSV 000139	07/18/1881
BRIGGS, JAMES	CSV 000800	09/08/1881
BRINLEE, WM R	CSV 000921	08/15/1881
BRISTER, F M	CSV 001608	01/20/1882
BROCK, I N	CSV 001459	11/14/1881
BROIN, P A	CSV 000670	08/08/1881
BRONAGH, WILLIAM	CSV 001826	04/15/1882
BRONLEE, C H	CSV 001864	04/20/1882
BROOKMAN, F C	CSV 000541	08/22/1881
BROOKS, F A	CSV 000432	08/08/1881
BROWN, B W	CSV 000476	08/12/1881
BROWN, CLARISSA	CSV 000310	BROWN, GARDNER, 08/09/1881
BROWN, GEORGE B	CSV 001065	10/12/1881

Confederate Scrip Vouchers-Alphabetical Listing

Name	Voucher	Date
BROWN, H C	CSV 000840	09/13/1881
BROWN, J B	CSV 000811	07/25/1881
BROWN, J M	CSV 000116	07/13/1881
BROWN, JAMES C	CSV 001410	11/14/1881
BROWN, MARY ANN	CSV 000863	09/21/1881
BROWN, N C	CSV 000327	08/12/1881
BROWN, PERRY	CSV 001369	11/26/1881
BROWN, W A	CSV 000946	08/15/1881
BRUCE, J T	CSV 001337	11/14/1881
BRUTON, P J	CSV 001420	11/18/1881
BRYAN, A H	CSV 000477	08/12/1881
BRYAN, JOHN L	CSV 000362	08/08/1881
BRYANT, A H R	CSV 000405	08/09/1881
BRYANT, C C	CSV 001942	05/09/1882
BUCHANAN, AMANDA	CSV 000460	08/17/1881
BULL, I M	CSV 000671	BULL, AUGUSTUS, 08/08/1881
BULLOCH, W W	CSV 001377	11/28/1881
BULLOCK, T T	CSV 000556	08/08/1881
BUMGARNER, TERREASY	CSV 001381	08/09/1881
BUNDRANT, PETER	CSV 000545	08/22/1881
BURCH, B D	CSV 001938	05/09/1882
BURCH, S M	CSV 001939	05/09/1881
BURDEN, CARROL	CSV 001345	11/14/1881
BURDEN, MATILDA	CSV 001267	11/23/1881
BURDETT, AUGUSTA H	CSV 000282	08/01/1881
BURGE, K F	CSV 000519	07/12/1881
BURGER, RICHARD	CSV 001063	08/09/1881
BURGES, WILLIAM	CSV 001229	11/21/1881
BURGESS, R J	CSV 000097	07/13/1881
BURLEW, C K	CSV 000975	08/09/1881
BURNS, J J	CSV 001660	02/18/1882
BURNS, T E	CSV 002021	10/16/1882
BURRIS, HENRIETTA	CSV 000121	BURRIS, L F, 07/23/1881
BURTILLO, ANTONIO	CSV 000708	08/30/1881
BURTIN, JOHN I	CSV 000032	07/11/1881
BURTON, THOMAS F	CSV 000799	09/08/1881
BUSSEY, ELIZABETH	CSV 000027	BUSSEY, THOMAS, 07/05/1881
BUTH, M A	CSV 000558	08/10/1881
BUTLER, JACOB	CSV 001975	06/26/1882
BUTLER, MARTHA	CSV 000204	BUTLER, JAMES, 07/11/1881
BUTLER, WADE H	CSV 000628	08/09/1881
BYBEE, F M	CSV 000244	08/06/1881
CADE, R R	CSV 000972	09/29/1881
CADLE, M A	CSV 001617	01/26/1882
CADWELL, J W	CSV 001226	11/21/1881
CAGE, BENJAMIN	CSV 001708	02/14/1882
CALLEY, JOHN T	CSV 001973	07/071882

Confederate Scrip Vouchers-Alphabetical Listing

CALVERY, J H	CSV 000154	07/24/1881
CALVIN, THOMAS	CSV 001592	01/12/1882
CAMERON, MARY	CSV 000001	CAMERON, ALLAN, 07/05/1881
CAMPBELL, JAMES	CSV 000597	08/15/1881
CAMPBELL, JAMES	CSV 001456	11/14/1881
CAMPBELL, K A	CSV 000199	07/20/1881
CAMPBELL, MARTHA	CSV 000633	07/13/1881
CANEY, LUNA	CSV 000379	CANEY, JOEL G, 08/13/1881
CANLTON, E J	CSV 000897	CANLTON, JOHN, 08/08/1881
CANNON, SARAH L	CSV 001390	CANNON, JOSEPHUS, 11/29/1881
CANON, A L	CSV 000517	08/20/1881
CANTRELL, J L	CSV 000060	07/14/1881
CANTRELL, J R	CSV 000291	08/08/1881
CARAWAY, MARY A	CSV 000672	CARAWAY, N J, 08/08/1881
CARDENAS, NICANOR	CSV 001669	02/15/1882
CARLTON, WILLIAM H	CSV 001129	10/31/1881
CAROUTH, T C	CSV 001223	11/16/1881
CARPENTER, W L	CSV 001655	02/13/1882
CARROLL, A F	CSV 001186	09/27/1881
CARROLL, T M	CSV 001204	11/14/1881
CARTER, E J	CSV 001195	11/18/1881
CARTER, ELBERT	CSV 001473	11/14/1881
CARTER, J A	CSV 000431	08/10/1881
CARTLOW, C B	CSV 001061	09/31/1881
CARTRIGHT, S C	CSV 001032	CARTRIGHT, J S, 10/12/1881
CARTWRIGHT, LEM C	CSV 000484	08/17/1881
CARTWRIGHT, SANFORD	CSV 001603	12/17/1881
CARTWRIGHT, THOMAS	CSV 000146	07/14/1881
CARVER, D L	CSV 001141	CARVER, LEVI, 11/12/1881
CASBEER, J L	CSV 000105	07/08/1881
CASE, SUSAN C	CSV 000459	08/17/1881
CASEY, HUGH	CSV 002006	09/11/1882
CASEY, MARS	CSV 001474	11/19/1881
CASPER, W L	CSV 001239	11/21/1881
CASTELBERRY, ELIZABETH	CSV 001831	CASTELBERRY, JOSHUA, 07/21/1881
CATE, D H	CSV 001999	06/13/1882
CAVINESS, W S	CSV 001181	11/17/1881
CAVITT, M A	CSV 000853	09/20/1881
CAVITT, W A	CSV 001431	11/14/1881
CECIL, WILLIAM	CSV 001972	07/21/1882
CELESTIN, C D	CSV 000915	09/05/1881
CELLUM, E J	CSV 002002	07/11/1882
CERVANTES, JULIAN	CSV 001539	12/29/1881
CHADICK, E M	CSV 000814	09/09/1881
CHAMBERLAIN, MINERVA	CSV 000613	CHAMBERLAIN, NICHOLAS, 08/10/1881

Confederate Scrip Vouchers-Alphabetical Listing

CHAMBERS, N L	CSV 000839	09/18/1881
CHAMBERS, WILLIAM	CSV 001295	11/23/1881
CHAMBLIS, ELKANAH	CSV 001333	11/25/1881
CHAMBSLIP, DELILAH ANN	CSV 000400	CHAMBSLIP, WILLIAM, 08/15/1881
CHANCE, DAVID	CSV 000987	10/03/1881
CHANDLER, L C	CSV 000206	CHANDLER, WILEY, 07/11/1881
CHASHUM, BETTIE	CSV 001403	11/16/11881
CHATHAM, MARY H	CSV 000896	08/08/1881
CHESTER, JOHN C	CSV 000078	07/18/1881
CHILDRESS, T A J	CSV 000481	07/07/1881
CHILES, P J	CSV 000695	08/08/1881
CHISM, W E	CSV 001114	09/26/1881
CHISUM, ELIJAH	CSV 001884	05/03/1882
CHOICE, W A	CSV 001113	08/08/1881
CHRISTIAN, JOHN R	CSV 001124	11/03/1881
CIRVARD, M M	CSV 001478	12/12/1881
CLACK, SARAH F	CSV 001359	CLACK, WILEY, 11/26/1881
CLANK, L J	CSV 001261	11/23/1881
CLARK, J M	CSV 001654	02/13/1882
CLARK, JOHN	CSV 000374	08/13/1881
CLARK, LESTER	CSV 001072	07/14/1881
CLAUNCH, JOHN	CSV 000419	08/10/1881
CLAUSEL, R H	CSV 001193	11/14/1881
CLAY, J M	CSV 000769	09/01/1881
CLAY, M A	CSV 001306	11/15/1881
CLAY, WILLIAM	CSV 000055	07/12/1881
CLEAVLAND, D A	CSV 000148	CLEAVLAND, J W, 07/18/1881
CLEMENTS, A Z	CSV 000548	08/22/1881
CLEVELAND, WILLIAM	CSV 001730	03/16/1882
CLIFFT, J S	CSV 000068	07/11/1881
CLIFTON, LEVIN	CSV 000570	08/08/1881
CLIFTON, S R	CSV 001756	08/09/1881
CLIFTON, THOMAS	CSV 000159	07/20/1881
CLOUD, JERRY	CSV 000520	08/20/1881
CLUCK, R J	CSV 001856	04/17/1882
COATS, HARRIET	CSV 000012	COATS, SAMUEL, 07/05/1881
COBB, AMANDA	CSV 000308	COBB, E, 08/08/1881
COCKBURN, CLARK	CSV 001759	03/21/1882
COCKERHAN, T E	CSV 000384	08/13/1881
CODY, J W	CSV 002054	12/13/1882
COFFMAN, PERMILIA	CSV 000387	07/01/1881
COGSWELL, M A	CSV 001022	09/15/1881
COKER, ALEXANDER	CSV 000752	08/29/1881
COLE, HENRY	CSV 001922	COLE, FRANCIS, 05/16/1882
COLE, JAMES	CSV 000992	08/09/1881
COLE, VINY	CSV 001321	COLE, WILLIAM, 11/1881
COLEMAN, LOUISE	CSV 000525	COLEMAN, J, 07/11/1881

Confederate Scrip Vouchers-Alphabetical Listing

COLEMAN, W G	CSV 001216	11/19/1881
COLESON, ABE	CSV 000951	09/27/1881
COLLIER, JOHN L	CSV 000509	08/08/1881
COLLINS, JAMES	CSV 000552	07/23/1881
COLLINS, R M	CSV 000833	09/17/1881
COLMAN, LOUIS	CSV 000655	08/27/1881
CONDRON, F M	CSV 001310	11/23/1881
CONROY, ANTHONY	CSV 001694	02/15/1882
COOK, F L	CSV 001002	10/04/1881
COOK, HULDAH	CSV 000229	07/19/1881
COOK, NANCY	CSV 001453	COOK, WESTY, 09/20/1881
COOK, REBECCA	CSV 001171	COOK, DAVID, 11/14/1881
COOKE, SAMUEL	CSV 000524	08/08/1881
COOKE, W G	CSV 001687	02/13/1882
COOMER, FREDERICK	CSV 000053	07/16/1881
COON, L W	CSV 001040	10/13/1881
COONER, F M	CSV 000727	09/02/1881
COOPER, HELEN M	CSV 000316	08/08/1881
COOPER, J F	CSV 001537	11/14/1881
COOPER, TALITHA	CSV 000892	07/11/1881
COOPER, TENABY	CSV 001622	01/31/1882
COOPER, W V L	CSV 000264	07/22/1881
COPELAND, SUSAN	CSV 002038	11/21/1882
COPELAND, THOMAS	CSV 000858	09/21/1881
COPELAND, THOMAS J	CSV 001462	12/09/1881
COPELAND, WILLIAM E	CSV 000667	08/22/1881
COPERING, JANE	CSV 001224	11/16/1881
COPPIDGE, MARY	CSV 000704	08/09/1881
CORBIN, D H	CSV 000547	08/22/1881
CORBRIE, G M	CSV 000209	07/15/1881
CORDOVA, MARY A	CSV 001640	02/13/1882
CORLEY, GEORGE	CSV 001612	01/23/1882
CORMELL, ASA	CSV 000538	08/12/1881
CORNELIAS, DANIEL	CSV 001800	04/10/1882
CORTHAN, T C	CSV 000217	08/04/1881
COTTON, J T	CSV 001814	11/15/1881
COUCH, J T	CSV 001471	12/10/1881
COUCH, W P	CSV 001470	12/10/1881
COULSON, O G	CSV 001647	02/14/1882
COUNT, LOUISA	CSV 001353	COUNT, CARL, 08/02/1881
COVIN, J W	CSV 000965	09/20/1881
COWTHORN, M E	CSV 001733	03/08/1882
COX, JOHN C	CSV 001597	01/12/1882
COX, MARY E	CSV 000155	07/11/1881
COY, C P	CSV 001376	11/17/1881
COYLE, EBBLINE	CSV 000054	COYLE, HENDERSON, 07/06/1881
CRADDOCK, E D	CSV 000652	08/27/1881
CRAIG, ALEXANDER P	CSV 001132	11/04/1881

Confederate Scrip Vouchers-Alphabetical Listing

CRAIG, S	CSV 001861	CRAIG, S R, 03/31/1882
CRAVER, JAMES P	CSV 001131	11/04/1881
CRAVY, A J	CSV 002000	08/25/1882
CRAWEN, JOE	CSV 002045	11/18/1882
CRAWFORD, H W	CSV 000875	08/08/1881
CRAWFORD, T K	CSV 000026	07/05/1881
CRAWSON, DELILAH	CSV 000320	08/08/1881
CRESS, ALFRED	CSV 001688	02/27/1882
CRISWELL, D E	CSV 002011	09/12/1882
CROOM, J W	CSV 001120	07/16/1881
CROSBY, MARY	CSV 001723	03/03/1882
CROSS, H	CSV 000595	08/09/1881
CROSS, V A	CSV 001976	08/11/1882
CROUCH, W H	CSV 001964	07/07/1882
CROW, N K	CSV 000746	08/08/1881
CROWDER, G H	CSV 001556	01/04/1882
CRYER, DANIEL W	CSV 000473	08/09/1881
CUDE, W J	CSV 001662	02/18/1882
CULBERSON, D E	CSV 001828	CULBERSON, J W, 07/22/1881
CULLEN, ED	CSV 000185	04/09/1881
CULLISON, J G	CSV 001780	03/31/1882
CULVER, MARTHA	CSV 002022	10/16/1882
CULWELL, A J	CSV 001092	10/25/1881
CUNNINGHAM, JAMES T	CSV 001191	11/14/1881
CUTHBERTSON, C D	CSV 001439	CUTHBERTSON, S J, 11/16/1881
DABNEY, JAMES A	CSV 001627	02/13/1882
DAGANT, JOHN	CSV 001004	10/07/1881
DANCE, JOHN T	CSV 001182	11/17/1881
DANIEL, JOHN W	CSV 002060	09/02/1882
DANIELS, FRANCIS	CSV 000299	DANIELS, GEORGE, 08/11/1881
DANIELS, JACK	CSV 001866	04/20/1882
DANNIELS, SALLIE	CSV 000233	DANIELS, JAMES, 07/12/1881
DARBOSON, MARY	CSV 001179	11/17/1881
DARCY, SAM J	CSV 000089	07/13/1881
DARDEN, E	CSV 001990	08/25/1882
DARK, W G	CSV 000779	08/24/1881
DAUGHERTY, GEO W	CSV 000783	08/08/1881
DAVENPORT, C C	CSV 001393	11/29/1881
DAVENPORT, ELIZABETH	CSV 000323	08/08/1881
DAVIDSON, ELIZA J L	CSV 000047	DAVIDSON, JOHN J, 07/11/1881
DAVIDSON, JNO	CSV 001721	03/01/1882
DAVIS, A M	CSV 001307	11/15/1881
DAVIS, ELIZABETH	CSV 000640	DAVIS, G T, 08/22/1881
DAVIS, H F	CSV 001830	02/14/1882
DAVIS, H H	CSV 001735	02/17/1882
DAVIS, J B	CSV 000945	09/24/1881

Confederate Scrip Vouchers-Alphabetical Listing

DAVIS, JOHN W	CSV 000649	08/26/1881
DAVIS, M E	CSV 000173	07/07/1881
DAVIS, MALINDA	CSV 000378	DAVIS, N L, 08/13/1881
DAVIS, NEWTON	CSV 001446	12/06/1881
DAVIS, RACHEL	CSV 000683	DAVIS, THOS D, 08/24/1881
DAVIS, THOMAS R	CSV 001440	12/06/1881
DAVIS, W C	CSV 000381	08/13/1881
DAVIS, WILLIAM	CSV 001301	11/15/1881
DAWSON, JOHN	CSV 001579	08/31/1881
DAWSON, JOHN	CSV 001824	09/19/1881
DAY, N R	CSV 001757	03/16/1882
DAY, S M	CSV 000135	07/14/1881
DAY, W C	CSV 001557	08/24/1881
DE BLANC, ANNA	CSV 001672	02/21/1882
DEAN, HENRY	CSV 000486	08/17/1881
DEAN, ROBERT	CSV 000034	07/15/1881
DEAN, WESLEY	CSV 000949	09/27/1881
DEATHERAGE, J W	CSV 000925	10/23/1881
DEAVERS, CHESTER	CSV 000359	08/08/1881
DEBORD, R	CSV 001877	11/28/1881
DECHARD, B S	CSV 001500	12/16/1881
DEEL, JOHN W	CSV 000051	07/16/1881
DEFEE, J J	CSV 001941	05/09/1882
DELANCY, T C	CSV 001279	11/23/1881
DELAY, HARRIET	CSV 001073	DELAY, JAMES, 10/21/1881
DENNIH, DAVID	CSV 001629	01/03/1882
DENNIS, ANGELINE E	CSV 000842	08/10/1881
DENSON, N A	CSV 000824	DENSON, W E, 08/09/1881
DENTON, MARY S	CSV 000536	DENTON, TIPTON, 07/28/1881
DENYS, JOHN H, RUDINGER, JOSEPH	CSV 000569	08/15/1881
DERMENT, L A	CSV 001484	11/15/1881
DESHONE, L E	CSV 000806	DESHONE, ENOCH, 09/09/1881
DESKIN, AMERICA	CSV 002046	04/08/1882
DEW, MARTHA	CSV 001039	DEW, B W, 10/13/1881
DEWEES, J M	CSV 001199	11/14/1881
DIAL, H C	CSV 000457	08/16/1881
DIAZ, ALEJOS	CSV 001706	02/27/1882
DIAZ, EMILIA	CSV 001887	02/11/1882
DICKEY, JONATHAN	CSV 001915	05/15/1882
DICKIE, JIM A	CSV 001175	11/17/1881
DILLARD, MARTHA S	CSV 000338	DILLARD, THOMAS J, 08/10/1881
DIXON, JOHN	CSV 001747	03/11/1882
DIXON, WILLIAM N	CSV 001928	05/08/1882
DOAK, J B	CSV 000518	07/12/1881
DOBBS, FRANCES	CSV 001707	02/28/1882
DOHERTY, ELIZABETH	CSV 000212	DOHERTY, JAMES M, 07/11/1881

Confederate Scrip Vouchers-Alphabetical Listing

DOLBY, H L	CSV 001133	11/04/1881
DOMINY, E A	CSV 000251	DOMINY, A B, 08/09/1881
DONAVAN, JAMES	CSV 001996	08/25/1882
DONEGAN, JNO	CSV 000095	07/13/1881
DOOLEY, JOHN E	CSV 001749	03/14/1882
DORSEY, MARY	CSV 001495	11/14/1881
DORWIN, W	CSV 000035	07/09/1881
DOSS, MARY	CSV 000090	DOSS, JOSEPH, 07/18/1881
DOTSON, L V	CSV 000516	08/10/1881
DOUGLASS, DAVID	CSV 001867	04/20/1882
DOUGLASS, W J	CSV 000954	09/20/1881
DRAKE, THOMAS B	CSV 001349	11/14/1881
DU BOIS, LUCAS	CSV 000496	08/08/1881
DUCE, D	CSV 001309	11/23/1881
DUFFEY, JOHN W	CSV 000588	08/08/1881
DUFFY, CLEMINTINE	CSV 001839	07/21/1881
DUKE, JAMES W	CSV 001955	06/20/1882
DUKE, N ELIZABETH	CSV 001545	09/09/1881
DUKE, W J	CSV 000175	07/22/1881
DUNCAN, ADELIA	CSV 000836	DUNCAN, GEORGE CLINTON, 09/13/1881
DUNKAN, JOHN	CSV 001767	03/21/1882
DUNLAP, D C	CSV 000283	08/08/1881
DUNMAN, ALGADA	CSV 000795	08/08/1881
DUNN, CHRISTINA MONTALVO	CSV 000763	DUNN, JAMES, 08/13/1881
DUNN, TELITHA	CSV 000318	04/05/1881
DURFEE, ALVIN A	CSV 001152	11/14/1881
DURRAND, GUS	CSV 001538	12/29/1881
DURRELT, R W	CSV 001042	10/14/1881
DWYER, WALIA	CSV 001734	03/08/1882
DYER, MARY ANN	CSV 000392	DYER, CHARLES, 08/15/1881
EARLES, T	CSV 000503	08/08/1881
EATON, J R	CSV 001768	03/22/1882
EATON, JOEL	CSV 001407	11/19/1881
EATON, RICHARD	CSV 000301	08/08/1881
EAVES, W R	CSV 001718	02/28/1882
EBERHARD, HENRY	CSV 001068	10/19/1881
ECCLES, MARY	CSV 001067	09/01/1881
EDDS, L W	CSV 000862	09/21/1881
EDINGTON, H F	CSV 001553	01/04/1882
EDISON, M T	CSV 001697	02/21/1882
EDNEY, F C	CSV 001001	10/04/1881
EDWARDS, J H	CSV 001742	03/11/1882
EGGLESTON, JOHN	CSV 000352	08/13/1881
EICKE, HENRY	CSV 000288	08/08/1881
ELDER, E P	CSV 000507	ELDER, I J
ELIZA, ASHLEY	CSV 000780	ASHLEY, JOHN H, 08/08/1881
ELLIOT, EDMOND	CSV 001499	12/16/1881
ELLIS, J T	CSV 001282	11/14/1881

Confederate Scrip Vouchers-Alphabetical Listing

Name	Voucher	Date
ELLIS, JOE	CSV 001201	09/30/1881
ELLIS, JOHN R	CSV 001614	01/23/1882
ELLISON, C E	CSV 000500	ELLISON, THOMAS, 08/18/1881
ELLISON, MINERVA	CSV 001497	08/08/1881
ELSON, M A	CSV 001906	05/12/1882
EMMONS, H R	CSV 001519	12/21/1881
EMMONS, MARY	CSV 000966	08/29/1881
EMMONS, RUFUS	CSV 000809	07/25/1881
ENGEL, CHRISTIAN	CSV 001121	11/03/1881
ENGLISH, JAMES D	CSV 001476	09/24/1881
ENKE, AUGUST	CSV 001565	01/05/1882
EPPERSON, JOSEPHINE	CSV 000958	EPPERSON, C N, 09/20/1881
ERCANBRACK, THOS T	CSV 001071	10/20/1881
ERSKIN, JAS D	CSV 000859	07/07/1881
ERVINE, SARAH	CSV 000305	08/08/1881
ERWIN, F M	CSV 000905	09/15/1881
ERWIN, MILES	CSV 000420	08/10/1881
ESHES, EDWARD	CSV 001463	12/09/1881
ESQUIVEL, LUIS	CSV 001599	01/14/1882
ESSARY, L Y	CSV 000469	08/17/1881
ESTES, EDWARD B	CSV 001060	*See* File CSV1059, TODD, W R
ESTES, M J	CSV 001404	11/15/1881
ESTES, WILLIAM E	CSV 000606	08/23/1881
ETHRIDGE, MARTHA	CSV 000866	ETHRIDGE, LEWIS, 08/08/1881
EULAE, JAMES	CSV 000367	08/09/1881
EVANS, C C	CSV 001931	05/10/1882
EVANS, J E	CSV 000397	08/08/1881
EVERETT, ELIZA	CSV 001525	12/23/1881
EVERETT, J C	CSV 000713	08/31/1881
EVERETT, MARY	CSV 001916	05/08/1882
EVERETT, NANCY	CSV 001555	09/09/1881
EVERETT, SAM	CSV 001987	08/16/1882
EVERSBERG, ALBERT	CSV 000019	07/09/1881
EWING, W Y	CSV 000418	08/10/1881
EYRES, GEORGE	CSV 000870	09/09/1881
FAIRCHILD, SARAH E	CSV 000734	09/02/1881
FALL, PHILIP H	CSV 000440	08/16/1881
FARE, ALBERT M	CSV 000346	08/08/1881
FARIAS, JOSE MARIA	CSV 001746	02/16/1882
FARMER, BRYMER J A G	CSV 000574	08/10/1881
FARMER, JOSEPH	CSV 000969	09/28/1881
FARR, JOSEPH	CSV 000851	09/07/1881
FAUBION, HENRY C	CSV 000738	09/03/1881
FAULKNER, VIRGINIA	CSV 000632	FAULKNER, ARCHIBALD, 08/25/1881
FENLEY, C W	CSV 000317	08/08/1881
FERGUSON, W H	CSV 000192	07/07/1881

Confederate Scrip Vouchers-Alphabetical Listing

Name	Voucher	Date
FIELD, D C	CSV 000553	08/22/1881
FILE EMPTY	CSV 000058	
FILE EMPTY	CSV 000527	
FILE EMPTY	CSV 000928	
FILE EMPTY	CSV 000929	
FILE EMPTY	CSV 000930	
FILE EMPTY	CSV 000931	
FILE EMPTY	CSV 000932	
FILE EMPTY	CSV 000933	
FILE EMPTY	CSV 000934	
FILE EMPTY	CSV 000935	
FILE EMPTY	CSV 000936	
FILE EMPTY	CSV 000937	
FILE EMPTY	CSV 000938	
FILE EMPTY	CSV 000939	
FILE EMPTY	CSV 000940	
FILE EMPTY	CSV 000942	
FILE EMPTY	CSV 001105	
FILE EMPTY	CSV 001106	
FILE EMPTY	CSV 001107	
FILE EMPTY	CSV 001108	
FILE EMPTY	CSV 001109	
FILE EMPTY	CSV 001110	
FILE EMPTY	CSV 001246	
FILE EMPTY	CSV 001247	
FILE EMPTY	CSV 001248	
FILE EMPTY	CSV 001249	
FILE EMPTY	CSV 001250	
FILE EMPTY	CSV 001251	
FILE EMPTY	CSV 001430	
FILE EMPTY	CSV 001744	
FILE EMPTY	CSV 001745	
FINCH, DANIEL	CSV 001184	11/17/1881
FINLEY, A T	CSV 001699	02/14/1882
FINN, DENNIS	CSV 001883	08/01/1882
FINNERTY, JOHN	CSV 001772	03/24/1882
FISCHER, H E	CSV 001868	04/22/1822
FISHER, STERLING	CSV 001048	10/14/1881
FITZGERALD, LUCUIS	CSV 001437	12/05/1881
FITZGERALD, MAHALA	CSV 000684	FITZGERALD, J A, 08/08/1881
FITZHUGH, GEORGE W	CSV 001502	11/18/1881
FITZHUGH, LEAL WILLIAM	CSV 001192	11/14/1881
FLEMING, SARAH	CSV 001434	FLEMING, JOHN, 09/20/1881
FLEPPIN, JULIA C	CSV 001018	FLEPPIN, THOMAS, 10/08/1881
FLETCHER, G W	CSV 002004	08/28/1882
FLETCHER, JOHN M	CSV 000128	07/18/1881
FLORES, CARLOS	CSV 001158	11/17/1881
FLORES, JESUS	CSV 002043	11/23/1882

Confederate Scrip Vouchers-Alphabetical Listing

FLOYD, R W	CSV 001217	11/19/1881
FLOYD, S S	CSV 000581	FLOYD, W A, 08/22/1881
FLOYD, T J	CSV 001444	11/14/1881
FORK, BATTLE	CSV 001136	10/08/1881
FORREST, R O	CSV 001078	10/22/1881
FORSYTH, Y P	CSV 001422	12/02/1881
FORSYTHE, Y F	CSV 001436	12/05/1881
FOSTER, CAROLINE	CSV 000989	07/21/1881
FOSTER, G R	CSV 001980	02/17/1882
FOSTER, GEORGE	CSV 000760	08/10/1881
FOSTER, J A	CSV 001189	11/15/1881
FOSTER, JOHN	CSV 001036	10/13/1881
FOSTER, L H	CSV 000564	08/16/1881
FOSTER, SARAH A	CSV 000996	08/08/1881
FOUNTAIN, J B	CSV 001666	02/13/1882
FOWLER, A W	CSV 001642	02/13/1882
FOWLER, J W	CSV 000971	09/15/1881
FOX, M J	CSV 001054	10/17/1881
FRANKLIN, P B	CSV 001164	11/14/1881
FRANKLIN, R L	CSV 001581	01/10/1882
FRANKS, HENRY	CSV 000874	07/07/1881
FRAZIER, I F	CSV 001442	11/15/1881
FRAZIER, SARAH	CSV 001896	05/06/1882
FRAZIOR, RACHEL	CSV 000847	FRAZIOR, JOSEPH E, 07/22/1881
FREDERICK, MARY ANN	CSV 001234	FREDERICK, JOHN, 11/21/1881
FREEMAN, J P	CSV 000730	09/02/1881
FREESTONE, ISABELLA	CSV 000837	09/14/1881
FRITH, N B	CSV 001464	12/09/1881
FROELICH, JOHN	CSV 000560	08/08/1881
FROST, W H	CSV 001045	09/26/1881
FRUGER, CLEMINTINE	CSV 000910	07/01/1881
FRYER, H C	CSV 000593	08/08/1881
FULLER, ALHMUND	CSV 001835	08/08/1881
FULLER, ALMOND	CSV 000368	08/08/1881
FULLER, J C	CSV 001243	11/21/1881
FULLER, M A	CSV 000196	FULLER, J K, 07/12/1881
FULLER, M J	CSV 001098	FULLER, L C, 08/08/1881
FULLER, R D	CSV 001388	11/29/1881
FULTON, D W	CSV 001635	02/13/1882
FURLOUGH, T A	CSV 001111	09/17/1881
FYFFE, S M	CSV 001015	10/08/1881
GAGE, MARION	CSV 000304	08/08/1881
GAGE, MARY E	CSV 000355	GAGE, HARRISON, 08/08/1881
GAHAHAGAN, THOMAS W	CSV 000676	08/29/1881
GARCIA, ALFONZO	CSV 001493	12/14/1881
GARCIA, ROBERT	CSV 001457	12/08/1881
GARDINER, C B	CSV 001978	08/14/1882

Confederate Scrip Vouchers-Alphabetical Listing

GARDNER, F M	CSV 000241	08/06/1881
GARDNER, W C	CSV 000571	08/08/1881
GARLAND, TILITHA	CSV 000567	GARLAND, ERASMUS N, 08/08/1881
GARNER, NATHANIEL	CSV 000761	08/09/1881
GARNER, W J	CSV 001807	02/15/1882
GARRETT, J C	CSV 000458	08/22/1881
GARRETT, JESSE	CSV 000426	08/10/1881
GARRETT, JOHN	CSV 001970	06/26/1882
GARRISON, H H	CSV 001784	04/05/1882
GARY, BALINDA	CSV 000267	GARY, A J, 08/10/1881
GASSETT, C T	CSV 000198	07/16/1881
GASTON, M E	CSV 001485	12/03/1881
GATES, C A	CSV 000775	08/22/1881
GAY, M A	CSV 000404	GAY, J H, 08/08/1881
GEASLIN, MARY A	CSV 000749	08/08/1881
GEE, J B	CSV 002049	12/12/1882
GEE, LEONARD G	CSV 001628	02/01/1882
GEORGE, A M	CSV 001344	11/14/1881
GIBBONS, AUSTIN	CSV 002047	11/20/1882
GIBBS, GEORGE	CSV 001773	01/14/1882
GIBBS, JNO M	CSV 000822	09/12/1881
GIBSON, A	CSV 000065	07/13/1881
GIBSON, GEORGE K	CSV 000395	08/09/1881
GILBERT, MARTHA	CSV 000461	08/17/1881
GILBERT, MORRIS	CSV 000712	08/31/1881
GILES, FANNIE A	CSV 000364	GILES, JOHN F, 06/08/1881
GILES, M J	CSV 001104	10/31/1881
GILES, MARY	CSV 001728	03/06/1882
GILL, JOSEPH	CSV 001093	10/25/1881
GILLARD, APPO	CSV 000907	09/21/1881
GILLEY, JANE	CSV 000778	GILLEY, W F, 08/08/1881
GILLIAND, SAM	CSV 001651	02/17/1882
GILMORE, MARGARET	CSV 001808	11/15/1881
GIPSON, LEROY	CSV 001822	11/14/1881
GISCHEIDLE, E	CSV 000789	09/02/1881
GISH, J P	CSV 000743	09/03/1881
GIVIN, THOMAS J	CSV 001187	11/14/1881
GLAP, S A	CSV 001299	11/23/1881
GLASER, JULIUS	CSV 000094	07/13/1881
GLASS, B F	CSV 001986	08/21/1882
GLASS, W S	CSV 000953	09/20/1881
GLASSON, ALVIS	CSV 000203	07/12/1881
GLENN, RHODA	CSV 001946	05/08/1882
GOAD, JAMES	CSV 001188	11/18/1881
GODFREY, JOHN	CSV 001070	10/11/1881
GODWIN, NANCY	CSV 000224	07/16/1881
GOLDMAN, MARGARET	CSV 001038	10/13/1881
GOLDSBERRY, MARY A	CSV 000927	09/24/1881

Confederate Scrip Vouchers-Alphabetical Listing

GOMEZ, MANUEL	CSV 001886	03/16/1882
GONZALES, MANUEL	CSV 001891	03/13/1882
GOODRUM, SEBORN	CSV 001373	10/14/1881
GOODWIN, JULIETTE	CSV 001781	03/13/1882
GOOLSBY, A C	CSV 000385	08/13/1881
GOOLSBY, IRA H	CSV 001914	05/15/1882
GORDAN, LEWIS	CSV 000964	08/08/1881
GORDON, L P	CSV 001527	12/21/1881
GORE, MARY J	CSV 000637	08/09/1881
GOSETT, F A	CSV 001564	11/14/1881
GRACE, JOHN W	CSV 000353	08/08/1881
GRAHAM, C G	CSV 000491	08/17/1881
GRAHAM, PRECILLA	CSV 000609	GRAHAM, JAMES, 08/31/1881
GRANT, G S	CSV 000017	07/12/1881
GRAVES, R C	CSV 000190	07/12/1881
GRAY, ELIZABETH	CSV 001185	11/15/1881
GRAY, JOHN	CSV 001011	10/07/1881
GRAY, SARAH J	CSV 000702	GRAY, JOHN F, 08/15/1881
GRAY, WILLIAM W	CSV 001491	07/01/1881
GRAYUM, MILTON	CSV 000008	07/02/1881
GREEAR, WILLIAM B	CSV 001765	03/21/1882
GREEN, J M	CSV 000351	08/08/1881
GREEN, JOHN A	CSV 001763	03/21/1882
GREEN, MARY	CSV 001815	04/15/1882
GREEN, W A	CSV 001222	11/21/1881
GREER, ARMINDA	CSV 001904	05/04/1882
GREER, J T	CSV 001816	04/15/1882
GREER, M H	CSV 000111	07/14/1881
GREGG, EDWARD	CSV 000657	08/10/1881
GREGG, SCYTHIA	CSV 001000	10/14/1881
GRIESE, ADAM	CSV 001962	04/09/1881
GRIFFIN, ELIZABETH	CSV 000247	GRIFFIN, A C, 07/19/1881
GRIFFIN, J B	CSV 000603	07/02/1881
GRIFFIN, J H	CSV 000169	07/11/1881
GRIFFIN, LUCINDA	CSV 000947	08/11/1881
GRIFFIS, J T	CSV 001169	11/17/1881
GRIFFITH, AMANDA	CSV 001336	GRIFFITH, GEORGE M, 11/15/1881
GRIGSBEL, J M	CSV 001917	05/16/1882
GRIMES, GEORGIA	CSV 002023	GRMES, DANIEL, 10/23/1882
GRIMES, LETTIS	CSV 000812	08/06/1881
GRIMES, NANCY H	CSV 000156	GRIMES, PLEASANT, 11/07/1881
GROIN, J S	CSV 000884	09/06/1881
GROOMS, E C	CSV 002007	08/08/1882
GROUNDS, JOHN	CSV 001961	06/27/1882
GRUBBS, B R	CSV 001760	03/21/1882
GRUN, WILLIAM	CSV 001995	11/07/1881
GUERERA, ANTONIO	CSV 001890	03/13/1882

Confederate Scrip Vouchers-Alphabetical Listing

Name	Voucher	Date
GUNSTANSON, R	CSV 001284	11/15/1881
GUNTER, I J	CSV 000867	09/02/1881
GUTHRIE, E J	CSV 001303	11/15/1881
GUTHRIE, JOHN F	CSV 000816	09/09/1881
GUTHRIE, S D	CSV 000623	08/08/1881
HAGAN, ELIZA	CSV 000468	HAGAN, A GREEN 08/17/1881
HAGGARD, SARAH	CSV 001847	04/17/1882
HAHN, JACOB	CSV 000855	08/08/1881
HAIL, JOHN S	CSV 001235	11/15/1881
HAIL, W G	CSV 000522	08/09/1880
HALE, J J	CSV 001043	10/08/1881
HALE, S M	CSV 000781	09/07/1881
HALL, M E	CSV 000136	HALL, JOHN H, 07/23/1881
HALL, MARTHA	CSV 000314	HALL, HARMON, 08/08/1881
HALL, MARY A E	CSV 001489	11/14/1881
HALL, W V	CSV 000744	09/03/1881
HALLEMON, PERRY	CSV 001406	11/30/1881
HALLMARK, T L	CSV 000551	08/22/1881
HALLUM, JOE A	CSV 001178	11/17/1881
HAMBLETON, JAMES	CSV 001912	05/15/1882
HAMILTON, C V	CSV 000592	HAMILTON, PAYTON, 08/19/1881
HAMILTON, EMILY C	CSV 000941	09/24/1881
HAMILTON, H	CSV 001477	12/12/1881
HAMILTON, J W W	CSV 001671	02/18/1882
HAMILTON, R S	CSV 000889	09/13/1881
HAMILTON, SAMUEL	CSV 001180	11/17/1881
HAMMER, W L	CSV 001161	11/14/1881
HAMMOND, J M	CSV 001785	03/30/1882
HAMPTON, W W	CSV 001509	12/20/1881
HANCOCK, J J	CSV 001849	08/10/1881
HANCOCK, JOHN P	CSV 001750	03/14/1882
HANDY, J H	CSV 001845	04/17/1882
HANES, JAMES J	CSV 001441	12/06/1881
HANEY, A N	CSV 001327	11/18/1881
HANKS, F M	CSV 001520	12/21/1881
HANSON, A	CSV 000828	HANSON, G W, 07/22/1881
HANSON, JOHN F	CSV 001348	11/25/1881
HARDIN, ASHER	CSV 001363	11/26/1881
HARDIN, JOHN	CSV 000330	08/09/1881
HARDIN, WILLIAM A	CSV 001207	11/14/1881
HARDING, WILLIAM	CSV 001148	11/14/1881
HARDWICK, J H	CSV 000664	08/27/1881
HARDWICK, WILLIAM L	CSV 001338	11/25/1881
HARLESS, F G	CSV 002058	09/02/1882
HARPER, MARY J	CSV 001827	HARPER, J P, 04/15/1882
HARRELL, ELIZABETH A	CSV 000927	09/24/1881
HARRELL, JAMES C	CSV 001075	10/22/1881
HARRELL, LITTLETON	CSV 000622	08/24/1881

Confederate Scrip Vouchers-Alphabetical Listing

HARRIS, ALFORD	CSV 001885	08/02/1881
HARRIS, AMANDA	CSV 000350	HARRIS, WILLIAM, 08/13/1881
HARRIS, ANN H	CSV 000759	HARRIS, J M, 09/05/1881
HARRIS, J N	CSV 000158	07/29/1881
HARRIS, MARY JANE	CSV 002057	09/02/1882
HARRIS, MELDORA A	CSV 000791	09/02/1881
HARRIS, S L	CSV 000025	07/05/1881
HARRIS, W A	CSV 000098	07/13/1881
HARRIS, W L	CSV 000788	08/20/1881
HARRISON, HILLIARD	CSV 001166	11/17/1881
HARRISON, J S	CSV 000978	09/30/1881
HARRISON, VINCENT	CSV 000587	08/08/1881
HART, A P	CSV 000701	08/15/1881
HART, W A	CSV 000887	09/13/1881
HARTLEY, JOHN D	CSV 000511	08/11/1881
HARVEY, W H H	CSV 001993	08/25/1882
HATCH, JOSEPH A	CSV 001405	11/30/1881
HATTON, W C	CSV 001704	08/08/1881
HAUGHTON, J F	CSV 000466	08/17/1881
HAVARD, C	CSV 002003	08/25/1882
HAVIS, SARAH J	CSV 000512	04/05/1881
HAWKINS, J EM	CSV 000577	07/18/1881
HAWKINS, J H	CSV 000741	09/03/1881
HAWKINS, MARY J	CSV 001041	10/14/1881
HAWKINS, SARAH O	CSV 000777	HAWKINS, C C, 08/08/1881
HAWLEY, HIRAM	CSV 000528	08/20/1881
HAYFORD, SAMUEL	CSV 000186	08/09/1881
HAYGOOD, MARTHA	CSV 000961	HAYGOOD, WM H, 09/20/1881
HAYS, E P	CSV 000612	08/13/1881
HAYS, J M	CSV 001281	11/14/1881
HEAD, JOHN H	CSV 000365	08/13/1881
HEAD, L M	CSV 000071	07/11/1881
HEARN, SEREPTA	CSV 001940	HEARN, J M, 09/20/1881
HEATH, W C	CSV 001589	11/14/1881
HEDICK, CAROLINE	CSV 000215	HEDICK, GEORGE, 07/18/1881
HEDRICK, A J	CSV 001280	HEADRICH, JAMES, 11/16/1881
HEFFERMAN, WILLIAM H	CSV 000130	07/12/1881
HEFFINGTON, ISAAC	CSV 000287	08/08/1881
HEFLIN, R A	CSV 001536	12/27/1881
HEFNER, W L	CSV 000666	08/27/1881
HEILL, JOHN W	CSV 002056	12/16/1882
HENDERSON, A	CSV 000531	HENDERSON, T W, 08/20/1881
HENDERSON, JOHN B	CSV 000962	09/20/1881
HENDRIX, SARAH C	CSV 001383	11/28/1881
HENLEY, WILLIAM D	CSV 000906	09/15/1881
HENLEY, WILLIAM D C	CSV 000909	07/01/1881
HENRY, JOHN	CSV 002009	02/13/1882

Confederate Scrip Vouchers-Alphabetical Listing

HENRY, WILLIAM	CSV 001984	08/18/1882
HENSLEY, J C	CSV 000699	08/15/1881
HENSON, W L	CSV 001659	02/17/1882
HERBERT, JAS H	CSV 001277	11/23/1881
HERNANDEZ, JOSE MARIA	CSV 001160	11/17/1881
HERRINGTON, J M	CSV 000559	08/10/1881
HERROD, GEORGE I	CSV 000480	08/12/1881
HERROD, JAMES M	CSV 000202	07/07/1881
HESS, JOHN H	CSV 001508	12/30/1881
HEWITT, W M	CSV 000773	08/10/1881
HIETT, J W	CSV 000627	08/22/1881
HIGGINBOTHAM, LIZZIE	CSV 000689	HIGGINBOTHAM, W W, 08/08/1881
HIGH, LEIGH	CSV 000514	08/20/1881
HIGH, R M	CSV 002034	11/20/1882
HILDENBRANDT, T	CSV 001200	11/18/1881
HILL, F	CSV 001705	02/14/1882
HILL, MARTHA A E	CSV 001147	HILL, HOLDEN, 07/22/1881
HILL, S R	CSV 000245	07/18/1881
HILL, SARAH	CSV 001287	HILL, THOMAS, 11/23/1881
HILLYER, JUNIUS	CSV 000108	07/04/1881
HINDEMAN, J K P	CSV 000922	09/23/1881
HINES, JAMES	CSV 001607	01/02/1882
HINES, M N	CSV 000745	09/03/1881
HOBBS, ISAAC	CSV 002032	11/18/1882
HODGES, SAMUEL	CSV 002018	10/11/1882
HODGES, T J	CSV 000315	08/12/1881
HODGES, W K	CSV 000398	HODGES, W K, 08/09/1881
HODGIN, H S	CSV 001752	08/31/1882
HOFFMAN, F M	CSV 001601	01/17/1882
HOGAN, ANDREW	CSV 000608	08/13/1881
HOGG, ELIZABETH	CSV 000757	HOGG, JAMES B, 08/09/1881
HOLBERT, J T	CSV 000785	09/07/1881
HOLBERT, R M	CSV 001875	08/08/1881
HOLCOMB, JOHN M	CSV 001429	12/01/1881
HOLCOME, LAURA	CSV 001274	11/23/1881
HOLLAND, C H	CSV 000758	08/08/1881
HOLLBROOK, G M	CSV 001944	05/30/1882
HOLT, J M	CSV 001950	06/12/1882
HONEA, NANCY	CSV 000830	08/08/1881
HONEY, SAM	CSV 001241	11/21/1881
HONEYCUT, W E	CSV 000625	08/08/1881
HOOD, ANDERSON B	CSV 000018	07/06/1881
HOOD, ELIZA	CSV 000162	HOOD, JOHN, 07/23/1881
HOOD, L A	CSV 001130	HOOD, ANDREW, 11/07/1881
HOOKER, HENRY G	CSV 000472	08/10/1881
HOOVER, E M	CSV 001829	HOOVER, PORTER, 04/17/1882
HOPE, MARTHA	CSV 001134	11/04/1881

Confederate Scrip Vouchers-Alphabetical Listing

HOPKINS, JOSLIN	CSV 002035	11/20/1882
HOPKINS, M E	CSV 000792	09/02/1881
HOPSON, S A	CSV 000386	08/13/1881
HORNBUCKLE, W	CSV 000736	08/29/1881
HORTON, EMILY C	CSV 001820	08/08/1881
HORTON, GEORGE	CSV 001460	12/09/1881
HOUSE, J S	CSV 001302	11/15/1881
HOUSTON, JAMES M	CSV 001360	11/14/1881
HOWARD, FLORIDA	CSV 001517	12/21/1881
HOWARD, GEORGE W	CSV 000988	10/03/1881
HOWARD, J W	CSV 000639	08/25/1881
HOWARD, SUSAN E	CSV 000865	HOWARD, JEPTHA, 09/21/1881
HOWARD, W J	CSV 000732	08/12/1881
HOWELL, J H	CSV 001510	11/18/1881
HUBERMACHER, STEPHEN	CSV 001860	04/18/1882
HUBERT, WILL	CSV 000494	08/08/1881
HUDDLE, CATHERIN	CSV 000576	08/22/1881
HUDGONS, JAMES	CSV 000117	07/14/1881
HUDSON, AMOS	CSV 000733	08/08/1881
HUDSON, GEO H	CSV 000620	08/10/1881
HUDSON, M V	CSV 000973	HUDSON, R L, 09/29/1881
HUFFMAN, ELI R	CSV 000823	08/08/1881
HUGHES, J N	CSV 001399	11/30/1881
HUGHES, RICHARD	CSV 001028	07/18/1881
HUGHES, ROBERT	CSV 000303	08/08/1881
HUGHES, WILLIAM	CSV 001127	09/09/1881
HULLUM, E J	CSV 001977	08/11/1882
HUMBLE, THOMAS	CSV 001423	12/02/1881
HUMPHREY, G W	CSV 001122	11/03/1881
HUSTEAD, C C	CSV 000120	07/13/1881
HUTCHERSON, H H	CSV 000879	09/08/1881
HUTCHINGS, S D	CSV 000344	08/13/1881
HYATT, J C	CSV 001214	09/09/1881
ICE, GEORGE	CSV 001967	06/19/1882
IVES, JAMES	CSV 000808	07/25/1881
JACKSON, D Y	CSV 001618	11/14/1881
JACKSON, GREEN	CSV 001398	11/15/1881
JACKSON, IKE	CSV 001664	02/18/1882
JACKSON, J F	CSV 001031	09/06/1881
JACKSON, J H	CSV 001726	03/04/1882
JACKSON, REUBEN	CSV 000917	09/23/1881
JACKSON, T M	CSV 001428	12/05/1881
JACOBS, MARY E	CSV 000881	09/08/1881
JAMES, AGNES	CSV 001602	01/20/1882
JAMES, B F	CSV 000631	08/08/1881
JAMES, M A	CSV 001283	11/14/1881
JENKINS, M J	CSV 000530	JENKINS, J W, 08/15/1881
JENNINGS, TOM	CSV 000407	08/10/1881

Confederate Scrip Vouchers-Alphabetical Listing

JOHNS, J D	CSV 001254	11/23/1881
JOHNSON, A G	CSV 001801	04/10/1882
JOHNSON, FELIX	CSV 000201	07/05/1881
JOHNSON, J W	CSV 001415	12/02/1881
JOHNSON, LUCINDA	CSV 000167	JOHNSON, H C, 07/12/1881
JOHNSON, P H	CSV 001340	11/25/1881
JOHNSON, SARAH	CSV 001389	11/29/1881
JOHNSON, SARAH	CSV 000101	JOHNSON, WILLIAM, 07/21/1881
JOHNSON, T J	CSV 000768	08/10/1881
JOHNSTON, A O	CSV 000817	08/08/1881
JOHNSTONE, L A	CSV 001770	03/23/1882
JONAS, HENRY	CSV 000993	10/03/1881
JONES, F M	CSV 000771	09/03/1881
JONES, GEORGE	CSV 001797	11/28/1881
JONES, H W	CSV 001901	05/11/1882
JONES, HARRIET	CSV 000615	JONES, T M, 08/24/1881
JONES, JOHN G	CSV 001700	02/27/1882
JONES, LEVITA ANN	CSV 000856	08/22/1881
JONES, M P	CSV 001653	02/13/1882
JONES, MARY ANN	CSV 001775	02/15/1882
JONES, MARY E	CSV 000449	JONES, JOHN W, 08/10/1881
JONES, NANCY	CSV 000529	JONES, J R, 08/20/1881
JONES, SUSAN	CSV 000636	08/09/1881
JONES, THOMAS	CSV 000226	07/20/1881
JONES, W S	CSV 001433	13/05/1881
JONES, WILLIAM	CSV 001720	02/13/1882
JONES, WILLIAM	CSV 001818	04/15/1882
JONES, WILLIAM E	CSV 000868	09/09/1881
JORDAN, M W	CSV 000091	07/11/1881
JOYNER, J H	CSV 000923	08/09/1881
JUDD, MARINDA	CSV 000433	JUDD, J L, 08/08/1881
KEENAN, W A	CSV 000439	08/16/1881
KELLY, J P	CSV 000268	07/13/1881
KELLY, MARY E	CSV 001019	10/08/1881
KELLY, W E	CSV 001174	11/14/1881
KENDRICK, ANN	CSV 000658	KENDRICK, DRURY, 08/08/1881
KENNEDY, G B	CSV 001099	07/07/1881
KENNEDY, J D	CSV 001725	08/09/1881
KESLERSON, MARY C	CSV 000643	KESLERSON, WILLIAM, 05/13/1881
KEY, WILLIAM	CSV 001255	11/16/1881
KIETH, JOHN	CSV 001872	04/25/1882
KILLIAN, W L W	CSV 001703	02/13/1882
KING, ELIZABETH	CSV 000532	KING, HENRY, 08/08/1881
KING, J W	CSV 000869	09/09/1881
KING, JAMES P	CSV 000210	07/15/1881
KING, M S	CSV 001871	04/25/1882

Confederate Scrip Vouchers-Alphabetical Listing

KING, MARY	CSV 000967	KING, NATHANIEL, 09/21/1881
KINGSBERRY, C H	CSV 000706	08/30/1881
KINGSTON, F H	CSV 000187	08/03/1881
KINGSTON, H C	CSV 000700	08/15/1881
KINMAN, P L	CSV 001142	07/16/1881
KIRBY, A J	CSV 001452	11/15/1881
KIRBY, L E	CSV 000401	KIRBY, J BERRY, 08/08/1881
KIRKBRIDE, F H	CSV 002028	08/29/1882
KIRKLAND, J P	CSV 000838	09/18/1881
KIRN, MICHAEL	CSV 000082	07/19/1881
KIRTLAND, D	CSV 000086	07/18/1881
KIZER, ENOCH	CSV 001774	03/24/1882
KNOWLS, K S	CSV 000686	KNOWLS, J B, 08/24/1881
KNOX, JAMES A	CSV 001714	02/28/1882
KNOX, M A	CSV 000218	07/14/1881
KOONCE, CHRISTOPHER	CSV 000313	08/08/1881
KOONCE, MARY C	CSV 000927	09/24/1881
KREUTZER, CARL	CSV 001936	05/08/1882
KRIEG, J H	CSV 000069	07/11/1881
KRUSE, HENRY J	CSV 000984	09/30/1881
KUYKENDALL, S C	CSV 001809	04/14/1882
LACK, L C	CSV 001144	09/15/1881
LACKLIN, J B	CSV 000624	08/08/1881
LAFFERTY, JOHN H	CSV 000084	07/02/1881
LAFLIN, J Y	CSV 000841	09/13/1881
LAICH, W F	CSV 000927	09/24/1881
LAMBERT, NATHANIEL	CSV 001709	02/15/1882
LANDRUM, L J	CSV 000447	LANDRUM, JOHN T, 08/08/1881
LANE, MARY	CSV 001548	LANE, JOSEPH, 07/21/1881
LANE, R P	CSV 001479	12/12/1881
LANEY, F M	CSV 001511	10/20/1881
LANG, J M	CSV 000147	07/21/1881
LANGLEY, G W	CSV 001320	11/25/1881
LANGSTON, E J	CSV 000941	09/24/1881
LANGSTON, SARAH	CSV 001443	LANGSTON, H V, 11/15/1881
LANHAM, L B	CSV 000329	08/08/1881
LANIER, C W	CSV 001953	06/17/1882
LANVENDER, E K	CSV 001992	08/25/1882
LARREMORE, SAM H	CSV 000891	08/08/1881
LASATER, JAS H	CSV 001558	01/04/1882
LATHAM, HOUSTON	CSV 001813	04/14/1882
LATHAM, P C	CSV 000927	09/24/1881
LAUDMAN, ISABELLA J	CSV 000260	LAUDMAN, MARTIN W, 08/09/1881
LAUGHTON, PAT M	CSV 001490	12/05/1881
LAWRENCE, J C	CSV 000195	07/12/1881
LAWSON, HARRIET	CSV 001748	03/14/1882

Confederate Scrip Vouchers-Alphabetical Listing

LAY, JOHN R.	CSV 001729	11/14/1881
LAZRONE, SARAH	CSV 000325	LAZRONE, HENRY, 08/09/1881
LE BLANC, OSCAR	CSV 001690	02/27/1882
LEACH, L	CSV 000252	07/05/1881
LEDGELY, J T	CSV 001788	11/15/1882
LEE, J L	CSV 001232	11/15/1881
LEE, L M	CSV 001215	11/15/1881
LEE, LEROY	CSV 001154	11/14/1881
LEE, NANCY A	CSV 000371	08/09/1881
LEE, WILLIAM	CSV 001521	12/03/1881
LEFTWICH, RUTH	CSV 000388	LEFTWICH, W H, 08/03/1881
LEHMAN, JOSEPH	CSV 000618	08/21/1881
LEMMONS, SARAH	CSV 001397	11/15/1881
LEMY, P H	CSV 000654	08/22/1881
LESTER, MARY E	CSV 000786	08/08/1881
LEVENTON, JOHN	CSV 001543	12/17/1881
LEVINGSTON, EDWARD D	CSV 000885	07/23/1881
LEWIS, LITTLE, JOHN	CSV 000411	08/15/1881
LEWIS, W A	CSV 000898	09/10/1881
LEWIS, W N B	CSV 000724	09/02/1881
LINDERY, SARAH	CSV 000835	09/12/1881
LINDLEY, MATILDA A	CSV 000482	08/12/1881
LINDLEY, R	CSV 001796	08/08/1881
LINDSAY, JOSH	CSV 001101	10/25/1881
LINDSAY, MAHALA	CSV 001305	11/15/1881
LITTLE, JOHN	CSV 000412	08/15/1881
LITTLEJOHN, J T	CSV 001853	07/21/1881
LITTLETON, ELIZA J	CSV 001794	04/10/1882
LIVINGSTON, MITT	CSV 001778	08/08/1881
LLOYD, S P	CSV 000834	09/15/1881
LOADER, JANE	CSV 000844	09/19/1881
LOGAN, JAMES	CSV 001802	03/13/1882
LOGAN, M T	CSV 001740	03/08/1882
LOGAN, Z L	CSV 000890	08/29/1881
LOGSDON, E J	CSV 001341	09/02/1881
LONDON, C M	CSV 000772	07/20/1881
LONG, EDWARD	CSV 001343	11/14/1881
LONG, F M	CSV 000402	08/15/1881
LONG, GEORGE T	CSV 000638	07/09/1881
LONG, LOUISA	CSV 001358	LONG, WILLIAM, 11/25/1881
LOPEZ, IGNACIO	CSV 001595	01/12/1882
LORILLARD, H M	CSV 000710	LORILLARD, WILLIAM, 08/13/1881
LOUT, JAMES	CSV 001291	11/23/1881
LOVE, H B	CSV 001695	02/27/1882
LOVELACE, D W	CSV 000901	09/15/1881
LOWRY, M S P	CSV 000793	07/07/1881

Confederate Scrip Vouchers-Alphabetical Listing

Name	Voucher	Date/Cross-reference
LUBBOCK, S	CSV 000363	LUBBOCK, THOMAS S, 08/04/1881
LUCE, SARAH H	CSV 000665	06/07/1881
LUCE, Z	CSV 000237	07/18/1881
LUMMUS, JAMES M	CSV 001190	11/15/1881
LUMPKIN, R D	CSV 000952	09/20/1881
LYSTER, C C	CSV 000112	LYSTER, JAMES, 07/16/1881
LYTTE, JNO J	CSV 001633	08/08/1882
MAC KAY, JACOB	CSV 001540	12/29/1881
MACHOST, HENRY	CSV 001948	06/09/1882
MACK, JESSE	CSV 001314	11/25/1881
MACKFARLIN, WILLIAM	CSV 000413	08/08/1881
MADDEN, B E	CSV 000873	07/11/1881
MADDOX, SARAH E	CSV 000255	MADDOX, M D A, 08/01/1881
MADEN, C P	CSV 000249	08/08/1881
MAFFETT, S B	CSV 001819	08/12/1881
MAGNESS, B A	CSV 001311	11/14/1881
MAHAN, J J W	CSV 001716	02/28/1882
MAIN, M J	CSV 002029	08/09/1882
MAIN, THOMAS	CSV 000956	09/27/1881
MAIZE, MARY E	CSV 000178	MAIZE, A G, 07/11/1881
MAKEIG, F M	CSV 000669	08/21/1881
MALDEN, A J	CSV 000920	08/15/1881
MALONEY, W H	CSV 000893	09/14/1881
MANCHACA, JOSE A	CSV 001675	02/18/1882
MANDUSON, JESSE	CSV 001512	12/17/1881
MANGNES, LUCIANNO	CSV 001804	02/17/1882
MANN, GREEN P	CSV 000451	08/11/1881
MARLEE, L J	CSV 000109	MARLEE, JACOB, 07/16/1881
MARRIS, MATILDA	CSV 000487	08/17/1881
MARSH, N B	CSV 001981	08/17/1882
MARSHALL, W W	CSV 000430	08/09/1881
MARTIN, J T	CSV 001231	11/21/1881
MARTIN, LUCINDA	CSV 000995	07/21/1881
MARTIN, M C	CSV 001908	05/15/1882
MARTIN, MARJAH	CSV 000766	08/10/1881
MARTIN, MARTHA	CSV 001162	MARTIN IRA, 11/14/1881
MARTIN, N	CSV 001219	11/15/1881
MARTIN, NANCY	CSV 000919	08/12/1881
MARTINEZ, ALEJOS	CSV 001541	12/29/1881
MASON, J G	CSV 001604	01/02/1882
MASSEY, ELIJAH E	CSV 000845	09/12/1881
MATA, ANDRES	CSV 001732	02/18/1882
MATHEWS, F M	CSV 000394	08/08/1881
MATHEWS, J W	CSV 000707	08/22/1881
MATHEWS, THOS R	CSV 001811	04/14/1882
MATTHEWS, ROSANAH	CSV 000562	MATTHEWS, JAMES C, 08/16/1881
MATTHEWS, WILLIAM	CSV 000194	08/03/1881

Confederate Scrip Vouchers-Alphabetical Listing

Name	Voucher	Date
MAULDIN, W	CSV 001528	11/16/1881
MAXWELL, ANDREW J	CSV 000345	08/08/1881
MAXWELL, JAS H	CSV 000774	08/08/1881
MAXWELL, RACHAL	CSV 000465	MAXWELL, REUBIN, 08/08/1881
MAY, D G	CSV 001386	11/15/1881
MAYES, DAVID H	CSV 000675	08/22/1881
MAYS, J W	CSV 001897	05/08/1882
MAYS, W A	CSV 001469	12/10/1881
MC AFEE, JOHN M	CSV 001952	06/12/1882
MC ANALLY, J P	CSV 001024	10/05/1881
MC ANELY, LAURA	CSV 001882	08/01/1882
MC ANINCH, E B	CSV 000300	08/11/1881
MC BRIDE, MARTHA D	CSV 000336	08/12/1881
MC CALL, ANGELINE	CSV 000916	09/22/1881
MC CANN, R H	CSV 001913	05/15/1882
MC CARTHY, I C	CSV 001203	11/14/1881
MC CARTY, JOHN	CSV 001418	11/15/1881
MC CAUGHAN, J T	CSV 001137	11/08/1881
MC CLAIN, JOHN	CSV 001636	02/13/1882
MC CLENDON, L M	CSV 001657	02/17/1882
MC CLINTOCK, S R	CSV 000764	08/08/1881
MC CLUNG, ANN	CSV 000425	08/15/1881
MC COLLUM, JANE M	CSV 000254	08/09/1881
MC CORGUALDALE, E A	CSV 002042	12/19/1883
MC CORMACK, WILLIAM	CSV 000403	08/11/1881
MC CORMICK, MARY	CSV 000373	MC CORMICK, DAVID R, 08/13/1881
MC COWEN, S C M	CSV 000376	MC COWEN, J B, 08/13/1881
MC CRIGHT, F P	CSV 001613	01/23/1882
MC CRIGHT, WILLIAM	CSV 001094	10/25/1881
MC CULLOCH, I J	CSV 000347	08/09/1881
MC DANIEL, M A	CSV 001194	11/15/1881
MC DANIEL, MARY E	CSV 001300	11/15/1881
MC DANIEL, W A	CSV 000680	08/30/1881
MC DONALD, DANIEL	CSV 000902	09/15/1881
MC DONALD, J M	CSV 000747	08/11/1881
MC DONALD, MARTHA	CSV 000805	MC DONALD, JAMES, 09/09/1881
MC DOUGAL, MARY	CSV 001919	05/16/1882
MC DOWELL, R E C	CSV 000656	08/08/1881
MC ELREATH, S H	CSV 001382	11/28/1881
MC FARLAN, ELIZABETH M	CSV 000802	MC FARLAN, MARVEL, 08/22/1881
MC FARLAND, JAMES R	CSV 000784	08/08/1881
MC GAHEY, NARCISSA	CSV 002016	10/07/1882
MC GEE, J A	CSV 000243	08/06/1881
MC GREGOR, M C	CSV 000957	09/23/1881
MC GREW, R W	CSV 001425	10/29/1881

Confederate Scrip Vouchers-Alphabetical Listing

Name	CSV	Date/Note
MC KAY, MARIA	CSV 001135	11/04/1881
MC KENZIE, JULIA	CSV 001793	04/10/1882
MC KINLEY, D M	CSV 001859	04/17/1882
MC KINLEY, L L	CSV 001588	04/09/1881
MC KINNEY, M A	CSV 000309	MC KINNEY, GEORGE W, 08/12/1881
MC KINNEY, W A	CSV 001758	11/14/1881
MC KNIGHT, E H	CSV 000046	07/15/1881
MC LAREN, M M	CSV 001263	MC LAREN, WILLIAM, 11/23/1881
MC LAUGHLIN, MARTIN	CSV 000016	07/11/1881
MC LAUGHLIN, THOMAS	CSV 000456	08/16/1881
MC LELAND, JOHN	CSV 001296	11/23/1881
MC LEOD, ISABELLA	CSV 001268	11/23/1881
MC MAHAN, W L	CSV 000926	09/19/1881
MC MICHAEL, J B	CSV 001894	05/08/1882
MC MICHAEL, ROBERT B	CSV 001346	11/25/1881
MC MILLAN, MARY	CSV 000488	08/16/1881
MC MURTRY, JAMES	CSV 001504	07/02/1881
MC NAMARA, DANIEL	CSV 001372	10/14/1881
MC PHEARSON, J H	CSV 001087	10/19/1881
MC RAE, W R	CSV 001900	05/11/1882
MEADOW, LUCINDA	CSV 001238	MEADOW, JAMES R, 11/17/1881
MEARS, J W	CSV 001202	11/14/1881
MEDLIN, MARTHA	CSV 000751	08/29/1881
MEEK, J W	CSV 000755	09/05/1881
MELTON, H P	CSV 001505	12/14/1881
MELTON, W A	CSV 000424	08/15/1881
MELTON, WILLIAM W	CSV 000927	09/24/1881
MENGER, OSCAR	CSV 000285	08/08/1881
MENLEY, VIRGINIA	CSV 000648	08/08/1881
MERCHANT, G A	CSV 001322	11/25/1881
MERCHANT, LOUISA	CSV 000505	08/09/1881
MERCHANT, S W	CSV 000871	08/08/1881
MERIWETHER, W M	CSV 000854	09/20/1881
METCALF, L R	CSV 001991	08/25/1882
MEYERS, ROZELIA	CSV 001324	11/17/1881
MIDYETT, MIRCANI	CSV 001119	08/10/1881
MILAM, B Y	CSV 000441	08/08/1881
MILAM, J B	CSV 000442	08/08/1881
MILES, AQUILLA	CSV 000010	07/02/1881
MILLARD, M A	CSV 000216	MILLARD, W H, 07/18/1881
MILLER, A C	CSV 001451	12/07/1881
MILLER, CARL	CSV 001594	01/12/1882
MILLER, JAMES H	CSV 000678	08/29/1881
MILLER, JOHN L	CSV 000118	07/05/1885
MILLER, JOHN P	CSV 000697	08/31/1881
MILLER, JOSHUA	CSV 001717	02/28/1882

Name	Voucher	Date / Reference
MILLER, THOMAS	CSV 001925	05/10/1882
MILLER, VICTORIA	CSV 001574	MILLER, THEOPHILIUS, 07/07/1881
MILLOWN, Y A	CSV 001168	11/17/1881
MILLS, A A	CSV 000415	MILLS, M C, 07/21/1881
MILLS, JAMES M	CSV 000375	08/13/1881
MILTON, MARTHA T	CSV 000170	MILTON, HENRY, 07/30/1881
MINGS, LAVINIA	CSV 001631	02/09/1882
MINGS, MARTHA	CSV 001562	01/04/1882
MITCHELL, J W	CSV 000031	07/15/1881
MITCHELL, JABEZ	CSV 000087	07/01/1881
MITCHELL, W J	CSV 001074	10/22/1881
MITCHELL, WILLIAM	CSV 001467	12/09/1881
MITCHERPIN, W E	CSV 000735	08/08/1881
MIXON, SARAH	CSV 000714	MIXON, HENRY, 07/11/1881
MOFFITH, J M	CSV 000448	08/16/1881
MONK, J R	CSV 000546	08/22/1881
MONTGOMERY, C A	CSV 000492	MONTGOMERY, JOHN, 08/11/1881
MONTGOMERY, JAMES	CSV 001090	10/11/1881
MONTGOMERY, JAMES M	CSV 002019	10/12/1882
MOON, JOHN	CSV 000490	08/04/1881
MOON, M J	CSV 001289	11/23/1881
MOON, R E	CSV 001766	10/22/1882
MOON, W J	CSV 001062	10/18/1881
MOORE, CHARLOTTE	CSV 000694	MOORE, JOHN, 08/25/1881
MOORE, D Y	CSV 001535	10/03/1881
MOORE, E T	CSV 001069	08/20/1881
MOORE, FRANCES	CSV 000236	MOORE, G W, 08/06/1881
MOORE, J S	CSV 000332	08/02/1881
MOORE, NANCY	CSV 001609	01/20/1882
MOORE, ROBERT	CSV 002005	08/22/1882
MOORE, S E	CSV 001227	11/21/1881
MOORE, THADDEUS	CSV 000257	08/09/1881
MOORE, THOMAS	CSV 000273	08/10/1881
MOORING, J S	CSV 001257	11/23/1881
MOORING, J W	CSV 000821	07/04/1881
MOORMAN, MARY	CSV 001170	11/17/1881
MOREAU, JULIUS	CSV 001230	11/21/1881
MORGAN, ABEL	CSV 000698	08/15/1881
MORGAN, G W	CSV 002037	11/14/1882
MORGAN, JAMES L	CSV 000455	08/16/1881
MORGAN, R L	CSV 001021	10/08/1881
MORGAN, T J	CSV 000804	MORGAN, ALLISON, 08/08/1881
MORPHIS, MARY	CSV 000266	MORPHIS, WILLIAM, 08/10/1881
MORRIS, BEN	CSV 001064	10/18/1881
MORRIS, JULIA ANN	CSV 001325	11/16/1881

Confederate Scrip Vouchers-Alphabetical Listing

MORRIS, MARY A	CSV 000474	07/07/1881
MORRIS, WILLIAM	CSV 000521	08/10/1881
MORRISON, JNO D	CSV 000762	08/09/1881
MORRISON, SUSAN	CSV 001943	05/30/1882
MORSE, DRURY	CSV 001316	11/25/1881
MORTON, M M	CSV 000372	MORTON, J G, 08/09/1881
MOSES, L G	CSV 001211	11/15/1881
MOSILEY, J B	CSV 000080	07/05/1881
MOULTON, A J	CSV 001696	02/21/1882
MOWRY, J T	CSV 001547	01/03/1882
MULLIN, W A	CSV 000630	08/08/1881
MULLINS, JANE	CSV 001899	MULLINS, A B, 05/08/1882
MULLINS, WILLIAM T	CSV 001326	11/18/1881
MUNK, RACHEL C	CSV 000679	08/09/1881
MURDOCK, JAMES H	CSV 000171	07/01/1881
MUREY, HARVEY	CSV 002010	09/18/1882
MURPHY, G S	CSV 001172	11/17/1881
MURPHY, J W	CSV 000815	08/08/1881
MURRAY, J W	CSV 000043	07/11/1881
MURRAY, M W	CSV 001128	10/31/1881
MURRAY, WILLIAM P	CSV 001394	11/29/1881
MURRIE, REBECCA	CSV 000002	MURRIE, ROBERT S, 07/01/1881
MYER, JOHN	CSV 001876	11/28/1881
MYERS, S E	CSV 000770	08/08/1881
MYRES, D D	CSV 001777	03/29/1882
NAGLE, JAMES E	CSV 000029	07/01/1881
NASH, WILLIAM	CSV 000903	09/15/1881
NEAL, ELIZABETH	CSV 000011	NEAL, THOMAS, 07/01/1881
NEAL, T K	CSV 000583	08/22/1881
NEELY, THOMAS J	CSV 001025	08/08/1881
NEFF, JOHN	CSV 001969	07/08/1882
NENENDOFF, MAX	CSV 000911	09/15/1881
NEULAND, JANE	CSV 000617	08/21/1881
NEVANS, MARGARET	CSV 000106	NEVANS, T C, 07/22/1881
NEVIL, A J	CSV 001010	07/18/1881
NEVILLS, D E	CSV 001285	11/14/1881
NEWBERRY, LUCY ANN	CSV 000591	NEWBERRY, JOHNSON, 08/23/1881
NEWBY, ELIZABETH	CSV 000296	NEWBY, WM H, 08/09/1881
NEWLAND, W W	CSV 001624	12/31/1881
NEWMAN, SIMPSON	CSV 001959	06/25/1882
NEWSOM, ELIAS	CSV 000396	08/09/1881
NEWTZE, ALBERT	CSV 001371	11/26/1881
NICHOLS, A W	CSV 001026	10/10/1881
NICHOLS, RICHARD	CSV 000537	08/08/1881
NICHOLSON, E M	CSV 000389	NICHOLSON, PETER, 08/15/1881
NICKLES, W W	CSV 000504	08/08/1881

Confederate Scrip Vouchers-Alphabetical Listing

NIDEVER, JOHN	CSV 000189	07/26/1881
NIEDERHOFER, CHARLES	CSV 001998	08/12/1881
NIGGLI, ROSINA	CSV 000493	NIGGLI, FERDINAND, 08/15/1881
NIXON, REBECCA	CSV 001855	04/17/1882
NIXON, SARAH	CSV 001843	07/21/1881
NIXON, W T	CSV 001842	07/21/1881
NOBLE, E A	CSV 000673	08/08/1881
NOBLE, ISAAC O	CSV 000756	08/08/1881
NOBLE, N M	CSV 000256	NOBLE, J C, 08/09/1881
NORFORD, Z W	CSV 001790	02/17/1882
NORMAN, M M	CSV 001623	01/31/1882
NORRIS, CHRISTINA	CSV 001269	11/23/1881
NORRIS, JOHN S	CSV 000341	08/08/1881
NORTH, SARAH	CSV 002020	NORTH, R R, 08/15/1882
NORVELL, T J	CSV 001050	08/08/1881
NORWOOD, JOHN H	CSV 000164	07/23/1881
NOTGRASS, T J	CSV 000041	07/15/1881
NOWLIN, MINERVA	CSV 000174	NOWLIN, BENJAMIN, 07/30/1881
O GUINN, E J	CSV 001932	05/11/1882
O REAR, J P	CSV 000127	07/01/1881
OATES, MARTHA E	CSV 000479	08/12/1881
ODOM, J W	CSV 001047	ODOM, JAS O, 10/01/1881
ODOM, JOSEPH	CSV 001857	12/27/1881
OGLESBEE, B H	CSV 001863	04/20/1882
OGLESBY, M J	CSV 001221	OGLESBY, CHARLES F, 11/15/1881
OLIVER, J J	CSV 001408	08/08/1881
ONEY, JOHN	CSV 001806	04/14/1882
ORR, C E	CSV 001009	10/07/1881
OTIS, THOMAS	CSV 000166	07/11/1881
OWENS, A M	CSV 001350	OWENS, J R, 11/25/1881
OWENS, J H	CSV 000417	08/10/1881
OWENS, M H	CSV 000634	08/15/1881
PACE, J H	CSV 000803	08/09/1881
PACE, SARAH	CSV 000584	PACE, JAMES B, 04/09/1881
PAGE, HEZAKIAH	CSV 001549	08/08/1881
PAIN, W D	CSV 001616	11/14/1881
PALLEY, J B	CSV 000042	07/16/1881
PALMER, ISAM	CSV 001005	10/07/1881
PANKEY, J B	CSV 000497	08/08/1881
PANTHER, L D	CSV 000176	08/18/1881
PANTHER, M F	CSV 001304	11/15/1881
PARCHMAN, W D	CSV 000997	08/08/1881
PARISH, J L	CSV 001851	04/17/1882
PARISH, JOHN D	CSV 001852	04/17/1882
PARKE, H	CSV 000742	09/03/1881
PARKER, ADA	CSV 000927	09/24/1881

Confederate Scrip Vouchers-Alphabetical Listing

PARKER, CHARLES .... CSV 001893 .... 03/13/1882
PARKER, F .... CSV 000445 .... 08/09/1881
PARKER, J P .... CSV 001722 .... 02/15/1882
PARKER, JOHN .... CSV 000092 .... 07/12/1881
PARKS, A B .... CSV 001632 .... 02/13/1882
PARKS, POLER .... CSV 001079 .... 10/22/1881
PARKS, VIRGINIA F .... CSV 001298 .... PARKS, W L, 11/15/1881
PARLAW, SUSAN .... CSV 001683 .... 02/24/1882
PARRIM, G W .... CSV 002015 .... 10/05/1882
PARRISH, SAPHRONIA .... CSV 000181 .... PARRISH, THOMAS,
                                                              07/22/1881
PATTERSON, E D .... CSV 000191 .... 07/07/1881
PATTERSON, W A .... CSV 002031 .... 11/17/1882
PATTERSON, WILLIAM C .... CSV 000324 .... 08/12/1881
PEDUTE, JOHN .... CSV 000281 .... 08/08/1881
PEEBLES, S P .... CSV 001586 .... 11/15/1881
PEEL, M J .... CSV 000265 .... PEEL, WILLIAM, 08/10/1881
PEEVEY, W D .... CSV 001909 .... 05/15/1882
PEMBERTON, C D .... CSV 000422 .... 08/15/1881
PENGE, PRISCILLA .... CSV 000298 .... BENGE, JAMES, 08/09/1881
PENN, D P .... CSV 001516 .... 11/14/1881
PERKINS, JAMES P .... CSV 001013 .... 10/07/1881
PERRY, MARTHA J .... CSV 000986 .... 10/01/1881
PERSONS, L R .... CSV 000165 .... 07/07/1881
PETIS, JAMES J .... CSV 000985 .... 09/30/1881
PETTY, HENRY .... CSV 001342 .... 11/25/1881
PETTY, M C .... CSV 000737 .... 08/09/1881
PETTYJOHN, J C .... CSV 000238 .... 07/18/1881
PEYTON, JOHN A .... CSV 000197 .... 07/02/1881
PFEIFER, JOHANN .... CSV 001560 .... 12/05/1881
PHARES, REUBEN .... CSV 000550 .... 08/22/1881
PHIFER, MARTHA .... CSV 001817 .... PHIFER, MATHEW, 08/08/1881
PHILIPPS, J H .... CSV 000333 .... 08/12/1881
PHILLIPS, E M .... CSV 001676 .... 02/18/1882
PHILLIPS, M S .... CSV 000172 .... 07/07/1881
PHILLIPS, REBECCA .... CSV 000677 .... PHILLIPS, JAMES B,
                                                              08/29/1881
PHILLIPS, WHIT .... CSV 000515 .... 08/20/1881
PHIPPS, MARY A .... CSV 000246 .... PHIPPS. G E, 08/06/1881
PIERCE, HUGH J .... CSV 000739 .... 08/13/1881
PIERCE, ROBERT .... CSV 001786 .... 02/18/1882
PIERCE, W M .... CSV 001918 .... 05/16/1882
PIKE, S A .... CSV 000470 .... PIKE, ISAAC, 08/11/1881
PINKNEY, R H .... CSV 001524 .... 12/23/1881
PISTOLE, THOMAS R .... CSV 000182 .... 07/18/1881
PLOWMAN, JOHN I .... CSV 000050 .... 07/16/1881
POLK, J L .... CSV 001030 .... 10/12/1881
POLK, JAMES .... CSV 001466 .... 11/15/1881
POLK, JOHN D .... CSV 000099 .... 07/16/1881

Confederate Scrip Vouchers-Alphabetical Listing

POLK, WILLIAM	CSV 001712	02/17/1882
POLLEY, ANGELINA	CSV 001367	POLLEY, OLIVER, 08/08/1881
POLSTER, GEORGE	CSV 001483	09/10/1881
POOL, E W	CSV 001228	11/21/1881
POOL, W M	CSV 000269	08/10/1881
POOL, WM	CSV 000134	07/12/1881
POOLE, HENRY	CSV 000776	08/22/1881
PORTMAN, E R	CSV 000753	08/29/1881
POSEY, MATILDA ANN	CSV 000114	POSEY, E D, 07/20/1881
POSEY, CAROLINE	CSV 001347	11/25/1881
POSTLETHWAIT, CHAS S	CSV 001083	10/10/1881
POTEET, H N	CSV 000262	POTEET, H N, 08/08/1881
POTTS, MARY	CSV 000161	POTTS, PAUL, 07/29/1881
POULSON, CHAS	CSV 000974	09/13/1881
POUNDS, J M D	CSV 000599	08/23/1881
POWELL, H S	CSV 000674	08/09/1881
POWELL, SARAH M	CSV 000948	POWELL, T D, 09/12/1881
POWELL, WILLIAM	CSV 000963	09/20/1881
POWER, NANCY	CSV 000409	08/15/1881
PRATER	CSV 002041	11/21/1882
PRESCOTT, LILITHA	CSV 000110	PRESCOTT, DAVIS, DAVID, 07/12/1881
PREWETT, J M	CSV 001297	11/23/1881
PREWITT, WILSON	CSV 000692	08/30/1881
PRICE, B H	CSV 001551	11/14/1881
PRICE, DAVID	CSV 000183	07/18/1881
PRICE, ELIZABETH	CSV 000878	09/08/1881
PRICE, G D	CSV 000133	07/01/1881
PRICE, JOHN	CSV 001413	11/14/1881
PRICE, JOHN ALLEN	CSV 001934	05/24/1882
PRICE, LUCINDA	CSV 001610	12/14/1881
PRICE, MORGAN	CSV 001625	12/31/1881
PRIDE, ANGELINA	CSV 001846	PRIDE, JOHN, 07/21/1881
PRIEST, JAMES T	CSV 000200	07/12/1881
PRIEST, LUCINDA	CSV 001834	PRIEST, JAMES, 11/14/1881
PRITCHARD, W D	CSV 000568	08/08/1881
PROTHRO, ELLEN C	CSV 000927	09/24/1881
PROTHRO, J M	CSV 002014	10/11/1882
PRUITT, ELIZABETH	CSV 001245	11/15/1881
PRUITT, RHODA	CSV 000534	08/20/1881
PRYOR, R N	CSV 000045	07/14/1881
PUCKETT, T E	CSV 000501	PUCKETT, J A, 08/20/1881
PULLIN, ALZADA	CSV 001272	PULLIN, THOMAS, 11/14/1881
PULLIN, R C	CSV 001472	12/10/1881
PURYEAR, J B	CSV 001554	12/27/1881
PYLRIS, ELIZABETH	CSV 000348	PYLRIS, AARON, 08/09/1881
QUAID, B W	CSV 001323	08/22/1881
RADAZ, FRANK	CSV 000651	08/18/1881
RAGSDALE, FRANCES	CSV 001445	RAGSDALE, JOHN, 07/16/1881

Confederate Scrip Vouchers-Alphabetical Listing

Name	Voucher	Date/Reference
RAIN, BENJAMIN	CSV 001461	12/06/1881
RAINE, M E	CSV 000295	RAINE, JIM, 08/08/1881
RAINEY, A T	CSV 000152	07/14/1881
RAINEY, E B	CSV 000093	07/12/1881
RAINS, R H	CSV 001526	12/23/1881
RAJE, LEAH	CSV 000292	08/09/1881
RAMSEY, G W	CSV 001402	11/30/1881
RAMSEY, JOHN	CSV 000072	07/18/1881
RANDOLPH, E J	CSV 001643	02/14/1882
RANEY, EMILY R	CSV 000523	07/22/1881
RANKIN, ROBERT	CSV 001212	11/15/1881
RAP, MARY	CSV 000444	RAP, EDWARD, 08/11/1881
RAPE, WILLIAM	CSV 000081	07/16/1881
RASCO, SOLON	CSV 000794	07/07/1881
RATCLIFF, MARY E	CSV 001271	11/14/1881
RATICAN, JOHN	CSV 000831	09/13/1881
RAWLS, THOMAS	CSV 001205	11/14/1881
RAY, JOHN W	CSV 000653	08/27/1881
REASONER, J W	CSV 001751	03/14/1882
REAVIS, W H	CSV 000542	08/22/1881
REDUS, JAMES	CSV 001236	11/21/1881
REED, ALEXANDER	CSV 000056	07/01/1881
REED, J A	CSV 001837	08/09/1881
REED, JOHN F	CSV 001352	11/25/1881
REED, WARRAN	CSV 001799	04/13/1882
REESE, E M	CSV 002008	03/23/1882
REESE, MARTHA	CSV 001361	REESE, CHARLES, 11/17/1881
REEVES, MARTHA	CSV 000100	REEVES, AGRIPPA, 04/09/1881
REID, B S	CSV 001209	11/14/1881
REUSHAW, SALLIE	CSV 000864	09/18/1881
REYES, ALEXANDER	CSV 001151	11/14/1881
REYES, JUAN	CSV 001150	11/14/1881
REYNOLDS, D R	CSV 001332	11/14/1881
REYNOLDS, J W B	CSV 001454	12/08/1881
REYNOLDS, WILLIAM	CSV 000994	09/12/1881
RHENDASIL, J C	CSV 001755	03/14/1882
RHODE, WILLIAM B	CSV 000416	08/15/1881
RHODES, MARTHA	CSV 001727	02/13/1882
RICE, J J	CSV 000312	08/12/1881
RICE, SUSANNAH	CSV 000061	07/11/1881
RICE, W P	CSV 000239	07/18/1881
RICHARDS, MARY E	CSV 000876	RICHARDS, R ADOLPHUS, 09/12/1881
RICHARDS, WILSON B	CSV 001177	11/17/1881
RICHARDSON, MARY F	CSV 000153	RICHARDSON, HENRY S, 07/15/1881
RICHARDSON, R C	CSV 001196	11/18/1881
RICHARDSON, W P	CSV 001218	11/16/1881

Confederate Scrip Vouchers-Alphabetical Listing

Name	Voucher	Date
RIDDLE, W S	CSV 000028	07/09/1881
RIDDLE, W S	CSV 001378	11/28/1881
RIDGAWAY, W P	CSV 000151	06/06/1881
RIFE, THOS C	CSV 000718	08/13/1881
RIGBY, R E	CSV 000235	07/18/1881
RIGGS, W S	CSV 001486	12/14/1881
RILEY, MARY	CSV 001016	RILEY, JOSEPH, 10/08/1881
RIPLEY, J W	CSV 001761	03/21/1882
RISINGER, AVARILLA P	CSV 000213	RISINGER, JAMES LAUDON, 08/04/1881
RISINGER, J J	CSV 001008	08/08/1881
RIVERSON, C N	CSV 001783	02/13/1882
ROACH, J F G	CSV 001833	07/21/1881
ROBBINS, FRANCES	CSV 000661	ROBBINS, JNO W, 08/08/1881
ROBBINS, LOUISA	CSV 001782	12/17/1881
ROBBINS, M J	CSV 000302	ROBBINS, ELIAS, 08/11/1881
ROBERTS, ELIJAH	CSV 001935	03/24/1882
ROBERTS, G R	CSV 001663	02/18/1882
ROBERTS, J E	CSV 001412	12/01/1881
ROBERTS, JOHN P	CSV 000179	07/21/1881
ROBERTS, T C	CSV 001411	12/01/1881
ROBERTSON, A B	CSV 001051	10/15/1881
ROBERTSON, D F	CSV 000232	08/06/1881
ROBERTSON, FRANCIS S	CSV 000059	07/14/1881
ROBERTSON, J F	CSV 001798	11/28/1881
ROBERTSON, JOHN	CSV 001095	10/30/1881
ROBERTSON, W H	CSV 001825	08/08/1881
ROBINETT, JAMES A	CSV 001293	11/23/1881
ROBINSON, E A	CSV 000979	08/08/1881
ROBINSON, J S	CSV 001012	09/29/1881
ROBINSON, JOHN C	CSV 000959	09/20/1881
ROBINSON, JOHN H	CSV 001902	05/04/1882
ROBINSON, MANERVA J	CSV 000895	ROBINSON, L J, 08/09/1881
ROBINSON, MATILDA	CSV 001573	01/09/1882
ROBINSON, N M	CSV 000356	ROBINSON, JESSE S, 08/08/1881
ROBINSON, R L	CSV 001315	11/25/1881
ROBINSON, T M	CSV 001294	11/23/1881
RODGERS, R M	CSV 001679	11/14/1881
RODMAN, H M	CSV 001275	11/15/1881
RODRIGUEZ, GREGORIA	CSV 001771	01/14/1882
RODRIGUEZ, JESUS	CSV 000610	08/08/1881
ROGENS, C C	CSV 000604	08/08/1881
ROGERS, DAVE	CSV 001869	04/22/1822
ROGERS, HILARY J C	CSV 000319	08/08/1881
ROGERS, I J	CSV 001240	11/21/1881
ROGERS, J B	CSV 002050	12/12/1882
ROGERS, J C	CSV 001242	11/21/1881
ROGERS, LOUISA	CSV 001848	07/07/1881

Confederate Scrip Vouchers-Alphabetical Listing

ROGERS, N B	CSV 000605	08/08/1881
ROGERS, NANCY	CSV 001898	ROGERS, JAMES, 05/09/1882
ROLAND, M A	CSV 001789	11/25/1881
ROME, W B	CSV 000696	08/08/1881
ROMERO, JUAN	CSV 001805	03/13/1882
ROMINE, J W	CSV 000228	07/20/1881
ROPER, T L	CSV 000284	08/08/1881
ROSE, G W	CSV 001053	10/15/1881
ROSSUN, T	CSV 001056	10/17/1881
ROTAN, W T	CSV 001081	08/21/1881
ROUNDTREE, W A	CSV 000478	08/12/1881
ROUNSAVOLL, W D	CSV 000767	08/10/1881
ROWLAND, T J	CSV 000565	08/16/1881
ROWLETT, JAMES	CSV 001648	02/14/1881
ROZELL, ELIZA	CSV 000502	08/08/1881
RUDDELL, ISAAC N	CSV 001146	08/08/1881
RUDINGER, JOSEPH	CSV 000748	09/01/1881
RUE, W B	CSV 001715	02/28/1882
RUIZ, GRANVIL	CSV 001159	11/18/1881
RUSHOU, JOHN	CSV 001937	05/08/1882
RUSSELL, J E S	CSV 001225	11/21/1881
RUSSELL, J J	CSV 001656	02/17/1882
RUSSELL, LAS E	CSV 001762	03/21/1882
RUSSELL, MILLY S	CSV 000349	RUSSELL, JESSEE, 08/13/1881
RUSSELL, S L	CSV 001354	11/14/1881
RUTLEDGE, WILLIAM	CSV 001213	11/19/1881
RUTTLEDGE, WILLIAM R	CSV 000370	08/09/1881
SALINAS, VICENTE	CSV 001692	02/17/1882
SAMS, MARGARET	CSV 001515	SAMS, JOSEPH, 12/21/1881
SANDELL, R S	CSV 000138	SANDELL, J O, 07/01/1881
SANDERS, CHARNEL	CSV 001220	11/15/1881
SANDERS, JOHN A	CSV 001795	12/21/1881
SANDERS, PHILIP	CSV 001584	01/10/1882
SANDERS, R M	CSV 000464	08/08/1881
SANDERS, S J	CSV 000886	08/10/1881
SANDOVAL, ADOLPHO	CSV 001370	11/26/1881
SANDOVAL, CARLOS	CSV 000912	09/21/1881
SANDOVAL, JESUS	CSV 001492	12/14/1881
SARRATT, LEVI	CSV 000124	07/01/1881
SAUNDERS, J M	CSV 001140	11/11/1881
SAVAGE, ELIZABETH	CSV 000438	SAVAGE, ROBERT, 08/08/1881
SAVAGE, JOSEPH	CSV 001580	01/10/1882
SAXON, H M E	CSV 001488	07/11/1881
SCALES, W G	CSV 000436	08/08/1881
SCHAEFER, DORIS	CSV 001923	SCHAEFER, LOUIS, 05/09/1882
SCHAFFER, JAMES	CSV 001593	01/12/1882
SCHERFFINS, JOHN A	CSV 000790	08/08/1881

Confederate Scrip Vouchers-Alphabetical Listing

SCHMIDT, ALBERT	CSV 000709	08/30/1881
SCHMIDT, FRANK	CSV 000968	08/08/1881
SCHMIT, HENRY	CSV 001889	03/13/1882
SCHNEIDER, E B H	CSV 000437	08/10/1881
SCHUCHERT, LUDWIG	CSV 000489	08/13/1881
SCHULTZ, HENRY	CSV 001126	08/08/1881
SCHULTZE, FRIEDRICH	CSV 000598	08/15/1881
SCOTT, A O	CSV 000499	SCOTT, J M, 08/08/1881
SCOTT, W T	CSV 001023	10/10/1881
SCROGGINS, LOUISA	CSV 000149	SCROGGINS, WILLIAM, 07/05/1881
SEARGENT, ANDREW	CSV 001278	11/23/1881
SEBASTIAN, SARAH	CSV 001895	05/06/1882
SEDBERRY, M A	CSV 000614	08/10/1881
SESSIONS, J M	CSV 001930	05/20/1882
SEWELL, JOHN J	CSV 000160	07/29/1881
SHADAIN, SARAH	CSV 001335	11/25/1881
SHARP, J H	CSV 000850	09/17/1881
SHARP, MALISA	CSV 001455	11/14/1881
SHARP, W C	CSV 001947	05/08/1882
SHARP, WILLIAM	CSV 001982	08/18/1882
SHARPE, T H	CSV 000208	07/07/1881
SHATTICK, J H	CSV 000234	SHATTICK, W M, 07/18/1881
SHEFFIELD, T J	CSV 000361	08/10/1881
SHELTON, F E	CSV 001769	02/13/1882
SHERRIL, J G	CSV 000272	08/10/1881
SHERWOOD, H T	CSV 001424	12/02/1881
SHIELDS, ISIAH	CSV 001427	12/03/1881
SHIPP, J M	CSV 000555	08/08/1881
SHORT, W H	CSV 000646	08/25/1881
SHROPSHIRE, WILLIAM	CSV 001639	02/13/1882
SHULER, GLENN	CSV 000335	08/08/1881
SIKES, ROBERT	CSV 000943	09/24/1881
SIMMONS, B P	CSV 001649	02/14/1881
SIMMONS, CARRIE	CSV 001812	04/14/1882
SIMMONS, MARY	CSV 000573	SIMMONS, JAMES J, 08/11/1881
SIMS, EDWARD	CSV 001088	04/19/1881
SIMS, J H	CSV 001701	02/13/1882
SIMS, MARY T E	CSV 000406	08/10/1881
SIMS, W B	CSV 000728	09/02/1881
SKEETERS, DAVID C	CSV 001713	02/28/1882
SKINNER, J E	CSV 001724	03/04/1882
SKINNER, JNO S	CSV 000443	08/11/1881
SKINNER, WILLIAM	CSV 001197	11/18/1881
SLADE, W C	CSV 001542	11/15/1881
SLAUGHTER, ARENA	CSV 001329	11/25/1881
SLEDGE, K C	CSV 000334	08/02/1881
SLOAN, JOHN V	CSV 000908	09/21/1881

Confederate Scrip Vouchers-Alphabetical Listing

SMALL, J B	CSV 001035	08/21/1881
SMILIE, JACOB	CSV 001681	02/24/1882
SMITH, A J	CSV 001328	11/18/1881
SMITH, B F	CSV 000960	09/20/1881
SMITH, B M	CSV 000023	07/01/1881
SMITH, FELIX JACKSON	CSV 000740	09/03/1881
SMITH, FRANK	CSV 000369	08/08/1881
SMITH, GEORGE	CSV 001149	11/14/1881
SMITH, J C	CSV 000716	08/22/1881
SMITH, J J	CSV 000290	08/08/1881
SMITH, J P	CSV 000231	07/20/1881
SMITH, J T	CSV 001691	02/27/1882
SMITH, JOHN	CSV 001983	08/16/1882
SMITH, JOHN H	CSV 000877	08/08/1881
SMITH, JOHN I	CSV 000038	07/15/1881
SMITH, JOSEPH	CSV 001686	02/13/1882
SMITH, LEW	CSV 000485	08/08/1881
SMITH, MARTHA	CSV 000137	SMITH, J B, 07/13/1881
SMITH, MARTHA A B	CSV 001058	10/17/1881
SMITH, MARY	CSV 000914	09/21/1881
SMITH, MARY	CSV 001570	SMITH, J R, 01/09/1882
SMITH, MARY A	CSV 000258	SMITH, T B, 08/09/1881
SMITH, MARY A	CSV 000535	08/20/1881
SMITH, N O	CSV 000826	08/08/1881
SMITH, RICHARD	CSV 001532	12/12/1881
SMITH, ROBERT	CSV 001112	10/31/1881
SMITH, S C	CSV 002001	08/25/1882
SMITH, SUSAN	CSV 000721	08/10/1881
SMITH, SUSAN	CSV 000662	SMITH, JOSEPH, 08/01/1881
SMITH, W K	CSV 001572	11/14/1881
SMITH, W R	CSV 000429	08/15/1881
SMITH, WILLIAM H	CSV 000277	08/11/1881
SMITH, WILLIAM R	CSV 000723	09/02/1881
SMITHERMAN, DOLLY	CSV 001052	10/15/1881
SMITHERS, G S	CSV 000720	08/26/1881
SNELGROVE, J P	CSV 000955	09/20/1881
SNIDER, W N	CSV 000380	08/13/1881
SNOW, EMILY	CSV 001731	03/07/1882
SOAPS, JOSEPH	CSV 000467	08/17/1881
SOLOMAN, MARY	CSV 000880	SOLOMAN, ALEXANDER, 09/12/1881
SOLOMAN, TABITHA E	CSV 000211	07/22/1881
SOWELL, JAMES A	CSV 000048	07/13/1881
SPANGENBERG, HENRY	CSV 001559	04/09/1881
SPARKMAN, M J	CSV 001165	SPARKMAN, S S, 11/14/1881
SPARKS, G A	CSV 000818	09/05/1881
SPEARS, MARTHA	CSV 001057	10/17/1881
SPELL, MARY	CSV 000125	SPELL, RICHARD H, 07/22/1881

Confederate Scrip Vouchers-Alphabetical Listing

Name	Voucher	Date/Reference
SPIDEL, M C	CSV 000357	SPIDEL, JOHN, 08/08/1881
SPIKES, MARTHA	CSV 001033	SPIKES, WILLIAM, 09/20/1881
SPINDLE, SAMUEL	CSV 001155	11/14/1881
SPITLER, WILLIAM M	CSV 000339	08/08/1881
SPOONAMORE, C L	CSV 000645	08/19/1881
SPOTTS, BASCOM	CSV 000703	08/30/1881
SPRADLING, G W	CSV 001318	11/25/1881
SPRINGER, G B	CSV 000040	07/11/1881
SPRINGER, W J	CSV 000240	07/18/1881
SPURLIER, W A	CSV 001989	08/24/1882
SQUIER, E	CSV 001988	08/20/1882
ST JOHN, H L	CSV 002040	11/21/1882
STACEY, J J	CSV 001260	11/15/1881
STACY, W A	CSV 001531	11/17/1881
STALCUP, J M	CSV 001971	07/18/1882
STAMPS, B F	CSV 000691	08/24/1881
STANFIELD, MARY F	CSV 001409	STANFIELD, E A, 08/08/1881
STANLEY, GEORGE R	CSV 000981	09/22/1881
STANLEY, J K	CSV 001840	08/08/1881
STANSBERRY, MARY	CSV 001810	04/14/1882
STAPLETON, SAM	CSV 002025	10/24/1882
STARKY, THOMAS	CSV 000483	08/12/1881
STARY, H G	CSV 000829	09/15/1881
STAUTS, G W	CSV 001702	02/27/1882
STEDMAN, ELY	CSV 000626	08/10/1881
STEEL, THOMAS	CSV 000322	08/08/1881
STEPHENS, CLARISA	CSV 000827	STEPHENS, G H, 08/08/1881
STEPHENS, D C	CSV 001598	01/16/1882
STEPHENS, JOHN	CSV 001384	11/28/1881
STEPHENS, JOHN	CSV 001385	11/28/1881
STEPHENS, THOMAS	CSV 000977	08/10/1881
STEPHENSON, C E	CSV 001737	02/17/1882
STEPHENSON, L	CSV 001661	02/18/1882
STEPHENSON, W D	CSV 001546	09/09/1881
STEUBING, FRED	CSV 001965	11/14/1881
STEVENS, MARY C	CSV 000998	10/04/1881
STEVERSON, W R	CSV 001252	11/21/1881
STEWART, CYNTHIA	CSV 001276	STEWART, ALEXANDER, 11/23/1881
STEWART, F C	CSV 001020	09/12/1881
STEWART, J D	CSV 001994	08/25/1882
STEWART, JAMES	CSV 000383	08/13/1881
STEWART, JAMES	CSV 002030	11/13/1882
STEWART, PETER	CSV 001438	12/05/1881
STIDHAM, CAROLINE	CSV 001046	STIDHAM, THOMAS, 08/08/1881
STILES, A B	CSV 000414	08/08/1881
STILLWELL, W	CSV 000393	STILLWELL, N B, 08/15/1881
STILWELL, C L	CSV 000399	STILWELL, J L H, 04/09/1881

Confederate Scrip Vouchers-Alphabetical Listing

STINNETT, HENRY	CSV 001356	11/15/1881
STINSON, JOHN H	CSV 000140	07/26/1881
STOCKTON, AMANDA	CSV 001416	07/11/1881
STOCKTON, WILLIAM W	CSV 001380	09/03/1881
STOKES, ELVIRA	CSV 001821	08/08/1881
STOKES, J G	CSV 000454	08/16/1881
STONE, EDWARD P	CSV 001364	08/09/1881
STONE, S T	CSV 000263	STONE, S T, 08/10/1881
STOOKS, JOSEPH S	CSV 001366	11/26/1881
STORY, D F	CSV 001533	12/12/1881
STORY, ISAAC	CSV 001926	05/09/1882
STORY, R D	CSV 001873	04/25/1882
STORY, SOPHRONIA	CSV 000261	STORY, WM M, 07/12/1881
STORY, THOMAS F	CSV 001874	08/08/1881
STOUT, JASPER	CSV 001313	11/25/1881
STOVALL, S T	CSV 000621	08/24/1881
STRANGE, CELIA	CSV 000498	STRANGE, O E W, 08/18/1881
STRICKLAND, M M	CSV 001339	11/25/1881
STRINGER, E A	CSV 001082	10/10/1881
STRODE, C E	CSV 001514	11/16/1881
STUART, JOHN E	CSV 000280	08/08/1881
STUBBELFIELD, S S	CSV 001911	05/15/1882
STUBBLEFIELD, M M	CSV 001684	02/24/1882
STUL, W C	CSV 000279	08/09/1881
STUSSY, MATT	CSV 000037	07/11/1881
STYLES, ELIZA	CSV 000693	STYLES, JOHN, 08/30/1881
SUBLETT, W C	CSV 001880	04/29/1882
SUCHART, FRITZ	CSV 000096	07/13/1881
SULLIVAN, W S	CSV 001507	11/21/1881
SURRATT, J M	CSV 001583	01/10/1882
SUTPHEN, W C	CSV 001529	11/14/1881
SUTTON, HUGH	CSV 001924	08/10/1881
SWAIN, THOMAS	CSV 000076	07/18/1881
SWEATT, EMALINE	CSV 001862	04/18/1882
SWENSON, MARY A	CSV 001116	SWENSON, H B, 10/24/1881
TALIAFERRO, LOUIS	CSV 001956	06/20/1882
TALLEY, CHARLOTTE	CSV 000036	TALLEY, CALVIN, 07/12/1881
TALLEY, REUBEN	CSV 000039	07/11/1881
TANKERSLEY, W H	CSV 000328	06/08/1881
TARKINGTON, G H	CSV 000641	07/30/1881
TARKINGTON, JOHN	CSV 001034	08/22/1881
TARVER, WILLIAM H	CSV 001029	09/18/1881
TATE, REBECCA	CSV 000145	TATE, JESSIE, 07/12/1881
TAYLOR, ANDREW	CSV 001097	10/10/1881
TAYLOR, B F	CSV 000991	08/09/1881
TAYLOR, C L	CSV 001265	11/23/1881
TAYLOR, F M	CSV 000150	07/06/1881
TAYLOR, H E	CSV 001522	11/15/1881
TAYLOR, J H	CSV 000446	08/09/1881

Confederate Scrip Vouchers-Alphabetical Listing

TAYLOR, J P	CSV 001206	11/14/1881
TAYLOR, JANE	CSV 000205	TAYLOR, OBE, 07/11/1881
TAYLOR, LEWIS H	CSV 000049	07/14/1881
TAYLOR, MARTHA	CSV 001958	06/12/1882
TAYLOR, MARY C	CSV 001259	11/23/1881
TAYLOR, PERRY S	CSV 000596	08/08/1881
TEAL, T A	CSV 001447	12/06/1881
TEAVER, W A	CSV 001432	12/05/1881
TEER, WILLIAM	CSV 000331	08/12/1881
TEMPLETON, JOHN S	CSV 002059	09/02/1882
TEN EYCK, H R	CSV 000005	TEN EYCK, ALFRED, 07/07/1887
TERRY, JOHN K	CSV 001741	03/10/1882
TERRY, JOHN W	CSV 001658	11/15/1881
TERRY, THOMAS	CSV 001518	12/21/1881
THARP, ELIZABETH	CSV 000131	THARP, R J, 07/01/1881
THIGPEN, JOHN	CSV 000726	09/02/1881
THOMAS, AOMINTA	CSV 001308	11/15/1881
THOMAS, J O	CSV 000410	08/15/1881
THOMAS, JOHN C	CSV 001365	11/26/1881
THOMAS, SARAH	CSV 000052	THOMAS, B P, 07/16/1881
THOMAS, W JASPER	CSV 000563	08/16/1881
THOMPSON, ALBERT	CSV 000063	07/14/1881
THOMPSON, D P	CSV 000057	07/01/1881
THOMPSON, GEORGE	CSV 001974	07/28/1882
THOMPSON, J	CSV 001115	08/09/1881
THOMPSON, JANE	CSV 000688	THOMPSON, JOHN T, 08/08/1881
THOMPSON, JULIA A	CSV 001600	THOMPSON, JOHN, 01/17/1882
THOMPSON, MAHALA W	CSV 000526	THOMPSON, MALCOMB, 07/11/1881
THOMPSON, MARTHA	CSV 000690	THOMPSON, T U, 08/08/1881
THOMPSON, MARY	CSV 001968	07/10/1882
THOMPSON, SUSAN	CSV 001465	12/09/1881
THOMPSON, W H	CSV 001587	04/09/1881
THOMTON, W J	CSV 001823	1/15/1881
THORNTON, VICTORIA	CSV 000729	09/02/1881
THORP, NANCY	CSV 001139	11/10/1881
TIDWELL, M E	CSV 000983	09/30/1881
TIERCE, J P	CSV 000888	09/13/1881
TIGERT, J M	CSV 001743	03/11/1882
TIMMINS, JOSEPHINE	CSV 000177	07/02/1881
TINNIN, WILLIAM	CSV 000248	08/08/1881
TIPPITT, GEORGIA	CSV 000927	09/24/1881
TISON, E J	CSV 001567	TYSON, WILLIAM, 12/21/1881
TITUS, E B	CSV 001673	02/21/1882
TODD, LOUISA	CSV 000508	TODD, J M, 08/08/1881
TODD, W R	CSV 001059	10/17/1881

Confederate Scrip Vouchers-Alphabetical Listing

TOSBER, EDWARD	CSV 001494	12/14/1881
TOWNSEND, J M	CSV 000848	08/08/1881
TOWNSEND, THOMAS	CSV 001596	01/12/1882
TRAMMEL, W B	CSV 000725	08/08/1881
TRANT, MARSHALL	CSV 001621	01/30/1882
TRAYNOR, JOHN	CSV 001513	11/15/1881
TREADWELL, S E	CSV 000582	TREADWELL, R L, 08/08/1881
TRIBBLE, ELIZABETH	CSV 000913	09/21/1881
TRIBBLE, MARY	CSV 000207	07/07/1881
TRISCHRMEYER, F	CSV 000337	08/12/1881
TROTTER, JOHN W	CSV 000650	08/27/1881
TRUITT, MARY A	CSV 001156	TRUITT, FRANCIS M, 07/11/1881
TRUITT, SUSAN	CSV 001157	TRUITT, THOMAS S, 07/11/1881
TUBBS, JOHN S	CSV 001055	09/20/1881
TUCKER, ALLEN J	CSV 000882	09/08/1881
TUCKER, EMILINE	CSV 000083	TUCKER, JEREWIOB, 07/18/1881
TUCKER, G W	CSV 001677	02/18/1882
TUCKER, J M	CSV 000894	09/10/1881
TULLY, MARY J F	CSV 000883	09/12/1881
TUNNELL, W B	CSV 001619	01/28/1882
TURLEY, G W	CSV 001933	05/22/1882
TURMAN, T G	CSV 000311	08/08/1881
TURNER, E P	CSV 001949	06/12/1882
TURNER, EMILIA, EMILY	CSV 000220	07/23/1881
TURNER, J T	CSV 001096	10/26/1881
TURNER, JAMES	CSV 000813	08/24/1881
TURNER, JESSE	CSV 001641	07/13/1881
TURNER, JOHN	CSV 001997	08/25/1882
TURNER, W B	CSV 000927	09/24/1881
TUTTLE, JAMES W	CSV 000275	08/08/1881
TYER, JOHN	CSV 001960	06/20/1882
TYLER, SARAH	CSV 001501	12/17/1881
UMPHREY, JOHN H	CSV 001951	06/12/1882
UPTON, GILES	CSV 001351	09/26/1881
UTZ, M C	CSV 000495	UTZ, JOE, 08/08/1881
VADER, ALLEN D	CSV 000113	07/20/1881
VALDEZ, JUAN ANTONIO	CSV 001667	02/15/1882
VAN OVER, SAMUEL	CSV 000594	08/09/1881
VAN SICKLE, THOMAS J	CSV 000572	08/18/1881
VANDERVEER, CHARLES S	CSV 000193	07/15/1881
VANNOY, SUSAN E	CSV 000157	07/07/1881
VASQUEZ, ANTONIO	CSV 001117	11/02/1881
VAUGHN, ELIZA J	CSV 000927	09/24/1881
VAUGHN, P H	CSV 000711	08/10/1881
VEAL, J C	CSV 000765	09/05/1881
VERMILLION, J H	CSV 000289	08/08/1881

Confederate Scrip Vouchers-Alphabetical Listing

Name	Voucher	Date / Related
VERNON, N A	CSV 000343	VERNON, THOS G, 08/08/1881
VICKENY, VANCE	CSV 001605	01/02/1882
VICKERY, HARDIN	CSV 000642	08/08/1881
VINSON, A H	CSV 001638	12/31/1881
VINSON, EVALINE	CSV 000801	VINSON, AUSTIN, 08/11/1881
VON DER DECKEN, CAROLINE	CSV 000860	VON DER DECKEN, OTTO, 09/15/1881
VOYLES, MARTHA	CSV 001017	VOYLES, SAM, 10/08/1881
WADE, ABRAHAM	CSV 001317	11/25/1881
WAGGONER, MARGARETT	CSV 000644	WAGGONER, GEORGE, 07/11/1881
WAGNER, JACOB	CSV 001125	08/08/1881
WAGNON, T J	CSV 001103	10/24/1881
WAKALEE, AUGUSTINE	CSV 002024	10/24/1882
WAKEFIELD, J H	CSV 001954	06/20/1882
WALDON, W M	CSV 000006	07/07/1881
WALDSCHMIDT, JACOB	CSV 000681	08/30/1881
WALKER, A D	CSV 001273	11/14/1881
WALKER, DICK	CSV 000668	08/11/1881
WALKER, E L	CSV 001792	11/14/1881
WALKER, JOHN W	CSV 001753	03/14/1882
WALKER, M J	CSV 000453	WALKER, W H, 08/08/1881
WALKER, MARTHA JANE	CSV 000340	WALKER, J WATTS, 08/08/1881
WALKER, S C	CSV 002017	12/17/1881
WALL, J T	CSV 000382	08/08/1881
WALLACE, AMANDA	CSV 001665	02/13/1882
WALLACE, H K	CSV 000970	09/01/1881
WALLACE, SARAH	CSV 001985	08/18/1882
WALLING, RICHARD	CSV 001198	11/18/1881
WALLS, LARKEN	CSV 000074	07/13/1881
WALSH, M F	CSV 001089	WALSH, W R, 08/27/1881
WALTERS, MARTHA	CSV 000578	WALTERS, PHILLIP A, 08/15/1881
WALTERS, TILMAN	CSV 000750	08/20/1881
WARD, H R	CSV 001014	10/07/1881
WARD, THOMAS	CSV 001803	04/13/1882
WARD, W S	CSV 000227	07/20/1881
WARREN, ORPA	CSV 000904	09/13/1881
WATKINS, JOHN W	CSV 000276	08/11/1881
WATKINS, PAUL JIM	CSV 000286	08/08/1881
WATSON, JOSIAH	CSV 001544	12/27/1881
WATTS, A J	CSV 000070	07/11/1881
WATTS, REBECCA	CSV 000062	WATTS, WILLIS, 07/18/1881
WATTS, WILLIS J	CSV 000064	07/14/1881
WEATHERSBY, NANCY	CSV 000421	WEATHERSBY, THOMAS, 08/09/1881
WEATHERSPOON, P W	CSV 000611	08/13/1881
WEAVER, J A	CSV 001319	11/25/1881

Confederate Scrip Vouchers-Alphabetical Listing

Name	Voucher	Date
WEAVER, J F	CSV 000717	08/16/1881
WEAVER, SALLIE	CSV 000225	08/06/1881
WEBB, JACOB	CSV 000366	07/08/1881
WEBB, MARY J	CSV 002027	11/09/1882
WEICHOLD, HENRY	CSV 001561	12/05/1881
WELBORN, A H	CSV 001498	12/16/1881
WELLAM, A C	CSV 000663	07/25/1881
WELLS, LOUIS	CSV 000003	07/07/1881
WELLS, W G	CSV 000115	07/20/1881
WELLS, W W	CSV 001258	11/14/1881
WEST, ALFRED	CSV 001650	02/16/1882
WEST, M M	CSV 000580	WEST, A J, 08/09/1881
WEYERS, F M	CSV 001266	11/23/1881
WHATLEY, J W	CSV 001006	10/07/1881
WHEAT, JOHN	CSV 002026	10/24/1882
WHEELER, A	CSV 001854	04/17/1882
WHEELER, HOUSTON	CSV 001449	12/07/1881
WHEELER, J P	CSV 001435	05/13/1881
WHEELER, M M	CSV 001850	04/17/1872
WHEELER, THOMAS	CSV 001450	12/07/1881
WHEELER, W J	CSV 001379	11/17/1881
WHITAKER, WILLIS	CSV 001085	10/24/1881
WHITE, ELIZA	CSV 001787	04/07/1882
WHITE, F W	CSV 000510	WHITE, DAVID, 08/11/1881
WHITE, FRANCIS C	CSV 000782	08/08/1881
WHITE, J A	CSV 001118	08/09/1881
WHITE, JOHN	CSV 000579	08/17/1881
WHITE, JOHN M	CSV 000872	08/08/1881
WHITE, JOHN O	CSV 000354	08/13/1881
WHITE, MARY	CSV 001905	05/12/1882
WHITE, R M	CSV 001764	03/21/1882
WHITE, W K	CSV 002033	11/20/1882
WHITE, W T	CSV 000102	07/02/1881
WHITEHEAD, JOE H	CSV 000635	07/29/1881
WHITEN, J D	CSV 001331	11/25/1881
WHITILY, J C	CSV 000543	08/22/1881
WHITNEY, MARY ANN	CSV 000980	WHITNEY, BENJAMIN AUGUSTUS, 09/17/1881
WHITSON, JAMES	CSV 001391	11/29/1881
WILBORN, M C	CSV 001286	11/23/1881
WILEY, ED	CSV 001481	12/12/1881
WILEY, MARY ANN	CSV 001838	11/14/1881
WILKES, A H	CSV 001927	05/18/1882
WILLIAMS, A J	CSV 001419	11/18/1881
WILLIAMS, CELETA	CSV 000163	WILLIAMS, E T, 07/23/1881
WILLIAMS, D F	CSV 001698	02/27/1882
WILLIAMS, E O	CSV 001468	12/10/1881
WILLIAMS, J F R	CSV 001183	11/17/1881
WILLIAMS, J S	CSV 001143	11/02/1881

Confederate Scrip Vouchers-Alphabetical Listing

Name	Voucher	Date / Notes
WILLIAMS, JAMES	CSV 001626	02/02/1882
WILLIAMS, JAMES T	CSV 001233	11/21/1881
WILLIAMS, LOUISA	CSV 001841	04/17/1882
WILLIAMS, M C	CSV 000659	WILLIAMS, A C, 08/08/1881
WILLIAMS, MARTIN	CSV 001244	10/3/1881
WILLIAMS, MATILDA	CSV 000927	09/24/1881
WILLIAMS, PARTHANA	CSV 000600	08/09/1881
WILLIAMS, SARAH J	CSV 001256	11/23/1881
WILLIAMS, T E	CSV 001417	11/15/1881
WILLIAMSON, N A	CSV 001288	WILLIAMSON, DANIEL, 1/16/1881
WILLIAMSON, W H	CSV 000471	08/07/1881
WILLIFORD, C J	CSV 001963	06/28/1882
WILLIS, M A	CSV 000377	WILLIS, J L, 08/03/1881
WILLIS, W B	CSV 000126	WILLIS, W B, 07/05/1881
WILLIYARDS, H C	CSV 001693	02/27/1882
WILLS, B N	CSV 000616	08/12/1881
WILLS, FRANCIS	CSV 000754	WILLS, ISAAC D, 08/08/1881
WILLS, JOSEPH	CSV 001552	01/04/1882
WILSON, A J	CSV 002039	11/21/1882
WILSON, E T	CSV 000807	09/09/1881
WILSON, J C	CSV 001458	07/12/1881
WILSON, JAMES	CSV 001530	12/24/1881
WILSON, L F	CSV 001577	01/10/1882
WILSON, R S	CSV 000797	08/08/1881
WILSON, W F	CSV 001563	01/04/1882
WILSON, W J	CSV 000230	07/21/1881
WILSON, W M	CSV 001534	12/27/1881
WILSON, WILLIAM	CSV 001080	10/11/1881
WINGO, W A	CSV 001374	11/28/1881
WINN, CASSANDRA	CSV 000321	08/08/1881
WINTON, J W	CSV 001487	12/14/1881
WISE, F J	CSV 001421	12/10/1881
WITHERSPOON, H E	CSV 000999	08/09/1881
WOLBERT, MARVEL	CSV 000066	07/11/1881
WOOD, CAMPBELL	CSV 001945	05/24/1882
WOOD, DAN A	CSV 001523	12/23/1881
WOOD, S M	CSV 001682	02/24/1882
WOOD, SARAH	CSV 000705	WOOD, ALEXANDER, 08/30/1881
WOOD, WILLIAM G	CSV 000141	07/07/1881
WOODALL, A C	CSV 000475	07/07/1881
WOODARD, J W	CSV 001355	11/25/1881
WOODARD, TYER	CSV 001979	08/14/1882
WOODHOUSER, JNO	CSV 000825	09/14/1881
WOODRUFF, D W	CSV 001044	10/08/1881
WOODS, KATE	CSV 001102	WOODS, BEN, 10/24/1881
WOODS, ROBERT	CSV 001689	12/12/1881
WOODSON, CHARLES	CSV 000360	07/24/1881

Name	Voucher	Date
WOODSON, W H	CSV 000143	07/09/1881
WOOLVERTON, E H	CSV 002051	11/08/1882
WOOLWORTH, J M	CSV 000221	07/25/1881
WOOTAN, A A	CSV 002036	11/20/1882
WORD, R J	CSV 001779	03/31/1882
WORRELL, JOHN	CSV 001414	11/18/1881
WORTHINGTON, MARY	CSV 001870	04/22/1882
WORTHY, JANE	CSV 001678	02/23/1882
WORTHY, M A	CSV 000144	07/12/1881
WRAY, MARTHA	CSV 001475	11/16/1881
WREN, PATHENA	CSV 000849	09/13/1881
WREN, W C	CSV 001652	02/17/1882
WRIGHT, DAVE	CSV 001634	08/22/1882
WRIGHT, J J T	CSV 000132	07/01/1881
WRIGHT, JOHN L	CSV 001844	04/17/1882
WYATT, WILLIAM H	CSV 001334	11/25/1881
WYNEKOOP, P C	CSV 001163	11/16/1881
YARBOROUGH, J W	CSV 000253	08/09/1881
YEAKLEY, M V	CSV 001100	10/29/1881
YEARY, J K	CSV 001966	07/08/1882
YEATMAN, J N	CSV 000513	07/18/1881
YORK, J T	CSV 000927	09/24/1881
YOUNG, H P	CSV 000293	08/09/1881
YOUNG, J F	CSV 000798	YOUNG, R B, 08/09/1881
YOUNG, J J	CSV 000549	08/22/1881
YOUNG, ROBERT	CSV 001208	11/14/1881
YOUNG, WILLIAM T	CSV 000391	08/01/1881
YOUNGBLOOD, M	CSV 000013	07/01/1881
ZACHERY, J U	CSV 000561	08/08/1881
ZEIGLER, JACOB	CSV 000274	08/08/1881
ZIRAMON, MANUEL	CSV 001368	11/26/1881

Index to Confederate Scrip Vouchers Numerical Listing

File Number	Grantee's Name	Description
CSV 000001	CAMERON, MARY	CAMERON, ALLAN, 07/05/1881
CSV 000002	MURRIE, REBECCA	MURRIE, ROBERT S, 07/01/1881
CSV 000003	WELLS, LOUIS	07/07/1881
CSV 000004	ALSTON, W W	07/07/1881
CSV 000005	TEN EYCK, H R	TEN EYCK, ALFRED, 07/07/1887
CSV 000006	WALDON, W M	07/07/1881
CSV 000007	BAUTWELL, A R	07/07/1881
CSV 000008	GRAYUM, MILTON	07/02/1881
CSV 000009	BLEDSOE, E W	BLEDSOE, JOHN, 07/07/1881
CSV 000010	MILES, AQUILLA	07/02/1881
CSV 000011	NEAL, ELIZABETH	NEAL, THOMAS, 07/01/1881
CSV 000012	COATS, HARRIET	COATS, SAMUEL, 07/05/1881
CSV 000013	YOUNGBLOOD, M	07/01/1881
CSV 000014	BABAR, THOS A	07/07/1881.
CSV 000015	BOASE, W J	07/07/1881.
CSV 000016	MC LAUGHLIN, MARTIN	07/11/1881
CSV 000017	GRANT, G S	07/12/1881
CSV 000018	HOOD, ANDERSON B	07/06/1881
CSV 000019	EVERSBERG, ALBERT	07/09/1881
CSV 000020	ATWOOD, MARY	ATWOOD, THOMAS, 07/02/1881
CSV 000021	BARKER, S A	BARKER, A J, 07/01/1881
CSV 000022	ADEMS, AMMAZILLA	ADEMS, BENJAMIN, 07/01/1881
CSV 000023	SMITH, B M	07/01/1881
CSV 000024	BAKER, SORILDA	BAKER, THOMAS, 07/05/1881
CSV 000025	HARRIS, S L	07/05/1881
CSV 000026	CRAWFORD, T K	07/05/1881
CSV 000027	BUSSEY, ELIZABETH	BUSSEY, THOMAS, 07/05/1881
CSV 000028	RIDDLE, W S	07/09/1881
CSV 000029	NAGLE, JAMES E	07/01/1881
CSV 000030	BIRDWELL, NANCY	BIRDWELL, J R, 07/11/1881
CSV 000031	MITCHELL, J W	07/15/1881
CSV 000032	BURTIN, JOHN I	07/11/1881
CSV 000033	BARRICK, BYRD M	BARRICK, S K, 07/02/1881
CSV 000034	DEAN, ROBERT	07/15/1881
CSV 000035	DORWIN, W	07/09/1881
CSV 000036	TALLEY, CHARLOTTE	TALLEY, CALVIN, 07/12/1881
CSV 000037	STUSSY, MATT	07/11/1881
CSV 000038	SMITH, JOHN I	07/15/1881
CSV 000039	TALLEY, REUBEN	07/11/1881
CSV 000040	SPRINGER, G B	07/11/1881
CSV 000041	NOTGRASS, T J	07/15/1881
CSV 000042	PALLEY. J B	07/16/1881

CSV 000043	MURRAY, J W	07/11/1881
CSV 000044	ALLEN, GEORGE	07/11/1881
CSV 000045	PRYOR, R N	07/14/1881
CSV 000046	MC KNIGHT, E H	07/15/1881
CSV 000047	DAVIDSON, ELIZA J L	DAVIDSON, JOHN J, 07/11/1881
CSV 000048	SOWELL, JAMES A	07/13/1881
CSV 000049	TAYLOR, LEWIS H	07/14/1881
CSV 000050	PLOWMAN, JOHN I	07/16/1881
CSV 000051	DEEL, JOHN W	07/16/1881
CSV 000052	THOMAS, SARAH	THOMAS, B P, 07/16/1881
CSV 000053	COOMER, FREDERICK	07/16/1881
CSV 000054	COYLE, EBBLINE	COYLE, HENDERSON, 07/06/1881
CSV 000055	CLAY, WILLIAM	07/12/1881
CSV 000056	REED, ALEXANDER	07/01/1881
CSV 000057	THOMPSON, D P	07/01/1881
CSV 000058	FILE EMPTY	
CSV 000059	ROBERTSON, FRANCIS S	07/14/1881
CSV 000060	CANTRELL, J L	07/14/1881
CSV 000061	RICE, SUSANNAH	07/11/1881
CSV 000062	WATTS, REBECCA	WATTS, WILLIS, 07/18/1881
CSV 000063	THOMPSON, ALBERT	07/14/1881
CSV 000064	WATTS, WILLIS J	07/14/1881
CSV 000065	GIBSON, A	07/13/1881
CSV 000066	WOLBERT, MARVEL	07/11/1881
CSV 000067	BIRMION, W A	07/11/1881
CSV 000068	CLIFFT, J S	07/11/1881
CSV 000069	KRIEG, J H	07/11/1881
CSV 000070	WATTS, A J	07/11/1881
CSV 000071	HEAD, L M	07/11/1881
CSV 000072	RAMSEY, JOHN	07/18/1881
CSV 000073	ARMSTRONG, G H	07/13/1881
CSV 000074	WALLS, LARKEN	07/13/1881
CSV 000075	BAKER, J H	07/18/1881
CSV 000076	SWAIN, THOMAS	07/18/1881
CSV 000077	ATCHLEY, MARTHA	07/18/1881
CSV 000078	CHESTER, JOHN C	07/18/1881
CSV 000079	BIRMINGHAM, E J	07/19/1881
CSV 000080	MOSILEY, J B	07/05/1881
CSV 000081	RAPE, WILLIAM	07/16/1881
CSV 000082	KIRN, MICHAEL	07/19/1881
CSV 000083	TUCKER, EMILINE	TUCKER, JEREWIOB, 07/18/1881
CSV 000084	LAFFERTY, JOHN H	07/02/1881
CSV 000085	BEAN, E M	07/18/1881
CSV 000086	KIRTLAND, D	07/18/1881
CSV 000087	MITCHELL, JABEZ	07/01/1881
CSV 000088	BAINES, J M	07/19/1881
CSV 000089	DARCY, SAM J	07/13/1881

CSV 000090	DOSS, MARY	DOSS, JOSEPH, 07/18/1881
CSV 000091	JORDAN, M W	07/11/1881
CSV 000092	PARKER, JOHN	07/12/1881
CSV 000093	RAINEY, E B	07/12/1881
CSV 000094	GLASER, JULIUS	07/13/1881
CSV 000095	DONEGAN, JNO	07/13/1881
CSV 000096	SUCHART, FRITZ	07/13/1881
CSV 000097	BURGESS, R J	07/13/1881
CSV 000098	HARRIS, W A	07/13/1881
CSV 000099	POLK, JOHN D	07/16/1881
CSV 000100	REEVES, MARTHA	REEVES, AGRIPPA, 04/09/1881
CSV 000101	JOHNSON, SARAH	JOHNSON, WILLIAM, 07/21/1881
CSV 000102	WHITE, W T	07/02/1881
CSV 000103	BARNWELL, SAMUEL M	07/06/1881
CSV 000104	BAILEY, A E	07/16/1881
CSV 000105	CASBEER, J L	07/08/1881
CSV 000106	NEVANS, MARGARET	NEVANS, T C, 07/22/1881
CSV 000107	BRADFIELD, JOHN W	07/22/1881
CSV 000108	HILLYER, JUNIUS	07/04/1881
CSV 000109	MARLEE, L J	MARLEE, JACOB, 07/16/1881
CSV 000110	PRESCOTT, LILITHA	PRESCOTT, DAVIS, DAVID, 07/12/1881
CSV 000111	GREER, M H	07/14/1881
CSV 000112	LYSTER, C C	LYSTER, JAMES, 07/16/1881
CSV 000113	VADER, ALLEN D	07/20/1881
CSV 000114	POSEY, MATILDA ANN	POSEY, E D, 07/20/1881
CSV 000115	WELLS, W G	07/20/1881
CSV 000116	BROWN, J M	07/13/1881
CSV 000117	HUDGONS, JAMES	07/14/1881
CSV 000118	MILLER, JOHN L	07/05/1885
CSV 000119	BOREN, FRANCIS	BOREN, PERRY, 07/05/1881
CSV 000120	HUSTEAD, C C	07/13/1881
CSV 000121	BURRIS, HENRIETTA	BURRIS, L F, 07/23/1881
CSV 000122	BEAVERS, R H	07/25/1881
CSV 000123	BEARD, JULIA	BEARD, WILLIAM, 07/11/1881
CSV 000124	SARRATT, LEVI	07/01/1881
CSV 000125	SPELL, MARY	SPELL, RICHARD H, 07/22/1881
CSV 000126	WILLIS, W B	WILLIS, W B, 07/05/1881
CSV 000127	O REAR, J P	07/01/1881
CSV 000128	FLETCHER, JOHN M	07/18/1881
CSV 000129	BARBER, NANCY	BARBER, GEORGE, 07/18/1881
CSV 000130	HEFFERMAN, WILLIAM H	07/12/1881
CSV 000131	THARP, ELIZABETH	THARP, R J, 07/01/1881
CSV 000132	WRIGHT, J J T	07/01/1881
CSV 000133	PRICE, G D	07/01/1881
CSV 000134	POOL, WM	07/12/1881
CSV 000135	DAY, S M	07/14/1881
CSV 000136	HALL, M E	HALL, JOHN H, 07/23/1881

Confederate Scrip Vouchers-Numerical Listing

CSV 000137	SMITH, MARTHA	SMITH, J B, 07/13/1881
CSV 000138	SANDELL, R S	SANDELL, J O, 07/01/1881
CSV 000139	BRIGAND, A L	07/18/1881
CSV 000140	STINSON, JOHN H	07/26/1881
CSV 000141	WOOD, WILLIAM G	07/07/1881
CSV 000142	BALDWIN, B J	07/07/1881
CSV 000143	WOODSON, W H	07/09/1881
CSV 000144	WORTHY, M A	07/12/1881
CSV 000145	TATE, REBECCA	TATE, JESSIE, 07/12/1881
CSV 000146	CARTWRIGHT, THOMAS	07/14/1881
CSV 000147	LANG, J M	07/21/1881
CSV 000148	CLEAVLAND, D A	CLEAVLAND, J W, 07/18/1881
CSV 000149	SCROGGINS, LOUISA	SCROGGINS, WILLIAM, 07/05/1881
CSV 000150	TAYLOR, F M	07/06/1881
CSV 000151	RIDGAWAY, W P	06/06/1881
CSV 000152	RAINEY, A T	07/14/1881
CSV 000153	RICHARDSON, MARY F	RICHARDSON, HENRY S, 07/15/1881
CSV 000154	CALVERY, J H	07/24/1881
CSV 000155	COX, MARY E	07/11/1881
CSV 000156	GRIMES, NANCY H	GRIMES, PLEASANT, 11/07/1881
CSV 000157	VANNOY, SUSAN E	07/07/1881
CSV 000158	HARRIS, J N	07/29/1881
CSV 000159	CLIFTON, THOMAS	07/20/1881
CSV 000160	SEWELL, JOHN J	07/29/1881
CSV 000161	POTTS, MARY	POTTS, PAUL, 07/29/1881
CSV 000162	HOOD, ELIZA	HOOD, JOHN, 07/23/1881
CSV 000163	WILLIAMS, CELETA	WILLIAMS, E T, 07/23/1881
CSV 000164	NORWOOD, JOHN H	07/23/1881
CSV 000165	PERSONS, L R	07/07/1881
CSV 000166	OTIS, THOMAS	07/11/1881
CSV 000167	JOHNSON, LUCINDA	JOHNSON, H C, 07/12/1881
CSV 000168	BRANSOM, JAMES W	07/12/1881
CSV 000169	GRIFFIN, J H	07/11/1881
CSV 000170	MILTON, MARTHA T	MILTON, HENRY, 07/30/1881
CSV 000171	MURDOCK, JAMES H	07/01/1881
CSV 000172	PHILLIPS, M S	07/07/1881
CSV 000173	DAVIS, M E	07/07/1881
CSV 000174	NOWLIN, MINERVA	NOWLIN, BENJAMIN, 07/30/1881
CSV 000175	DUKE, W J	07/22/1881
CSV 000176	PANTHER, L D	08/18/1881
CSV 000177	TIMMINS, JOSEPHINE	07/02/1881
CSV 000178	MAIZE, MARY E	MAIZE, A G, 07/11/1881
CSV 000179	ROBERTS, JOHN P	07/21/1881
CSV 000180	ANGAN, THOMAS	08/01/1881
CSV 000181	PARRISH, SAPHRONIA	PARRISH, THOMAS, 07/22/1881

CSV 000182	PISTOLE, THOMAS R	07/18/1881
CSV 000183	PRICE, DAVID	07/18/1881
CSV 000184	BLAKE, A M	07/28/1881
CSV 000185	CULLEN, ED	04/09/1881
CSV 000186	HAYFORD, SAMUEL	08/09/1881
CSV 000187	KINGSTON, F H	08/03/1881
CSV 000188	BILLS, J W	07/26/1881
CSV 000189	NIDEVER, JOHN	07/26/1881
CSV 000190	GRAVES, R C	07/12/1881
CSV 000191	PATTERSON, E D	07/07/1881
CSV 000192	FERGUSON, W H	07/07/1881
CSV 000193	VANDERVEER, CHARLES S	07/15/1881
CSV 000194	MATTHEWS, WILLIAM	08/03/1881
CSV 000195	LAWRENCE, J C	07/12/1881
CSV 000196	FULLER, M A	FULLER, J K, 07/12/1881
CSV 000197	PEYTON, JOHN A	07/02/1881
CSV 000198	GASSETT, C T	07/16/1881
CSV 000199	CAMPBELL, K A	07/20/1881
CSV 000200	PRIEST, JAMES T	07/12/1881
CSV 000201	JOHNSON, FELIX	07/05/1881
CSV 000202	HERROD, JAMES M	07/07/1881
CSV 000203	GLASSON, ALVIS	07/12/1881
CSV 000204	BUTLER, MARTHA	BUTLER, JAMES, 07/11/1881
CSV 000205	TAYLOR, JANE	TAYLOR, OBE, 07/11/1881
CSV 000206	CHANDLER, L C	CHANDLER, WILEY, 07/11/1881
CSV 000207	TRIBBLE, MARY	07/07/1881
CSV 000208	SHARPE, T H	07/07/1881
CSV 000209	CORBRIE, G M	07/15/1881
CSV 000210	KING, JAMES P	07/15/1881
CSV 000211	SOLOMAN, TABITHA E	07/22/1881
CSV 000212	DOHERTY, ELIZABETH	DOHERTY, JAMES M, 07/11/1881
CSV 000213	RISINGER, AVARILLA P	RISINGER, JAMES LAUDON, 08/04/1881
CSV 000214	AMOX, SARAH A	AMOX, CORNELIUS, 07/18/1881
CSV 000215	HEDICK, CAROLINE	HEDICK, GEORGE, 07/18/1881
CSV 000216	MILLARD, M A	MILLARD, W H, 07/18/1881
CSV 000217	CORTHAN, T C	08/04/1881
CSV 000218	KNOX, M A	07/14/1881
CSV 000219	ADAM, E R	07/01/1881
CSV 000220	TURNER, EMILIA, EMILY	07/23/1881
CSV 000221	WOOLWORTH, J M	07/25/1881
CSV 000222	ALLEN, JOHN W	08/06/1881
CSV 000223	BEAL, D R	07/09/1881
CSV 000224	GODWIN, NANCY	07/16/1881
CSV 000225	WEAVER, SALLIE	08/06/1881
CSV 000226	JONES, THOMAS	07/20/1881
CSV 000227	WARD, W S	07/20/1881
CSV 000228	ROMINE, J W	07/20/1881

Confederate Scrip Vouchers-Numerical Listing

CSV 000229	COOK, HULDAH	07/19/1881
CSV 000230	WILSON, W J	07/21/1881
CSV 000231	SMITH, J P	07/20/1881
CSV 000232	ROBERTSON, D F	08/06/1881
CSV 000233	DANNIELS, SALLIE	DANIELS, JAMES, 07/12/1881
CSV 000234	SHATTICK, J H	SHATTICK, W M, 07/18/1881
CSV 000235	RIGBY, R E	07/18/1881
CSV 000236	MOORE, FRANCES	MOORE, G W, 08/06/1881
CSV 000237	LUCE, Z	07/18/1881
CSV 000238	PETTYJOHN, J C	07/18/1881
CSV 000239	RICE, W P	07/18/1881
CSV 000240	SPRINGER, W J	07/18/1881
CSV 000241	GARDNER, F M	08/06/1881
CSV 000242	ALLEN, B F	07/18/1881
CSV 000243	MC GEE, J A	08/06/1881
CSV 000244	BYBEE, F M	08/06/1881
CSV 000245	HILL, S R	07/18/1881
CSV 000246	PHIPPS, MARY A	PHIPPS. G E, 08/06/1881
CSV 000247	GRIFFIN, ELIZABETH	GRIFFIN, A C, 07/19/1881
CSV 000248	TINNIN, WILLIAM	08/08/1881
CSV 000249	MADEN, C P	08/08/1881
CSV 000250	BARNES, JOSEPH	07/02/1881
CSV 000251	DOMINY, E A	DOMINY, A B, 08/09/1881
CSV 000252	LEACH, L	07/05/1881
CSV 000253	YARBOROUGH, J W	08/09/1881
CSV 000254	MC COLLUM, JANE M	08/09/1881
CSV 000255	MADDOX, SARAH E	MADDOX, M D A, 08/01/1881
CSV 000256	NOBLE, N M	NOBLE, J C, 08/09/1881
CSV 000257	MOORE, THADDEUS	08/09/1881
CSV 000258	SMITH, MARY A	SMITH, T B, 08/09/1881
CSV 000259	BLACKWELL, SARAH P	BLACKWELL, H F, 08/09/1881
CSV 000260	LAUDMAN, ISABELLA J	LAUDMAN, MARTIN W, 08/09/1881
CSV 000261	STORY, SOPHRONIA	STORY, WM M, 07/12/1881
CSV 000262	POTEET, H N	POTEET, H N, 08/08/1881
CSV 000263	STONE, S T	STONE, S T, 08/10/1881
CSV 000264	COOPER, W V L	07/22/1881
CSV 000265	PEEL, M J	PEEL, WILLIAM, 08/10/1881
CSV 000266	MORPHIS, MARY	MORPHIS, WILLIAM, 08/10/1881
CSV 000267	GARY, BALINDA	GARY, A J, 08/10/1881
CSV 000268	KELLY, J P	07/13/1881
CSV 000269	POOL, W M	08/10/1881
CSV 000270	ALLEN, MARTHA A	ALLEN, THOMAS J, 08/08/1881
CSV 000271	ATTAWAY, DAVID	08/08/1881
CSV 000272	SHERRIL, J G	08/10/1881
CSV 000273	MOORE, THOMAS	08/10/1881
CSV 000274	ZEIGLER, JACOB	08/08/1881
CSV 000275	TUTTLE, JAMES W	08/08/1881

CSV 000276	WATKINS, JOHN W	08/11/1881
CSV 000277	SMITH, WILLIAM H	08/11/1881
CSV 000278	BAMPLIN, W A	07/22/1881
CSV 000279	STUL, W C	08/09/1881
CSV 000280	STUART, JOHN E	08/08/1881
CSV 000281	PEDUTE, JOHN	08/08/1881
CSV 000282	BURDETT, AUGUSTA H	08/01/1881
CSV 000283	DUNLAP, D C	08/08/1881
CSV 000284	ROPER, T L	08/08/1881
CSV 000285	MENGER, OSCAR	08/08/1881
CSV 000286	WATKINS, PAUL JIM	08/08/1881
CSV 000287	HEFFINGTON, ISAAC	08/08/1881
CSV 000288	EICKE, HENRY	08/08/1881
CSV 000289	VERMILLION, J H	08/08/1881
CSV 000290	SMITH, J J	08/08/1881
CSV 000291	CANTRELL, J R	08/08/1881
CSV 000292	RAJE, LEAH	08/09/1881
CSV 000293	YOUNG, H P	08/09/1881
CSV 000294	ASHWORTH, MONROE	08/08/1881
CSV 000295	RAINE, M E	RAINE, JIM, 08/08/1881
CSV 000296	NEWBY, ELIZABETH	NEWBY, WM H, 08/09/1881
CSV 000297	BLUE, JNO W	08/11/1881
CSV 000298	PENGE, PRISCILLA	BENGE, JAMES, 08/09/1881
CSV 000299	DANIELS, FRANCIS	DANIELS, GEORGE, 08/11/1881
CSV 000300	MC ANINCH, E B	08/11/1881
CSV 000301	EATON, RICHARD	08/08/1881
CSV 000302	ROBBINS, M J	ROBBINS, ELIAS, 08/11/1881
CSV 000303	HUGHES, ROBERT	08/08/1881
CSV 000304	GAGE, MARION	08/08/1881
CSV 000305	ERVINE, SARAH	08/08/1881
CSV 000306	ADER, GORDON	GORDON, L C, 08/08/1881
CSV 000307	ADAMS, T F	08/08/1881
CSV 000308	COBB, AMANDA	COBB, E, 08/08/1881
CSV 000309	MC KINNEY, M A	MC KINNEY, GEORGE W, 08/12/1881
CSV 000310	BROWN, CLARISSA	BROWN, GARDNER, 08/09/1881
CSV 000311	TURMAN, T G	08/08/1881
CSV 000312	RICE, J J	08/12/1881
CSV 000313	KOONCE, CHRISTOPHER	08/08/1881
CSV 000314	HALL, MARTHA	HALL, HARMON, 08/08/1881
CSV 000315	HODGES, T J	08/12/1881
CSV 000316	COOPER, HELEN M	08/08/1881
CSV 000317	FENLEY, C W	08/08/1881
CSV 000318	DUNN, TELITHA	04/05/1881
CSV 000319	ROGERS, HILARY J C	08/08/1881
CSV 000320	CRAWSON, DELILAH	08/08/1881
CSV 000321	WINN, CASSANDRA	08/08/1881
CSV 000322	STEEL, THOMAS	08/08/1881
CSV 000323	DAVENPORT, ELIZABETH	08/08/1881

Confederate Scrip Vouchers-Numerical Listing

CSV 000324	PATTERSON, WILLIAM C	08/12/1881
CSV 000325	LAZRONE, SARAH	LAZRONE, HENRY, 08/09/1881
CSV 000326	BARTON, LEM	08/08/1881
CSV 000327	BROWN, N C	08/12/1881
CSV 000328	TANKERSLEY, W H	06/08/1881
CSV 000329	LANHAM, L B	08/08/1881
CSV 000330	HARDIN, JOHN	08/09/1881
CSV 000331	TEER, WILLIAM	08/12/1881
CSV 000332	MOORE, J S	08/02/1881
CSV 000333	PHILIPPS, J H	08/12/1881
CSV 000334	SLEDGE, K C	08/02/1881
CSV 000335	SHULER, GLENN	08/08/1881
CSV 000336	MC BRIDE, MARTHA D	08/12/1881
CSV 000337	TRISCHRMEYER, F	08/12/1881
CSV 000338	DILLARD, MARTHA S	DILLARD, THOMAS J, 08/10/1881
CSV 000339	SPITLER, WILLIAM M	08/08/1881
CSV 000340	WALKER, MARTHA JANE	WALKER, J WATTS, 08/08/1881
CSV 000341	NORRIS, JOHN S	08/08/1881
CSV 000342	ARLEDGE, WILLIAM M	08/08/1881
CSV 000343	VERNON, N A	VERNON, THOS G, 08/08/1881
CSV 000344	HUTCHINGS, S D	08/13/1881
CSV 000345	MAXWELL, ANDREW J	08/08/1881
CSV 000346	FARE, ALBERT M	08/08/1881
CSV 000347	MC CULLOCH, I J	08/09/1881
CSV 000348	PYLRIS, ELIZABETH	PYLRIS, AARON, 08/09/1881
CSV 000349	RUSSELL, MILLY S	RUSSELL, JESSEE, 08/13/1881
CSV 000350	HARRIS, AMANDA	HARRIS, WILLIAM, 08/13/1881
CSV 000351	GREEN, J M	08/08/1881
CSV 000352	EGGLESTON, JOHN	08/13/1881
CSV 000353	GRACE, JOHN W	08/08/1881
CSV 000354	WHITE, JOHN O	08/13/1881
CSV 000355	GAGE, MARY E	GAGE, HARRISON, 08/08/1881
CSV 000356	ROBINSON, N M	ROBINSON, JESSE S, 08/08/1881
CSV 000357	SPIDEL, M C	SPIDEL, JOHN, 08/08/1881
CSV 000358	BARRON, MILDRED	08/09/1881
CSV 000359	DEAVERS, CHESTER	08/08/1881
CSV 000360	WOODSON, CHARLES	07/24/1881
CSV 000361	SHEFFIELD, T J	08/10/1881
CSV 000362	BRYAN, JOHN L	08/08/1881
CSV 000363	LUBBOCK, S	LUBBOCK, THOMAS S, 08/04/1881
CSV 000364	GILES, FANNIE A	GILES, JOHN F, 06/08/1881
CSV 000365	HEAD, JOHN H	08/13/1881
CSV 000366	WEBB, JACOB	07/08/1881
CSV 000367	EULAE, JAMES	08/09/1881
CSV 000368	FULLER, ALMOND	08/08/1881
CSV 000369	SMITH, FRANK	08/08/1881
CSV 000370	RUTTLEDGE, WILLIAM R	08/09/1881

CSV 000371	LEE, NANCY A	08/09/1881
CSV 000372	MORTON, M M	MORTON, J G, 08/09/1881
CSV 000373	MC CORMICK, MARY	MC CORMICK, DAVID R, 08/13/1881
CSV 000374	CLARK, JOHN	08/13/1881
CSV 000375	MILLS, JAMES M	08/13/1881
CSV 000376	MC COWEN, S C M	MC COWEN, J B, 08/13/1881
CSV 000377	WILLIS, M A	WILLIS, J L, 08/03/1881
CSV 000378	DAVIS, MALINDA	DAVIS, N L, 08/13/1881
CSV 000379	CANEY, LUNA	CANEY, JOEL G, 08/13/1881
CSV 000380	SNIDER, W N	08/13/1881
CSV 000381	DAVIS, W C	08/13/1881
CSV 000382	WALL, J T	08/08/1881
CSV 000383	STEWART, JAMES	08/13/1881
CSV 000384	COCKERHAN, T E	08/13/1881
CSV 000385	GOOLSBY, A C	08/13/1881
CSV 000386	HOPSON, S A	08/13/1881
CSV 000387	COFFMAN, PERMILIA	07/01/1881
CSV 000388	LEFTWICH, RUTH	LEFTWICH, W H, 08/03/1881
CSV 000389	NICHOLSON, E M	NICHOLSON, PETER, 08/15/1881
CSV 000390	ALLISON, RACHAEL	ALLISON, W M, 07/13/1881
CSV 000391	YOUNG, WILLIAM T	08/01/1881
CSV 000392	DYER, MARY ANN	DYER, CHARLES, 08/15/1881
CSV 000393	STILLWELL, W	STILLWELL, N B, 08/15/1881
CSV 000394	MATHEWS, F M	08/08/1881
CSV 000395	GIBSON, GEORGE K	08/09/1881
CSV 000396	NEWSOM, ELIAS	08/09/1881
CSV 000397	EVANS, J E	08/08/1881
CSV 000398	HODGES, W K	HODGES, W K, 08/09/1881
CSV 000399	STILWELL, C L	STILWELL, J L H, 04/09/1881
CSV 000400	CHAMBSLIP, DELILAH ANN	CHAMBSLIP, WILLIAM, 08/15/1881
CSV 000401	KIRBY, L E	KIRBY, J BERRY, 08/08/1881
CSV 000402	LONG, F M	08/15/1881
CSV 000403	MC CORMACK, WILLIAM	08/11/1881
CSV 000404	GAY, M A	GAY, J H, 08/08/1881
CSV 000405	BRYANT, A H R	08/09/1881
CSV 000406	SIMS, MARY T E	08/10/1881
CSV 000407	JENNINGS, TOM	08/10/1881
CSV 000408	BRACKEN, T E	08/15/1881
CSV 000409	POWER, NANCY	08/15/1881
CSV 000410	THOMAS, J O	08/15/1881
CSV 000411	LEWIS, LITTLE, JOHN	08/15/1881
CSV 000412	LITTLE, JOHN	08/15/1881
CSV 000413	MACKFARLIN, WILLIAM	08/08/1881
CSV 000414	STILES, A B	08/08/1881
CSV 000415	MILLS, A A	MILLS, M C, 07/21/1881
CSV 000416	RHODE, WILLIAM B	08/15/1881

Confederate Scrip Vouchers-Numerical Listing

CSV 000417	OWENS, J H	08/10/1881
CSV 000418	EWING, W Y	08/10/1881
CSV 000419	CLAUNCH, JOHN	08/10/1881
CSV 000420	ERWIN, MILES	08/10/1881
CSV 000421	WEATHERSBY, NANCY	WEATHERSBY, THOMAS, 08/09/1881
CSV 000422	PEMBERTON, C D	08/15/1881
CSV 000423	BIRDWELL, S L	08/15/1881
CSV 000424	MELTON, W A	08/15/1881
CSV 000425	MC CLUNG, ANN	08/15/1881
CSV 000426	GARRETT, JESSE	08/10/1881
CSV 000427	ANDERSON, W V	08/08/1881
CSV 000428	BLAKE, JAMES C	08/15/1881
CSV 000429	SMITH, W R	08/15/1881
CSV 000430	MARSHALL, W W	08/09/1881
CSV 000431	CARTER, J A	08/10/1881
CSV 000432	BROOKS, F A	08/08/1881
CSV 000433	JUDD, MARINDA	JUDD, J L, 08/08/1881
CSV 000434	BAUTA, WILLIAM	08/11/1881
CSV 000435	BLUNDELL, MILES F	08/09/1881
CSV 000436	SCALES, W G	08/08/1881
CSV 000437	SCHNEIDER, E B H	08/10/1881
CSV 000438	SAVAGE, ELIZABETH	SAVAGE, ROBERT, 08/08/1881
CSV 000439	KEENAN, W A	08/16/1881
CSV 000440	FALL, PHILIP H	08/16/1881
CSV 000441	MILAM, B Y	08/08/1881
CSV 000442	MILAM, J B	08/08/1881
CSV 000443	SKINNER, JNO S	08/11/1881
CSV 000444	RAP, MARY	RAP, EDWARD, 08/11/1881
CSV 000445	PARKER, F	08/09/1881
CSV 000446	TAYLOR, J H	08/09/1881
CSV 000447	LANDRUM, L J	LANDRUM, JOHN T, 08/08/1881
CSV 000448	MOFFITH, J M	08/16/1881
CSV 000449	JONES, MARY E	JONES, JOHN W, 08/10/1881
CSV 000450	BARGAINER, VINA	BARGAINER, JAMES, 08/09/1881
CSV 000451	MANN, GREEN P	08/11/1881
CSV 000452	AUSTIN, J L	07/01/1881
CSV 000453	WALKER, M J	WALKER, W H, 08/08/1881
CSV 000454	STOKES, J G	08/16/1881
CSV 000455	MORGAN, JAMES L	08/16/1881
CSV 000456	MC LAUGHLIN, THOMAS	08/16/1881
CSV 000457	DIAL, H C	08/16/1881
CSV 000458	GARRETT, J C	08/22/1881
CSV 000459	CASE, SUSAN C	08/17/1881
CSV 000460	BUCHANAN, AMANDA	08/17/1881
CSV 000461	GILBERT, MARTHA	08/17/1881
CSV 000462	BOATWRIGHT, R	BOATWRIGHT, D T, 08/08/1881
CSV 000463	BELL, JACKSON	08/13/1881

CSV 000464	SANDERS, R M	08/08/1881
CSV 000465	MAXWELL, RACHAL	MAXWELL, REUBIN, 08/08/1881
CSV 000466	HAUGHTON, J F	08/17/1881
CSV 000467	SOAPS, JOSEPH	08/17/1881
CSV 000468	HAGAN, ELIZA	HAGAN, A GREEN 08/17/1881
CSV 000469	ESSARY, L Y	08/17/1881
CSV 000470	PIKE, S A	PIKE, ISAAC, 08/11/1881
CSV 000471	WILLIAMSON, W H	08/07/1881
CSV 000472	HOOKER, HENRY G	08/10/1881
CSV 000473	CRYER, DANIEL W	08/09/1881
CSV 000474	MORRIS, MARY A	07/07/1881
CSV 000475	WOODALL, A C	07/07/1881
CSV 000476	BROWN, B W	08/12/1881
CSV 000477	BRYAN, A H	08/12/1881
CSV 000478	ROUNDTREE, W A	08/12/1881
CSV 000479	OATES, MARTHA E	08/12/1881
CSV 000480	HERROD, GEORGE I	08/12/1881
CSV 000481	CHILDRESS, T A J	07/07/1881
CSV 000482	LINDLEY, MATILDA A	08/12/1881
CSV 000483	STARKY, THOMAS	08/12/1881
CSV 000484	CARTWRIGHT, LEM C	08/17/1881
CSV 000485	SMITH, LEW	08/08/1881
CSV 000486	DEAN, HENRY	08/17/1881
CSV 000487	MARRIS, MATILDA	08/17/1881
CSV 000488	MC MILLAN, MARY	08/16/1881
CSV 000489	SCHUCHERT, LUDWIG	08/13/1881
CSV 000490	MOON, JOHN	08/04/1881
CSV 000491	GRAHAM, C G	08/17/1881
CSV 000492	MONTGOMERY, C A	MONTGOMERY, JOHN, 08/11/1881
CSV 000493	NIGGLI, ROSINA	NIGGLI, FERDINAND, 08/15/1881
CSV 000494	HUBERT, WILL	08/08/1881
CSV 000495	UTZ, M C	UTZ, JOE, 08/08/1881
CSV 000496	DU BOIS, LUCAS	08/08/1881
CSV 000497	PANKEY, J B	08/08/1881
CSV 000498	STRANGE, CELIA	STRANGE, O E W, 08/18/1881
CSV 000499	SCOTT, A O	SCOTT, J M, 08/08/1881
CSV 000500	ELLISON, C E	ELLISON, THOMAS, 08/18/1881
CSV 000501	PUCKETT, T E	PUCKETT, J A, 08/20/1881
CSV 000502	ROZELL, ELIZA	08/08/1881
CSV 000503	EARLES, T	08/08/1881
CSV 000504	NICKLES, W W	08/08/1881
CSV 000505	MERCHANT, LOUISA	08/09/1881
CSV 000506	ANSILEU, CLARISSA	08/20/1881
CSV 000507	ELDER, E P	ELDER, I J
CSV 000508	TODD, LOUISA	TODD, J M, 08/08/1881
CSV 000509	COLLIER, JOHN L	08/08/1881

CSV 000510	WHITE, F W	WHITE, DAVID, 08/11/1881
CSV 000511	HARTLEY, JOHN D	08/11/1881
CSV 000512	HAVIS, SARAH J	04/05/1881
CSV 000513	YEATMAN, J N	07/18/1881
CSV 000514	HIGH, LEIGH	08/20/1881
CSV 000515	PHILLIPS, WHIT	08/20/1881
CSV 000516	DOTSON, L V	08/10/1881
CSV 000517	CANON, A L	08/20/1881
CSV 000518	DOAK, J B	07/12/1881
CSV 000519	BURGE, K F	07/12/1881
CSV 000520	CLOUD, JERRY	08/20/1881
CSV 000521	MORRIS, WILLIAM	08/10/1881
CSV 000522	HAIL, W G	08/09/1880
CSV 000523	RANEY, EMILY R	07/22/1881
CSV 000524	COOKE, SAMUEL	08/08/1881
CSV 000525	COLEMAN, LOUISE	COLEMAN, J, 07/11/1881
CSV 000526	THOMPSON, MAHALA W	THOMPSON, MALCOMB, 07/11/1881
CSV 000527	FILE EMPTY	
CSV 000528	HAWLEY, HIRAM	08/20/1881
CSV 000529	JONES, NANCY	JONES, J R, 08/20/1881
CSV 000530	JENKINS, M J	JENKINS, J W, 08/15/1881
CSV 000531	HENDERSON, A	HENDERSON, T W, 08/20/1881
CSV 000532	KING, ELIZABETH	KING, HENRY, 08/08/1881
CSV 000533	BLAUD, B F	08/20/1881
CSV 000534	PRUITT, RHODA	08/20/1881
CSV 000535	SMITH, MARY A	08/20/1881
CSV 000536	DENTON, MARY S	DENTON, TIPTON, 07/28/1881
CSV 000537	NICHOLS, RICHARD	08/08/1881
CSV 000538	CORMELL, ASA	08/12/1881
CSV 000539	BARNETT, W F G	08/10/1881
CSV 000540	ASHMORE, M J	07/14/1881
CSV 000541	BROOKMAN, F C	08/22/1881
CSV 000542	REAVIS, W H	08/22/1881
CSV 000543	WHITILY, J C	08/22/1881
CSV 000544	BLAIR, J D	08/22/1881
CSV 000545	BUNDRANT, PETER	08/22/1881
CSV 000546	MONK, J R	08/22/1881
CSV 000547	CORBIN, D H	08/22/1881
CSV 000548	CLEMENTS, A Z	08/22/1881
CSV 000549	YOUNG, J J	08/22/1881
CSV 000550	PHARES, REUBEN	08/22/1881
CSV 000551	HALLMARK, T L	08/22/1881
CSV 000552	COLLINS, JAMES	07/23/1881
CSV 000553	FIELD, D C	08/22/1881
CSV 000554	BALLARD, SARAH A	08/08/1881
CSV 000555	SHIPP, J M	08/08/1881
CSV 000556	BULLOCK, T T	08/08/1881
CSV 000557	ARMSTRONG, J M	07/11/1881

Voucher	Name	Additional/Date
CSV 000558	BUTH, M A	08/10/1881
CSV 000559	HERRINGTON, J M	08/10/1881
CSV 000560	FROELICH, JOHN	08/08/1881
CSV 000561	ZACHERY, J U	08/08/1881
CSV 000562	MATTHEWS, ROSANAH	MATTHEWS, JAMES C, 08/16/1881
CSV 000563	THOMAS, W JASPER	08/16/1881
CSV 000564	FOSTER, L H	08/16/1881
CSV 000565	ROWLAND, T J	08/16/1881
CSV 000566	ALLEN, P M	08/18/1881
CSV 000567	GARLAND, TILITHA	GARLAND, ERASMUS N, 08/08/1881
CSV 000568	PRITCHARD, W D	08/08/1881
CSV 000569	DENYS, JOHN H, RUDINGER, JOSEPH	08/15/1881
CSV 000570	CLIFTON, LEVIN	08/08/1881
CSV 000571	GARDNER, W C	08/08/1881
CSV 000572	VAN SICKLE, THOMAS J	08/18/1881
CSV 000573	SIMMONS, MARY	SIMMONS, JAMES J, 08/11/1881
CSV 000574	FARMER, BRYMER J A G	08/10/1881
CSV 000575	BOHAMON, NANCY	08/22/1881
CSV 000576	HUDDLE, CATHERIN	08/22/1881
CSV 000577	HAWKINS, J EM	07/18/1881
CSV 000578	WALTERS, MARTHA	WALTERS, PHILLIP A, 08/15/1881
CSV 000579	WHITE, JOHN	08/17/1881
CSV 000580	WEST, M M	WEST, A J, 08/09/1881
CSV 000581	FLOYD, S S	FLOYD, W A, 08/22/1881
CSV 000582	TREADWELL, S E	TREADWELL, R L, 08/08/1881
CSV 000583	NEAL, T K	08/22/1881
CSV 000584	PACE, SARAH	PACE, JAMES B, 04/09/1881
CSV 000585	BAXLEY, A E	BAXLEY, R W, 08/08/1881
CSV 000586	BRANMONT, JACOB	08/19/1881
CSV 000587	HARRISON, VINCENT	08/08/1881
CSV 000588	DUFFEY, JOHN W	08/08/1881
CSV 000589	BAKER, E A	BAKER, JOSEPH, 07/07/1881
CSV 000590	ALLEN, SARAH	ALLEN, D Y, 08/23/1881
CSV 000591	NEWBERRY, LUCY ANN	NEWBERRY, JOHNSON, 08/23/1881
CSV 000592	HAMILTON, C V	HAMILTON, PAYTON, 08/19/1881
CSV 000593	FRYER, H C	08/08/1881
CSV 000594	VAN OVER, SAMUEL	08/09/1881
CSV 000595	CROSS, H	08/09/1881
CSV 000596	TAYLOR, PERRY S	08/08/1881
CSV 000597	CAMPBELL, JAMES	08/15/1881
CSV 000598	SCHULTZE, FRIEDRICH	08/15/1881
CSV 000599	POUNDS, J M D	08/23/1881
CSV 000600	WILLIAMS, PARTHANA	08/09/1881
CSV 000601	BLOUNT, B F	08/09/1881

CSV 000602	AYRES, NANCY	AYRES, WILLIAM A, 08/23/1881
CSV 000603	GRIFFIN, J B	07/02/1881
CSV 000604	ROGENS, C C	08/08/1881
CSV 000605	ROGERS, N B	08/08/1881
CSV 000606	ESTES, WILLIAM E	08/23/1881
CSV 000607	BOYLE, W H	08/08/1881
CSV 000608	HOGAN, ANDREW	08/13/1881
CSV 000609	GRAHAM, PRECILLA	GRAHAM, JAMES, 08/31/1881
CSV 000610	RODRIGUEZ, JESUS	08/08/1881
CSV 000611	WEATHERSPOON, P W	08/13/1881
CSV 000612	HAYS, E P	08/13/1881
CSV 000613	CHAMBERLAIN, MINERVA	CHAMBERLAIN, NICHOLAS, 08/10/1881
CSV 000614	SEDBERRY, M A	08/10/1881
CSV 000615	JONES, HARRIET	JONES, T M, 08/24/1881
CSV 000616	WILLS, B N	08/12/1881
CSV 000617	NEULAND, JANE	08/21/1881
CSV 000618	LEHMAN, JOSEPH	08/21/1881
CSV 000619	BELL, GEORGE P	08/21/1881
CSV 000620	HUDSON, GEO H	08/10/1881
CSV 000621	STOVALL, S T	08/24/1881
CSV 000622	HARRELL, LITTLETON	08/24/1881
CSV 000623	GUTHRIE, S D	08/08/1881
CSV 000624	LACKLIN, J B	08/08/1881
CSV 000625	HONEYCUT, W E	08/08/1881
CSV 000626	STEDMAN, ELY	08/10/1881
CSV 000627	HIETT, J W	08/22/1881
CSV 000628	BUTLER, WADE H	08/09/1881
CSV 000629	ASHLEY, ROBERT A	08/08/1881
CSV 000630	MULLIN, W A	08/08/1881
CSV 000631	JAMES, B F	08/08/1881
CSV 000632	FAULKNER, VIRGINIA	FAULKNER, ARCHIBALD, 08/25/1881
CSV 000633	CAMPBELL, MARTHA	07/13/1881
CSV 000634	OWENS, M H	08/15/1881
CSV 000635	WHITEHEAD, JOE H	07/29/1881
CSV 000636	JONES, SUSAN	08/09/1881
CSV 000637	GORE, MARY J	08/09/1881
CSV 000638	LONG, GEORGE T	07/09/1881
CSV 000639	HOWARD, J W	08/25/1881
CSV 000640	DAVIS, ELIZABETH	DAVIS, G T, 08/22/1881
CSV 000641	TARKINGTON, G H	07/30/1881
CSV 000642	VICKERY, HARDIN	08/08/1881
CSV 000643	KESLERSON, MARY C	KESLERSON, WILLIAM, 05/13/1881
CSV 000644	WAGGONER, MARGARETT	WAGGONER, GEORGE, 07/11/1881
CSV 000645	SPOONAMORE, C L	08/19/1881
CSV 000646	SHORT, W H	08/25/1881

CSV 000647	BARTON, JOHN M	07/01/1881
CSV 000648	MENLEY, VIRGINIA	08/08/1881
CSV 000649	DAVIS, JOHN W	08/26/1881
CSV 000650	TROTTER, JOHN W	08/27/1881
CSV 000651	RADAZ, FRANK	08/18/1881
CSV 000652	CRADDOCK, E D	08/27/1881
CSV 000653	RAY, JOHN W	08/27/1881
CSV 000654	LEMY, P H	08/22/1881
CSV 000655	COLMAN, LOUIS	08/27/1881
CSV 000656	MC DOWELL, R E C	08/08/1881
CSV 000657	GREGG, EDWARD	08/10/1881
CSV 000658	KENDRICK, ANN	KENDRICK, DRURY, 08/08/1881
CSV 000659	WILLIAMS, M C	WILLIAMS, A C, 08/08/1881
CSV 000660	BARBEE, A E	BARBEE, J P, 08/08/1881
CSV 000661	ROBBINS, FRANCES	ROBBINS, JNO W, 08/08/1881
CSV 000662	SMITH, SUSAN	SMITH, JOSEPH, 08/01/1881
CSV 000663	WELLAM, A C	07/25/1881
CSV 000664	HARDWICK, J H	08/27/1881
CSV 000665	LUCE, SARAH H	06/07/1881
CSV 000666	HEFNER, W L	08/27/1881
CSV 000667	COPELAND, WILLIAM E	08/22/1881
CSV 000668	WALKER, DICK	08/11/1881
CSV 000669	MAKEIG, F M	08/21/1881
CSV 000670	BROIN, P A	08/08/1881
CSV 000671	BULL, I M	BULL, AUGUSTUS, 08/08/1881
CSV 000672	CARAWAY, MARY A	CARAWAY, N J, 08/08/1881
CSV 000673	NOBLE, E A	08/08/1881
CSV 000674	POWELL, H S	08/09/1881
CSV 000675	MAYES, DAVID H	08/22/1881
CSV 000676	GAHAHAGAN, THOMAS W	08/29/1881
CSV 000677	PHILLIPS, REBECCA	PHILLIPS, JAMES B, 08/29/1881
CSV 000678	MILLER, JAMES H	08/29/1881
CSV 000679	MUNK, RACHEL C	08/09/1881
CSV 000680	MC DANIEL, W A	08/30/1881
CSV 000681	WALDSCHMIDT, JACOB	08/30/1881
CSV 000682	BREWSTER, A M	BREWSTER, B F S, 08/14/1881
CSV 000683	DAVIS, RACHEL	DAVIS, THOS D, 08/24/1881
CSV 000684	FITZGERALD, MAHALA	FITZGERALD, J A, 08/08/1881
CSV 000685	BARRON, M	BARRON, J J, 08/08/1881
CSV 000686	KNOWLS, K S	KNOWLS, J B, 08/24/1881
CSV 000687	BELCHER, ROBERT	08/24/1881
CSV 000688	THOMPSON, JANE	THOMPSON, JOHN T, 08/08/1881
CSV 000689	HIGGINBOTHAM, LIZZIE	HIGGINBOTHAM, W W, 08/08/1881
CSV 000690	THOMPSON, MARTHA	THOMPSON, T U, 08/08/1881
CSV 000691	STAMPS, B F	08/24/1881
CSV 000692	PREWITT, WILSON	08/30/1881
CSV 000693	STYLES, ELIZA	STYLES, JOHN, 08/30/1881

Voucher	Name	Details
CSV 000694	MOORE, CHARLOTTE	MOORE, JOHN, 08/25/1881
CSV 000695	CHILES, P J	08/08/1881
CSV 000696	ROME, W B	08/08/1881
CSV 000697	MILLER, JOHN P	08/31/1881
CSV 000698	MORGAN, ABEL	08/15/1881
CSV 000699	HENSLEY, J C	08/15/1881
CSV 000700	KINGSTON, H C	08/15/1881
CSV 000701	HART, A P	08/15/1881
CSV 000702	GRAY, SARAH J	GRAY, JOHN F, 08/15/1881
CSV 000703	SPOTTS, BASCOM	08/30/1881
CSV 000704	COPPIDGE, MARY	08/09/1881
CSV 000705	WOOD, SARAH	WOOD, ALEXANDER, 08/30/1881
CSV 000706	KINGSBERRY, C H	08/30/1881
CSV 000707	MATHEWS, J W	08/22/1881
CSV 000708	BURTILLO, ANTONIO	08/30/1881
CSV 000709	SCHMIDT, ALBERT	08/30/1881
CSV 000710	LORILLARD, H M	LORILLARD, WILLIAM, 08/13/1881
CSV 000711	VAUGHN, P H	08/10/1881
CSV 000712	GILBERT, MORRIS	08/31/1881
CSV 000713	EVERETT, J C	08/31/1881
CSV 000714	MIXON, SARAH	MIXON, HENRY, 07/11/1881
CSV 000715	BARNES, ELIZABETH	BARNES, ROBERT, 08/26/1881
CSV 000716	SMITH, J C	08/22/1881
CSV 000717	WEAVER, J F	08/16/1881
CSV 000718	RIFE, THOS C	08/13/1881
CSV 000719	ANDERSON, M B	08/08/1881
CSV 000720	SMITHERS, G S	08/26/1881
CSV 000721	SMITH, SUSAN	08/10/1881
CSV 000722	BALDEREE, JANE	BALDREE, STERLING, 08/08/1881
CSV 000723	SMITH, WILLIAM R	09/02/1881
CSV 000724	LEWIS, W N B	09/02/1881
CSV 000725	TRAMMEL, W B	08/08/1881
CSV 000726	THIGPEN, JOHN	09/02/1881
CSV 000727	COONER, F M	09/02/1881
CSV 000728	SIMS, W B	09/02/1881
CSV 000729	THORNTON, VICTORIA	09/02/1881
CSV 000730	FREEMAN, J P	09/02/1881
CSV 000731	ATKINSON, LOUIS	08/11/1881
CSV 000732	HOWARD, W J	08/12/1881
CSV 000733	HUDSON, AMOS	08/08/1881
CSV 000734	FAIRCHILD, SARAH E	09/02/1881
CSV 000735	MITCHERPIN, W E	08/08/1881
CSV 000736	HORNBUCKLE, W	08/29/1881
CSV 000737	PETTY, M C	08/09/1881
CSV 000738	FAUBION, HENRY C	09/03/1881
CSV 000739	PIERCE, HUGH J	08/13/1881

CSV 000740	SMITH, FELIX JACKSON	09/03/1881
CSV 000741	HAWKINS, J H	09/03/1881
CSV 000742	PARKE, H	09/03/1881
CSV 000743	GISH, J P	09/03/1881
CSV 000744	HALL, W V	09/03/1881
CSV 000745	HINES, M N	09/03/1881
CSV 000746	CROW, N K	08/08/1881
CSV 000747	MC DONALD, J M	08/11/1881
CSV 000748	RUDINGER, JOSEPH	09/01/1881
CSV 000749	GEASLIN, MARY A	08/08/1881
CSV 000750	WALTERS, TILMAN	08/20/1881
CSV 000751	MEDLIN, MARTHA	08/29/1881
CSV 000752	COKER, ALEXANDER	08/29/1881
CSV 000753	PORTMAN, E R	08/29/1881
CSV 000754	WILLS, FRANCIS	WILLS, ISAAC D, 08/08/1881
CSV 000755	MEEK, J W	09/05/1881
CSV 000756	NOBLE, ISAAC O	08/08/1881
CSV 000757	HOGG, ELIZABETH	HOGG, JAMES B, 08/09/1881
CSV 000758	HOLLAND, C H	08/08/1881
CSV 000759	HARRIS, ANN H	HARRIS, J M, 09/05/1881
CSV 000760	FOSTER, GEORGE	08/10/1881
CSV 000761	GARNER, NATHANIEL	08/09/1881
CSV 000762	MORRISON, JNO D	08/09/1881
CSV 000763	DUNN, CHRISTINA MONTALVO	DUNN, JAMES, 08/13/1881
CSV 000764	MC CLINTOCK, S R	08/08/1881
CSV 000765	VEAL, J C	09/05/1881
CSV 000766	MARTIN, MARJAH	08/10/1881
CSV 000767	ROUNSAVOLL, W D	08/10/1881
CSV 000768	JOHNSON, T J	08/10/1881
CSV 000769	CLAY, J M	09/01/1881
CSV 000770	MYERS, S E	08/08/1881
CSV 000771	JONES, F M	09/03/1881
CSV 000772	LONDON, C M	07/20/1881
CSV 000773	HEWITT, W M	08/10/1881
CSV 000774	MAXWELL, JAS H	08/08/1881
CSV 000775	GATES, C A	08/22/1881
CSV 000776	POOLE, HENRY	08/22/1881
CSV 000777	HAWKINS, SARAH O	HAWKINS, C C, 08/08/1881
CSV 000778	GILLEY, JANE	GILLEY, W F, 08/08/1881
CSV 000779	DARK, W G	08/24/1881
CSV 000780	ELIZA, ASHLEY	ASHLEY, JOHN H, 08/08/1881
CSV 000781	HALE, S M	09/07/1881
CSV 000782	WHITE, FRANCIS C	08/08/1881
CSV 000783	DAUGHERTY, GEO W	08/08/1881
CSV 000784	MC FARLAND, JAMES R	08/08/1881
CSV 000785	HOLBERT, J T	09/07/1881
CSV 000786	LESTER, MARY E	08/08/1881
CSV 000787	BASHAM, W R	08/20/1881
CSV 000788	HARRIS, W L	08/20/1881

Voucher	Name	Additional / Date
CSV 000789	GISCHEIDLE, E	09/02/1881
CSV 000790	SCHERFFINS, JOHN A	08/08/1881
CSV 000791	HARRIS, MELDORA A	09/02/1881
CSV 000792	HOPKINS, M E	09/02/1881
CSV 000793	LOWRY, M S P	07/07/1881
CSV 000794	RASCO, SOLON	07/07/1881
CSV 000795	DUNMAN, ALGADA	08/08/1881
CSV 000796	ANDERSON, A D	08/08/1881
CSV 000797	WILSON, R S	08/08/1881
CSV 000798	YOUNG, J F	YOUNG, R B, 08/09/1881
CSV 000799	BURTON, THOMAS F	09/08/1881
CSV 000800	BRIGGS, JAMES	09/08/1881
CSV 000801	VINSON, EVALINE	VINSON, AUSTIN, 08/11/1881
CSV 000802	MC FARLAN, ELIZABETH M	MC FARLAN, MARVEL, 08/22/1881
CSV 000803	PACE, J H	08/09/1881
CSV 000804	MORGAN, T J	MORGAN, ALLISON, 08/08/1881
CSV 000805	MC DONALD, MARTHA	MC DONALD, JAMES, 09/09/1881
CSV 000806	DESHONE, L E	DESHONE, ENOCH, 09/09/1881
CSV 000807	WILSON, E T	09/09/1881
CSV 000808	IVES, JAMES	07/25/1881
CSV 000809	EMMONS, RUFUS	07/25/1881
CSV 000810	ANDERSON, JAMES	07/25/1881
CSV 000811	BROWN, J B	07/25/1881
CSV 000812	GRIMES, LETTIS	08/06/1881
CSV 000813	TURNER, JAMES	08/24/1881
CSV 000814	CHADICK, E M	09/09/1881
CSV 000815	MURPHY, J W	08/08/1881
CSV 000816	GUTHRIE, JOHN F	09/09/1881
CSV 000817	JOHNSTON, A O	08/08/1881
CSV 000818	SPARKS, G A	09/05/1881
CSV 000819	BOYD, OLLIVER	09/05/1881
CSV 000820	BRASWELL, W N	09/15/1881
CSV 000821	MOORING, J W	07/04/1881
CSV 000822	GIBBS, JNO M	09/12/1881
CSV 000823	HUFFMAN, ELI R	08/08/1881
CSV 000824	DENSON, N A	DENSON, W E, 08/09/1881
CSV 000825	WOODHOUSER, JNO	09/14/1881
CSV 000826	SMITH, N O	08/08/1881
CSV 000827	STEPHENS, CLARISA	STEPHENS, G H, 08/08/1881
CSV 000828	HANSON, A	HANSON, G W, 07/22/1881
CSV 000829	STARY, H G	09/15/1881
CSV 000830	HONEA, NANCY	08/08/1881
CSV 000831	RATICAN, JOHN	09/13/1881
CSV 000832	ALEXANDER, H	09/17/1881
CSV 000833	COLLINS, R M	09/17/1881
CSV 000834	LLOYD, S P	09/15/1881

CSV 000835..... LINDERY, SARAH 09/12/1881
CSV 000836..... DUNCAN, ADELIA .... DUNCAN, GEORGE CLINTON, 09/13/1881
CSV 000837..... FREESTONE, ISABELLA 09/14/1881
CSV 000838..... KIRKLAND, J P 09/18/1881
CSV 000839..... CHAMBERS, N L 09/18/1881
CSV 000840..... BROWN, H C 09/13/1881
CSV 000841..... LAFLIN, J Y 09/13/1881
CSV 000842..... DENNIS, ANGELINE E 08/10/1881
CSV 000843..... BRACK, HENDERSON 08/09/1881
CSV 000844..... LOADER, JANE 09/19/1881
CSV 000845..... MASSEY, ELIJAH E 09/12/1881
CSV 000846..... BEUL, JOHN, BOIL, HONAS 09/12/1881
CSV 000847..... FRAZIOR, RACHEL .... FRAZIOR, JOSEPH E, 07/22/1881
CSV 000848..... TOWNSEND, J M 08/08/1881
CSV 000849..... WREN, PATHENA 09/13/1881
CSV 000850..... SHARP, J H 09/17/1881
CSV 000851..... FARR, JOSEPH 09/07/1881
CSV 000852..... BENNATT, BEN M 09/12/1881
CSV 000853..... CAVITT, M A 09/20/1881
CSV 000854..... MERIWETHER, W M 09/20/1881
CSV 000855..... HAHN, JACOB 08/08/1881
CSV 000856..... JONES, LEVITA ANN 08/22/1881
CSV 000857..... ADAM, ANTON 09/15/1881
CSV 000858..... COPELAND, THOMAS 09/21/1881
CSV 000859..... ERSKIN, JAS D 07/07/1881
CSV 000860..... VON DER DECKEN, CAROLINE .... VON DER DECKEN, OTTO, 09/15/1881
CSV 000861..... BAUER, ANDERSON 09/21/1881
CSV 000862..... EDDS, L W 09/21/1881
CSV 000863..... BROWN, MARY ANN 09/21/1881
CSV 000864..... REUSHAW, SALLIE 09/18/1881
CSV 000865..... HOWARD, SUSAN E .... HOWARD, JEPTHA, 09/21/1881
CSV 000866..... ETHRIDGE, MARTHA .... ETHRIDGE, LEWIS, 08/08/1881
CSV 000867..... GUNTER, I J 09/02/1881
CSV 000868..... JONES, WILLIAM E 09/09/1881
CSV 000869..... KING, J W 09/09/1881
CSV 000870..... EYRES, GEORGE 09/09/1881
CSV 000871..... MERCHANT, S W 08/08/1881
CSV 000872..... WHITE, JOHN M 08/08/1881
CSV 000873..... MADDEN, B E 07/11/1881
CSV 000874..... FRANKS, HENRY 07/07/1881
CSV 000875..... CRAWFORD, H W 08/08/1881
CSV 000876..... RICHARDS, MARY E .... RICHARDS, R ADOLPHUS, 09/12/1881
CSV 000877..... SMITH, JOHN H 08/08/1881
CSV 000878..... PRICE, ELIZABETH 09/08/1881
CSV 000879..... HUTCHERSON, H H 09/08/1881

CSV Number	Name	Additional Info / Date
CSV 000880	SOLOMAN, MARY	SOLOMAN, ALEXANDER, 09/12/1881
CSV 000881	JACOBS, MARY E	09/08/1881
CSV 000882	TUCKER, ALLEN J	09/08/1881
CSV 000883	TULLY, MARY J F	09/12/1881
CSV 000884	GROIN, J S	09/06/1881
CSV 000885	LEVINGSTON, EDWARD D	07/23/1881
CSV 000886	SANDERS, S J	08/10/1881
CSV 000887	HART, W A	09/13/1881
CSV 000888	TIERCE, J P	09/13/1881
CSV 000889	HAMILTON, R S	09/13/1881
CSV 000890	LOGAN, Z L	08/29/1881
CSV 000891	LARREMORE, SAM H	08/08/1881
CSV 000892	COOPER, TALITHA	07/11/1881
CSV 000893	MALONEY, W H	09/14/1881
CSV 000894	TUCKER, J M	09/10/1881
CSV 000895	ROBINSON, MANERVA J	ROBINSON, L J, 08/09/1881
CSV 000896	CHATHAM, MARY H	08/08/1881
CSV 000897	CANLTON, E J	CANLTON, JOHN, 08/08/1881
CSV 000898	LEWIS, W A	09/10/1881
CSV 000899	ANDERSON, CATHERINE	ANDERSON, WILLIAM P, 09/13/1881
CSV 000900	BELLAMY, J F	09/08/1881
CSV 000901	LOVELACE, D W	09/15/1881
CSV 000902	MC DONALD, DANIEL	09/15/1881
CSV 000903	NASH, WILLIAM	09/15/1881
CSV 000904	WARREN, ORPA	09/13/1881
CSV 000905	ERWIN, F M	09/15/1881
CSV 000906	HENLEY, WILLIAM D	09/15/1881
CSV 000907	GILLARD, APPO	09/21/1881
CSV 000908	SLOAN, JOHN V	09/21/1881
CSV 000909	HENLEY, WILLIAM D C	07/01/1881
CSV 000910	FRUGER, CLEMINTINE	07/01/1881
CSV 000911	NENENDOFF, MAX	09/15/1881
CSV 000912	SANDOVAL, CARLOS	09/21/1881
CSV 000913	TRIBBLE, ELIZABETH	09/21/1881
CSV 000914	SMITH, MARY	09/21/1881
CSV 000915	CELESTIN, C D	09/05/1881
CSV 000916	MC CALL, ANGELINE	09/22/1881
CSV 000917	JACKSON, REUBEN	09/23/1881
CSV 000918	BLACK, E M	09/23/1881
CSV 000919	MARTIN, NANCY	08/12/1881
CSV 000920	MALDEN, A J	08/15/1881
CSV 000921	BRINLEE, WM R	08/15/1881
CSV 000922	HINDEMAN, J K P	09/23/1881
CSV 000923	JOYNER, J H	08/09/1881
CSV 000924	BREWER, ELISHA K	09/23/1881
CSV 000925	DEATHERAGE, J W	10/23/1881
CSV 000926	MC MAHAN, W L	09/19/1881

CSV 000927.....	BLACKWELL, MARY L............................	09/24/1881
CSV 000927.....	GOLDSBERRY, MARY A	09/24/1881
CSV 000927.....	HARRELL, ELIZABETH A	09/24/1881
CSV 000927.....	KOONCE, MARY C	09/24/1881
CSV 000927.....	LAICH, W F	09/24/1881
CSV 000927.....	LATHAM, P C..	09/24/1881
CSV 000927.....	MELTON, WILLIAM W	09/24/1881
CSV 000927.....	PARKER, ADA	09/24/1881
CSV 000927.....	PROTHRO, ELLEN C.............................	09/24/1881
CSV 000927.....	TIPPITT, GEORGIA	09/24/1881
CSV 000927.....	TURNER, W B	09/24/1881
CSV 000927.....	VAUGHN, ELIZA J	09/24/1881
CSV 000927.....	WILLIAMS, MATILDA	09/24/1881
CSV 000927.....	YORK, J T	09/24/1881
CSV 000928.....	FILE EMPTY	
CSV 000929.....	FILE EMPTY	
CSV 000930.....	FILE EMPTY	
CSV 000931.....	FILE EMPTY	
CSV 000932.....	FILE EMPTY	
CSV 000933.....	FILE EMPTY	
CSV 000934.....	FILE EMPTY	
CSV 000935.....	FILE EMPTY	
CSV 000936.....	FILE EMPTY	
CSV 000937.....	FILE EMPTY	
CSV 000938.....	FILE EMPTY	
CSV 000939.....	FILE EMPTY	
CSV 000940.....	FILE EMPTY	
CSV 000941.....	HAMILTON, EMILY C	09/24/1881
CSV 000941.....	LANGSTON, E J	09/24/1881
CSV 000942.....	FILE EMPTY	
CSV 000943.....	SIKES, ROBERT	09/24/1881
CSV 000944.....	BLUNDELL, J A	09/03/1881
CSV 000945.....	DAVIS, J B	09/24/1881
CSV 000946.....	BROWN, W A	08/15/1881
CSV 000947.....	GRIFFIN, LUCINDA	08/11/1881
CSV 000948.....	POWELL, SARAH M	POWELL, T D, 09/12/1881
CSV 000949.....	DEAN, WESLEY	09/27/1881
CSV 000950.....	BARKER, HENRY...................................	09/27/1881
CSV 000951.....	COLESON, ABE	09/27/1881
CSV 000952.....	LUMPKIN, R D..	09/20/1881
CSV 000953.....	GLASS, W S	09/20/1881
CSV 000954.....	DOUGLASS, W J	09/20/1881
CSV 000955.....	SNELGROVE, J P	09/20/1881
CSV 000956.....	MAIN, THOMAS	09/27/1881
CSV 000957.....	MC GREGOR, M C	09/23/1881
CSV 000958.....	EPPERSON, JOSEPHINE	EPPERSON, C N, 09/20/1881
CSV 000959.....	ROBINSON, JOHN C	09/20/1881
CSV 000960.....	SMITH, B F	09/20/1881
CSV 000961.....	HAYGOOD, MARTHA	HAYGOOD, WM H, 09/20/1881

CSV 000962	HENDERSON, JOHN B	09/20/1881
CSV 000963	POWELL, WILLIAM	09/20/1881
CSV 000964	GORDAN, LEWIS	08/08/1881
CSV 000965	COVIN, J W	09/20/1881
CSV 000966	EMMONS, MARY	08/29/1881
CSV 000967	KING, MARY	KING, NATHANIEL, 09/21/1881
CSV 000968	SCHMIDT, FRANK	08/08/1881
CSV 000969	FARMER, JOSEPH	09/28/1881
CSV 000970	WALLACE, H K	09/01/1881
CSV 000971	FOWLER, J W	09/15/1881
CSV 000972	CADE, R R	09/29/1881
CSV 000973	HUDSON, M V	HUDSON, R L, 09/29/1881
CSV 000974	POULSON, CHAS	09/13/1881
CSV 000975	BURLEW, C K	08/09/1881
CSV 000976	BERRYMAN, H W	09/26/1881
CSV 000977	STEPHENS, THOMAS	08/10/1881
CSV 000978	HARRISON, J S	09/30/1881
CSV 000979	ROBINSON, E A	08/08/1881
CSV 000980	WHITNEY, MARY ANN	WHITNEY, BENJAMIN AUGUSTUS, 09/17/1881
CSV 000981	STANLEY, GEORGE R	09/22/1881
CSV 000982	ALLDAY, M A	ALLDAY, J F, 09/20/1881
CSV 000983	TIDWELL, M E	09/30/1881
CSV 000984	KRUSE, HENRY J	09/30/1881
CSV 000985	PETIS, JAMES J	09/30/1881
CSV 000986	PERRY, MARTHA J	10/01/1881
CSV 000987	CHANCE, DAVID	10/03/1881
CSV 000988	HOWARD, GEORGE W	10/03/1881
CSV 000989	FOSTER, CAROLINE	07/21/1881
CSV 000990	BLANKENSHIP, F M	08/08/1881
CSV 000991	TAYLOR, B F	08/09/1881
CSV 000992	COLE, JAMES	08/09/1881
CSV 000993	JONAS, HENRY	10/03/1881
CSV 000994	REYNOLDS, WILLIAM	09/12/1881
CSV 000995	MARTIN, LUCINDA	07/21/1881
CSV 000996	FOSTER, SARAH A	08/08/1881
CSV 000997	PARCHMAN, W D	08/08/1881
CSV 000998	STEVENS, MARY C	10/04/1881
CSV 000999	WITHERSPOON, H E	08/09/1881
CSV 001000	GREGG, SCYTHIA	10/14/1881
CSV 001001	EDNEY, F C	10/04/1881
CSV 001002	COOK, F L	10/04/1881
CSV 001003	BANDY, PIKE	10/03/1881
CSV 001004	DAGANT, JOHN	10/07/1881
CSV 001005	PALMER, ISAM	10/07/1881
CSV 001006	WHATLEY, J W	10/07/1881
CSV 001007	BAGLEY, T G	10/01/1881
CSV 001008	RISINGER, J J	08/08/1881
CSV 001009	ORR, C E	10/07/1881

Confederate Scrip Vouchers-Numerical Listing

CSV 001010	NEVIL, A J	07/18/1881
CSV 001011	GRAY, JOHN	10/07/1881
CSV 001012	ROBINSON, J S	09/29/1881
CSV 001013	PERKINS, JAMES P	10/07/1881
CSV 001014	WARD, H R	10/07/1881
CSV 001015	FYFFE, S M	10/08/1881
CSV 001016	RILEY, MARY	RILEY, JOSEPH, 10/08/1881
CSV 001017	VOYLES, MARTHA	VOYLES, SAM, 10/08/1881
CSV 001018	FLEPPIN, JULIA C	FLEPPIN, THOMAS, 10/08/1881
CSV 001019	KELLY, MARY E	10/08/1881
CSV 001020	STEWART, F C	09/12/1881
CSV 001021	MORGAN, R L	10/08/1881
CSV 001022	COGSWELL, M A	09/15/1881
CSV 001023	SCOTT, W T	10/10/1881
CSV 001024	MC ANALLY, J P	10/05/1881
CSV 001025	NEELY, THOMAS J	08/08/1881
CSV 001026	NICHOLS, A W	10/10/1881
CSV 001027	ANDREWS, G A	10/11/1881
CSV 001028	HUGHES, RICHARD	07/18/1881
CSV 001029	TARVER, WILLIAM H	09/18/1881
CSV 001030	POLK, J L	10/12/1881
CSV 001031	JACKSON, J F	09/06/1881
CSV 001032	CARTRIGHT, S C	CARTRIGHT, J S, 10/12/1881
CSV 001033	SPIKES, MARTHA	SPIKES, WILLIAM, 09/20/1881
CSV 001034	TARKINGTON, JOHN	08/22/1881
CSV 001035	SMALL, J B	08/21/1881
CSV 001036	FOSTER, JOHN	10/13/1881
CSV 001037	BAILEY, SALLY	BAILEY, AUTHOR NILE, 10/13/1881
CSV 001038	GOLDMAN, MARGARET	10/13/1881
CSV 001039	DEW, MARTHA	DEW, B W, 10/13/1881
CSV 001040	COON, L W	10/13/1881
CSV 001041	HAWKINS, MARY J	10/14/1881
CSV 001042	DURRELT, R W	10/14/1881
CSV 001043	HALE, J J	10/08/1881
CSV 001044	WOODRUFF, D W	10/08/1881
CSV 001045	FROST, W H	09/26/1881
CSV 001046	STIDHAM, CAROLINE	STIDHAM, THOMAS, 08/08/1881
CSV 001047	ODOM, J W	ODOM, JAS O, 10/01/1881
CSV 001048	FISHER, STERLING	10/14/1881
CSV 001049	BARNETT, R G	10/15/1881
CSV 001050	NORVELL, T J	08/08/1881
CSV 001051	ROBERTSON, A B	10/15/1881
CSV 001052	SMITHERMAN, DOLLY	10/15/1881
CSV 001053	ROSE, G W	10/15/1881
CSV 001054	FOX, M J	10/17/1881
CSV 001055	TUBBS, JOHN S	09/20/1881
CSV 001056	ROSSUN, T	10/17/1881

Confederate Scrip Vouchers-Numerical Listing

CSV 001057	SPEARS, MARTHA	10/17/1881
CSV 001058	SMITH, MARTHA A B	10/17/1881
CSV 001059	TODD, W R	10/17/1881
CSV 001060	ESTES, EDWARD B	SEE FILE CSV1059
CSV 001061	CARTLOW, C B	09/31/1881
CSV 001062	MOON, W J	10/18/1881
CSV 001063	BURGER, RICHARD	08/09/1881
CSV 001064	MORRIS, BEN	10/18/1881
CSV 001065	BROWN, GEORGE B	10/12/1881
CSV 001066	BAZINETT, S W	BAZINETT, WILLIAM, 10/11/1881
CSV 001067	ECCLES, MARY	09/01/1881
CSV 001068	EBERHARD, HENRY	10/19/1881
CSV 001069	MOORE, E T	08/20/1881
CSV 001070	GODFREY, JOHN	10/11/1881
CSV 001071	ERCANBRACK, THOS T	10/20/1881
CSV 001072	CLARK, LESTER	07/14/1881
CSV 001073	DELAY, HARRIET	DELAY, JAMES, 10/21/1881
CSV 001074	MITCHELL, W J	10/22/1881
CSV 001075	HARRELL, JAMES C	10/22/1881
CSV 001076	ALLEN, CATHERIN	ALLEN, BERRY, 07/11/1881
CSV 001077	ALLEN, ADAMIRAM	07/11/1881
CSV 001078	FORREST, R O	10/22/1881
CSV 001079	PARKS, POLER	10/22/1881
CSV 001080	WILSON, WILLIAM	10/11/1881
CSV 001081	ROTAN, W T	08/21/1881
CSV 001082	STRINGER, E A	10/10/1881
CSV 001083	POSTLETHWAIT, CHAS S	10/10/1881
CSV 001084	BERRYMAN, FREDERICK	08/08/1881
CSV 001085	WHITAKER, WILLIS	10/24/1881
CSV 001086	BREWER, WILLIAM M	10/15/1881
CSV 001087	MC PHEARSON, J H	10/19/1881
CSV 001088	SIMS, EDWARD	04/19/1881
CSV 001089	WALSH, M F	WALSH, W R, 08/27/1881
CSV 001090	MONTGOMERY, JAMES	10/11/1881
CSV 001091	BOOZMAN, AMANDA	BOOZMAN, EZEKIEL, 10/17/1881
CSV 001092	CULWELL, A J	10/25/1881
CSV 001093	GILL, JOSEPH	10/25/1881
CSV 001094	MC CRIGHT, WILLIAM	10/25/1881
CSV 001095	ROBERTSON, JOHN	10/30/1881
CSV 001096	TURNER, J T	10/26/1881
CSV 001097	TAYLOR, ANDREW	10/10/1881
CSV 001098	FULLER, M J	FULLER, L C, 08/08/1881
CSV 001099	KENNEDY, G B	07/07/1881
CSV 001100	YEAKLEY, M V	10/29/1881
CSV 001101	LINDSAY, JOSH	10/25/1881
CSV 001102	WOODS, KATE	WOODS, BEN, 10/24/1881
CSV 001103	WAGNON, T J	10/24/1881

CSV 001104	GILES, M J	10/31/1881
CSV 001105	FILE EMPTY	
CSV 001106	FILE EMPTY	
CSV 001107	FILE EMPTY	
CSV 001108	FILE EMPTY	
CSV 001109	FILE EMPTY	
CSV 001110	FILE EMPTY	
CSV 001111	FURLOUGH, T A	09/17/1881
CSV 001112	SMITH, ROBERT	10/31/1881
CSV 001113	CHOICE, W A	08/08/1881
CSV 001114	CHISM, W E	09/26/1881
CSV 001115	THOMPSON, J	08/09/1881
CSV 001116	SWENSON, MARY A	SWENSON, H B, 10/24/1881
CSV 001117	VASQUEZ, ANTONIO	11/02/1881
CSV 001118	WHITE, J A	08/09/1881
CSV 001119	MIDYETT, MIRCANI	08/10/1881
CSV 001120	CROOM, J W	07/16/1881
CSV 001121	ENGEL, CHRISTIAN	11/03/1881
CSV 001122	HUMPHREY, G W	11/03/1881
CSV 001123	BLAKWAY, W T	08/12/1881
CSV 001124	CHRISTIAN, JOHN R	11/03/1881
CSV 001125	WAGNER, JACOB	08/08/1881
CSV 001126	SCHULTZ, HENRY	08/08/1881
CSV 001127	HUGHES, WILLIAM	09/09/1881
CSV 001128	MURRAY, M W	10/31/1881
CSV 001129	CARLTON, WILLIAM H	10/31/1881
CSV 001130	HOOD, L A	HOOD, ANDREW, 11/07/1881
CSV 001131	CRAVER, JAMES P	11/04/1881
CSV 001132	CRAIG, ALEXANDER P	11/04/1881
CSV 001133	DOLBY, H L	11/04/1881
CSV 001134	HOPE, MARTHA	11/04/1881
CSV 001135	MC KAY, MARIA	11/04/1881
CSV 001136	FORK, BATTLE	10/08/1881
CSV 001137	MC CAUGHAN, J T	11/08/1881
CSV 001138	BAKER, J W S	11/08/1881
CSV 001139	THORP, NANCY	11/10/1881
CSV 001140	SAUNDERS, J M	11/11/1881
CSV 001141	CARVER, D L	CARVER, LEVI, 11/12/1881
CSV 001142	KINMAN, P L	07/16/1881
CSV 001143	WILLIAMS, J S	11/02/1881
CSV 001144	LACK, L C	09/15/1881
CSV 001145	BOWLES, TOM	09/20/1881
CSV 001146	RUDDELL, ISAAC N	08/08/1881
CSV 001147	HILL, MARTHA A E	HILL, HOLDEN, 07/22/1881
CSV 001148	HARDING, WILLIAM	11/14/1881
CSV 001149	SMITH, GEORGE	11/14/1881
CSV 001150	REYES, JUAN	11/14/1881
CSV 001151	REYES, ALEXANDER	11/14/1881
CSV 001152	DURFEE, ALVIN A	11/14/1881

CSV 001153	BENSON, J W	11/16/1881
CSV 001154	LEE, LEROY	11/14/1881
CSV 001155	SPINDLE, SAMUEL	11/14/1881
CSV 001156	TRUITT, MARY A	TRUITT, FRANCIS M, 07/11/1881
CSV 001157	TRUITT, SUSAN	TRUITT, THOMAS S, 07/11/1881
CSV 001158	FLORES, CARLOS	11/17/1881
CSV 001159	RUIZ, GRANVIL	11/18/1881
CSV 001160	HERNANDEZ, JOSE MARIA	11/17/1881
CSV 001161	HAMMER, W L	11/14/1881
CSV 001162	MARTIN, MARTHA	MARTIN IRA, 11/14/1881
CSV 001163	WYNEKOOP, P C	11/16/1881
CSV 001164	FRANKLIN, P B	11/14/1881
CSV 001165	SPARKMAN, M J	SPARKMAN, S S, 11/14/1881
CSV 001166	HARRISON, HILLIARD	11/17/1881
CSV 001167	BASSETT, NOAH	11/17/1881
CSV 001168	MILLOWN, Y A	11/17/1881
CSV 001169	GRIFFIS, J T	11/17/1881
CSV 001170	MOORMAN, MARY	11/17/1881
CSV 001171	COOK, REBECCA	COOK, DAVID, 11/14/1881
CSV 001172	MURPHY, G S	11/17/1881
CSV 001173	BISHOP, J R	11/14/1881
CSV 001174	KELLY, W E	11/14/1881
CSV 001175	DICKIE, JIM A	11/17/1881
CSV 001176	ATWOOD, C M	11/17/1881
CSV 001177	RICHARDS, WILSON B	11/17/1881
CSV 001178	HALLUM, JOE A	11/17/1881
CSV 001179	DARBOSON, MARY	11/17/1881
CSV 001180	HAMILTON, SAMUEL	11/17/1881
CSV 001181	CAVINESS, W S	11/17/1881
CSV 001182	DANCE, JOHN T	11/17/1881
CSV 001183	WILLIAMS, J F R	11/17/1881
CSV 001184	FINCH, DANIEL	11/17/1881
CSV 001185	GRAY, ELIZABETH	11/15/1881
CSV 001186	CARROLL, A F	09/27/1881
CSV 001187	GIVIN, THOMAS J	11/14/1881
CSV 001188	GOAD, JAMES	11/18/1881
CSV 001189	FOSTER, J A	11/15/1881
CSV 001190	LUMMUS, JAMES M	11/15/1881
CSV 001191	CUNNINGHAM, JAMES T	11/14/1881
CSV 001192	FITZHUGH, LEAL WILLIAM	11/14/1881
CSV 001193	CLAUSEL, R H	11/14/1881
CSV 001194	MC DANIEL, M A	11/15/1881
CSV 001195	CARTER, E J	11/18/1881
CSV 001196	RICHARDSON, R C	11/18/1881
CSV 001197	SKINNER, WILLIAM	11/18/1881
CSV 001198	WALLING, RICHARD	11/18/1881
CSV 001199	DEWEES, J M	11/14/1881
CSV 001200	HILDENBRANDT, T	11/18/1881

Confederate Scrip Vouchers-Numerical Listing

Voucher	Name	Date
CSV 001201	ELLIS, JOE	09/30/1881
CSV 001202	MEARS, J W	11/14/1881
CSV 001203	MC CARTHY, I C	11/14/1881
CSV 001204	CARROLL, T M	11/14/1881
CSV 001205	RAWLS, THOMAS	11/14/1881
CSV 001206	TAYLOR, J P	11/14/1881
CSV 001207	HARDIN, WILLIAM A	11/14/1881
CSV 001208	YOUNG, ROBERT	11/14/1881
CSV 001209	REID, B S	11/14/1881
CSV 001210	BOESE, CHARLES	11/19/1881
CSV 001211	MOSES, L G	11/15/1881
CSV 001212	RANKIN, ROBERT	11/15/1881
CSV 001213	RUTLEDGE, WILLIAM	11/19/1881
CSV 001214	HYATT, J C	09/09/1881
CSV 001215	LEE, L M	11/15/1881
CSV 001216	COLEMAN, W G	11/19/1881
CSV 001217	FLOYD, R W	11/19/1881
CSV 001218	RICHARDSON, W P	11/16/1881
CSV 001219	MARTIN, N	11/15/1881
CSV 001220	SANDERS, CHARNEL	11/15/1881
CSV 001221	OGLESBY, M J	OGLESBY, CHARLES F, 11/15/1881
CSV 001222	GREEN, W A	11/21/1881
CSV 001223	CAROUTH, T C	11/16/1881
CSV 001224	COPERING, JANE	11/16/1881
CSV 001225	RUSSELL, J E S	11/21/1881
CSV 001226	CADWELL, J W	11/21/1881
CSV 001227	MOORE, S E	11/21/1881
CSV 001228	POOL, E W	11/21/1881
CSV 001229	BURGES, WILLIAM	11/21/1881
CSV 001230	MOREAU, JULIUS	11/21/1881
CSV 001231	MARTIN, J T	11/21/1881
CSV 001232	LEE, J L	11/15/1881
CSV 001233	WILLIAMS, JAMES T	11/21/1881
CSV 001234	FREDERICK, MARY ANN	FREDERICK, JOHN, 11/21/1881
CSV 001235	HAIL, JOHN S	11/15/1881
CSV 001236	REDUS, JAMES	11/21/1881
CSV 001237	AUTREY, E A	11/21/1881
CSV 001238	MEADOW, LUCINDA	MEADOW, JAMES R, 11/17/1881
CSV 001239	CASPER, W L	11/21/1881
CSV 001240	ROGERS, I J	11/21/1881
CSV 001241	HONEY, SAM	11/21/1881
CSV 001242	ROGERS, J C	11/21/1881
CSV 001243	FULLER, J C	11/21/1881
CSV 001244	WILLIAMS, MARTIN	10/3/1881
CSV 001245	PRUITT, ELIZABETH	11/15/1881
CSV 001246	FILE EMPTY	
CSV 001247	FILE EMPTY	

Confederate Scrip Vouchers-Numerical Listing

CSV 001248..... FILE EMPTY
CSV 001249..... FILE EMPTY
CSV 001250..... FILE EMPTY
CSV 001251..... FILE EMPTY
CSV 001252..... STEVERSON, W R 11/21/1881
CSV 001253..... ALVERY, D S 11/14/1881
CSV 001254..... JOHNS, J D.. 11/23/1881
CSV 001255..... KEY, WILLIAM.. 11/16/1881
CSV 001256..... WILLIAMS, SARAH J...................................... 11/23/1881
CSV 001257..... MOORING, J S.. 11/23/1881
CSV 001258..... WELLS, W W... 11/14/1881
CSV 001259..... TAYLOR, MARY C... 11/23/1881
CSV 001260..... STACEY, J J... 11/15/1881
CSV 001261..... CLANK, L J... 11/23/1881
CSV 001262..... ABSHEAR, WILLIAM 11/23/1881
CSV 001263..... MC LAREN, M M .... MC LAREN, WILLIAM, 11/23/1881
CSV 001264..... BLAIR, J J.. 11/17/1881
CSV 001265..... TAYLOR, C L 11/23/1881
CSV 001266..... WEYERS, F M 11/23/1881
CSV 001267..... BURDEN, MATILDA.. 11/23/1881
CSV 001268..... MC LEOD, ISABELLA 11/23/1881
CSV 001269..... NORRIS, CHRISTINA....................................... 11/23/1881
CSV 001270..... ACKER, W H 11/23/1881
CSV 001271..... RATCLIFF, MARY E 11/14/1881
CSV 001272..... PULLIN, ALZADA .... PULLIN, THOMAS, 11/14/1881
CSV 001273..... WALKER, A D 11/14/1881
CSV 001274..... HOLCOME, LAURA 11/23/1881
CSV 001275..... RODMAN, H M 11/15/1881
CSV 001276..... STEWART, CYNTHIA....................................... STEWART, ALEXANDER, 11/23/1881
CSV 001277..... HERBERT, JAS H... 11/23/1881
CSV 001278..... SEARGENT, ANDREW 11/23/1881
CSV 001279..... DELANCY, T C 11/23/1881
CSV 001280..... HEDRICK, A J .... HEADRICH, JAMES, 11/16/1881
CSV 001281..... HAYS, J M.. 11/14/1881
CSV 001282..... ELLIS, J T 11/14/1881
CSV 001283..... JAMES, M A... 11/14/1881
CSV 001284..... GUNSTANSON, R.. 11/15/1881
CSV 001285..... NEVILLS, D E.. 11/14/1881
CSV 001286..... WILBORN, M C... 11/23/1881
CSV 001287..... HILL, SARAH .... HILL, THOMAS, 11/23/1881
CSV 001288..... WILLIAMSON, N A .... WILLIAMSON, DANIEL, 1/16/1881
CSV 001289..... MOON, M J.. 11/23/1881
CSV 001290..... AINSWORTH, DAVID H................................... 11/23/1881
CSV 001291..... LOUT, JAMES 11/23/1881
CSV 001292..... BARRON, JASPER.. 11/23/1881
CSV 001293..... ROBINETT, JAMES A 11/23/1881

CSV 001294	ROBINSON, T M	11/23/1881
CSV 001295	CHAMBERS, WILLIAM	11/23/1881
CSV 001296	MC LELAND, JOHN	11/23/1881
CSV 001297	PREWETT, J M	11/23/1881
CSV 001298	PARKS, VIRGINIA F	PARKS, W L, 11/15/1881
CSV 001299	GLAP, S A	11/23/1881
CSV 001300	MC DANIEL, MARY E	11/15/1881
CSV 001301	DAVIS, WILLIAM	11/15/1881
CSV 001302	HOUSE, J S	11/15/1881
CSV 001303	GUTHRIE, E J	11/15/1881
CSV 001304	PANTHER, M F	11/15/1881
CSV 001305	LINDSAY, MAHALA	11/15/1881
CSV 001306	CLAY, M A	11/15/1881
CSV 001307	DAVIS, A M	11/15/1881
CSV 001308	THOMAS, AOMINTA	11/15/1881
CSV 001309	DUCE, D	11/23/1881
CSV 001310	CONDRON, F M	11/23/1881
CSV 001311	MAGNESS, B A	11/14/1881
CSV 001312	ATKINS, W A	11/14/1881
CSV 001313	STOUT, JASPER	11/25/1881
CSV 001314	MACK, JESSE	11/25/1881
CSV 001315	ROBINSON, R L	11/25/1881
CSV 001316	MORSE, DRURY	11/25/1881
CSV 001317	WADE, ABRAHAM	11/25/1881
CSV 001318	SPRADLING, G W	11/25/1881
CSV 001319	WEAVER, J A	11/25/1881
CSV 001320	LANGLEY, G W	11/25/1881
CSV 001321	COLE, VINY	COLE, WILLIAM, 11/1881
CSV 001322	MERCHANT, G A	11/25/1881
CSV 001323	QUAID, B W	08/22/1881
CSV 001324	MEYERS, ROZELIA	11/17/1881
CSV 001325	MORRIS, JULIA ANN	11/16/1881
CSV 001326	MULLINS, WILLIAM T	11/18/1881
CSV 001327	HANEY, A N	11/18/1881
CSV 001328	SMITH, A J	11/18/1881
CSV 001329	SLAUGHTER, ARENA	11/25/1881
CSV 001330	BRANTLY, R A	11/25/1881
CSV 001331	WHITEN, J D	11/25/1881
CSV 001332	REYNOLDS, D R	11/14/1881
CSV 001333	CHAMBLIS, ELKANAH	11/25/1881
CSV 001334	WYATT, WILLIAM H	11/25/1881
CSV 001335	SHADAIN, SARAH	11/25/1881
CSV 001336	GRIFFITH, AMANDA	GRIFFITH, GEORGE M, 11/15/1881
CSV 001337	BRUCE, J T	11/14/1881
CSV 001338	HARDWICK, WILLIAM L	11/25/1881
CSV 001339	STRICKLAND, M M	11/25/1881
CSV 001340	JOHNSON, P H	11/25/1881
CSV 001341	LOGSDON, E J	09/02/1881

Confederate Scrip Vouchers-Numerical Listing

CSV 001342	PETTY, HENRY	11/25/1881
CSV 001343	LONG, EDWARD	11/14/1881
CSV 001344	GEORGE, A M	11/14/1881
CSV 001345	BURDEN, CARROL	11/14/1881
CSV 001346	MC MICHAEL, ROBERT B	11/25/1881
CSV 001347	POSEY, CAROLINE	11/25/1881
CSV 001348	HANSON, JOHN F	11/25/1881
CSV 001349	DRAKE, THOMAS B	11/14/1881
CSV 001350	OWENS, A M	OWENS, J R, 11/25/1881
CSV 001351	UPTON, GILES	09/26/1881
CSV 001352	REED, JOHN F	11/25/1881
CSV 001353	COUNT, LOUISA	COUNT, CARL, 08/02/1881
CSV 001354	RUSSELL, S L	11/14/1881
CSV 001355	WOODARD, J W	11/25/1881
CSV 001356	STINNETT, HENRY	11/15/1881
CSV 001357	ALSOP, MARY	ALSOP, ARTHUR, 11/16/1881
CSV 001358	LONG, LOUISA	LONG, WILLIAM, 11/25/1881
CSV 001359	CLACK, SARAH F	CLACK, WILEY, 11/26/1881
CSV 001360	HOUSTON, JAMES M	11/14/1881
CSV 001361	REESE, MARTHA	REESE, CHARLES, 11/17/1881
CSV 001362	BOWDEN, W R	11/26/1881
CSV 001363	HARDIN, ASHER	11/26/1881
CSV 001364	STONE, EDWARD P	08/09/1881
CSV 001365	THOMAS, JOHN C	11/26/1881
CSV 001366	STOOKS, JOSEPH S	11/26/1881
CSV 001367	POLLEY, ANGELINA	POLLEY, OLIVER, 08/08/1881
CSV 001368	ZIRAMON, MANUEL	11/26/1881
CSV 001369	BROWN, PERRY	11/26/1881
CSV 001370	SANDOVAL, ADOLPHO	11/26/1881
CSV 001371	NEWTZE, ALBERT	11/26/1881
CSV 001372	MC NAMARA, DANIEL	10/14/1881
CSV 001373	GOODRUM, SEBORN	10/14/1881
CSV 001374	WINGO, W A	11/28/1881
CSV 001375	BERRY, MILES	10/22/1881
CSV 001376	COY, C P	11/17/1881
CSV 001377	BULLOCH, W W	11/28/1881
CSV 001378	RIDDLE, W S	11/28/1881
CSV 001379	WHEELER, W J	11/17/1881
CSV 001380	STOCKTON, WILLIAM W	09/03/1881
CSV 001381	BUMGARNER, TERREASY	08/09/1881
CSV 001382	MC ELREATH, S H	11/28/1881
CSV 001383	HENDRIX, SARAH C	11/28/1881
CSV 001384	STEPHENS, JOHN	11/28/1881
CSV 001385	STEPHENS, JOHN	11/28/1881
CSV 001386	MAY, D G	11/15/1881
CSV 001387	BOLTON, E W	11/29/1881
CSV 001388	FULLER, R D	11/29/1881
CSV 001389	JOHNSON, SARAH	11/29/1881

Voucher	Name	Additional / Date
CSV 001390	CANNON, SARAH L	CANNON, JOSEPHUS, 11/29/1881
CSV 001391	WHITSON, JAMES	11/29/1881
CSV 001392	BLAIR, CHARLES W	11/29/1881
CSV 001393	DAVENPORT, C C	11/29/1881
CSV 001394	MURRAY, WILLIAM P	11/29/1881
CSV 001395	AGUILAR, NEPOMUCENO	11/29/1881
CSV 001396	BALLARD, FRANCIS	BALLARD, MATT, 11/30/1881
CSV 001397	LEMMONS, SARAH	11/15/1881
CSV 001398	JACKSON, GREEN	11/15/1881
CSV 001399	HUGHES, J N	11/30/1881
CSV 001400	BLOODSWORTH, J N	11/30/1881
CSV 001401	ALEXANDER, J S	11/30/1881
CSV 001402	RAMSEY, G W	11/30/1881
CSV 001403	CHASHUM, BETTIE	11/16/11881
CSV 001404	ESTES, M J	11/15/1881
CSV 001405	HATCH, JOSEPH A	11/30/1881
CSV 001406	HALLEMON, PERRY	11/30/1881
CSV 001407	EATON, JOEL	11/19/1881
CSV 001408	OLIVER, J J	08/08/1881
CSV 001409	STANFIELD, MARY F	STANFIELD, E A, 08/08/1881
CSV 001410	BROWN, JAMES C	11/14/1881
CSV 001411	ROBERTS, T C	12/01/1881
CSV 001412	ROBERTS, J E	12/01/1881
CSV 001413	PRICE, JOHN	11/14/1881
CSV 001414	WORRELL, JOHN	11/18/1881
CSV 001415	JOHNSON, J W	12/02/1881
CSV 001416	STOCKTON, AMANDA	07/11/1881
CSV 001417	WILLIAMS, T E	11/15/1881
CSV 001418	MC CARTY, JOHN	11/15/1881
CSV 001419	WILLIAMS, A J	11/18/1881
CSV 001420	BRUTON, P J	11/18/1881
CSV 001421	WISE, F J	12/10/1881
CSV 001422	FORSYTH, Y P	12/02/1881
CSV 001423	HUMBLE, THOMAS	12/02/1881
CSV 001424	SHERWOOD, H T	12/02/1881
CSV 001425	MC GREW, R W	10/29/1881
CSV 001426	BLANTON, W W	12/03/1881
CSV 001427	SHIELDS, ISIAH	12/03/1881
CSV 001428	JACKSON, T M	12/05/1881
CSV 001429	HOLCOMB, JOHN M	12/01/1881
CSV 001430	FILE EMPTY	
CSV 001431	CAVITT, W A	11/14/1881
CSV 001432	TEAVER, W A	12/05/1881
CSV 001433	JONES, W S	13/05/1881
CSV 001434	FLEMING, SARAH	FLEMING, JOHN, 09/20/1881
CSV 001435	WHEELER, J P	05/13/1881
CSV 001436	FORSYTHE, Y F	12/05/1881
CSV 001437	FITZGERALD, LUCUIS	12/05/1881

CSV 001438	STEWART, PETER	12/05/1881
CSV 001439	CUTHBERTSON, C D	CUTHBERTSON, S J, 11/16/1881
CSV 001440	DAVIS, THOMAS R	12/06/1881
CSV 001441	HANES, JAMES J	12/06/1881
CSV 001442	FRAZIER, I F	11/15/1881
CSV 001443	LANGSTON, SARAH	LANGSTON, H V, 11/15/1881
CSV 001444	FLOYD, T J	11/14/1881
CSV 001445	RAGSDALE, FRANCES	RAGSDALE, JOHN, 07/16/1881
CSV 001446	DAVIS, NEWTON	12/06/1881
CSV 001447	TEAL, T A	12/06/1881
CSV 001448	BAKER, G C	12/06/1881
CSV 001449	WHEELER, HOUSTON	12/07/1881
CSV 001450	WHEELER, THOMAS	12/07/1881
CSV 001451	MILLER, A C	12/07/1881
CSV 001452	KIRBY, A J	11/15/1881
CSV 001453	COOK, NANCY	COOK, WESTY, 09/20/1881
CSV 001454	REYNOLDS, J W B	12/08/1881
CSV 001455	SHARP, MALISA	11/14/1881
CSV 001456	CAMPBELL, JAMES	11/14/1881
CSV 001457	GARCIA, ROBERT	12/08/1881
CSV 001458	WILSON, J C	07/12/1881
CSV 001459	BROCK, I N	11/14/1881
CSV 001460	HORTON, GEORGE	12/09/1881
CSV 001461	RAIN, BENJAMIN	12/06/1881
CSV 001462	COPELAND, THOMAS J	12/09/1881
CSV 001463	ESHES, EDWARD	12/09/1881
CSV 001464	FRITH, N B	12/09/1881
CSV 001465	THOMPSON, SUSAN	12/09/1881
CSV 001466	POLK, JAMES	11/15/1881
CSV 001467	MITCHELL, WILLIAM	12/09/1881
CSV 001468	WILLIAMS, E O	12/10/1881
CSV 001469	MAYS, W A	12/10/1881
CSV 001470	COUCH, W P	12/10/1881
CSV 001471	COUCH, J T	12/10/1881
CSV 001472	PULLIN, R C	12/10/1881
CSV 001473	CARTER, ELBERT	11/14/1881
CSV 001474	CASEY, MARS	11/19/1881
CSV 001475	WRAY, MARTHA	11/16/1881
CSV 001476	ENGLISH, JAMES D	09/24/1881
CSV 001477	HAMILTON, H	12/12/1881
CSV 001478	CIRVARD, M M	12/12/1881
CSV 001479	LANE, R P	12/12/1881
CSV 001480	ANNBOYLE, MARY	12/12/1881
CSV 001481	WILEY, ED	12/12/1881
CSV 001482	BARNES, FRANK	12/13/1881
CSV 001483	POLSTER, GEORGE	09/10/1881
CSV 001484	DERMENT, L A	11/15/1881
CSV 001485	GASTON, M E	12/03/1881
CSV 001486	RIGGS, W S	12/14/1881

Confederate Scrip Vouchers-Numerical Listing

CSV 001487.....	WINTON, J W	12/14/1881
CSV 001488.....	SAXON, H M E	07/11/1881
CSV 001489.....	HALL, MARY A E	11/14/1881
CSV 001490.....	LAUGHTON, PAT M	12/05/1881
CSV 001491.....	GRAY, WILLIAM W	07/01/1881
CSV 001492.....	SANDOVAL, JESUS	12/14/1881
CSV 001493.....	GARCIA, ALFONZO	12/14/1881
CSV 001494.....	TOSBER, EDWARD	12/14/1881
CSV 001495.....	DORSEY, MARY	11/14/1881
CSV 001496.....	BADER, CHRISTINA	11/16/1881
CSV 001497.....	ELLISON, MINERVA	08/08/1881
CSV 001498.....	WELBORN, A H	12/16/1881
CSV 001499.....	ELLIOT, EDMOND	12/16/1881
CSV 001500.....	DECHARD, B S	12/16/1881
CSV 001501.....	TYLER, SARAH	12/17/1881
CSV 001502.....	FITZHUGH, GEORGE W	11/18/1881
CSV 001503.....	BARBEE, JON	11/16/1881
CSV 001504.....	MC MURTRY, JAMES	07/02/1881
CSV 001505.....	MELTON, H P	12/14/1881
CSV 001506.....	BAILEY, S P	11/26/1881
CSV 001507.....	SULLIVAN, W S	11/21/1881
CSV 001508.....	HESS, JOHN H	12/30/1881
CSV 001509.....	HAMPTON, W W	12/20/1881
CSV 001510.....	HOWELL, J H	11/18/1881
CSV 001511.....	LANEY, F M	10/20/1881
CSV 001512.....	MANDUSON, JESSE	12/17/1881
CSV 001513.....	TRAYNOR, JOHN	11/15/1881
CSV 001514.....	STRODE, C E	11/16/1881
CSV 001515.....	SAMS, MARGARET	SAMS, JOSEPH, 12/21/1881
CSV 001516.....	PENN, D P	11/14/1881
CSV 001517.....	HOWARD, FLORIDA	12/21/1881
CSV 001518.....	TERRY, THOMAS	12/21/1881
CSV 001519.....	EMMONS, H R	12/21/1881
CSV 001520.....	HANKS, F M	12/21/1881
CSV 001521.....	LEE, WILLIAM	12/03/1881
CSV 001522.....	TAYLOR, H E	11/15/1881
CSV 001523.....	WOOD, DAN A	12/23/1881
CSV 001524.....	PINKNEY, R H	12/23/1881
CSV 001525.....	EVERETT, ELIZA	12/23/1881
CSV 001526.....	RAINS, R H	12/23/1881
CSV 001527.....	GORDON, L P	12/21/1881
CSV 001528.....	MAULDIN, W	11/16/1881
CSV 001529.....	SUTPHEN, W C	11/14/1881
CSV 001530.....	WILSON, JAMES	12/24/1881
CSV 001531.....	STACY, W A	11/17/1881
CSV 001532.....	SMITH, RICHARD	12/12/1881
CSV 001533.....	STORY, D F	12/12/1881
CSV 001534.....	WILSON, W M	12/27/1881
CSV 001535.....	MOORE, D Y	10/03/1881

Confederate Scrip Vouchers-Numerical Listing

CSV 001536	HEFLIN, R A	12/27/1881
CSV 001537	COOPER, J F	11/14/1881
CSV 001538	DURRAND, GUS	12/29/1881
CSV 001539	CERVANTES, JULIAN	12/29/1881
CSV 001540	MAC KAY, JACOB	12/29/1881
CSV 001541	MARTINEZ, ALEJOS	12/29/1881
CSV 001542	SLADE, W C	11/15/1881
CSV 001543	LEVENTON, JOHN	12/17/1881
CSV 001544	WATSON, JOSIAH	12/27/1881
CSV 001545	DUKE, N ELIZABETH	09/09/1881
CSV 001546	STEPHENSON, W D	09/09/1881
CSV 001547	MOWRY, J T	01/03/1882
CSV 001548	LANE, MARY	LANE, JOSEPH, 07/21/1881
CSV 001549	PAGE, HEZAKIAH	08/08/1881
CSV 001550	ANDREWS, E B	11/14/1881
CSV 001551	PRICE, B H	11/14/1881
CSV 001552	WILLS, JOSEPH	01/04/1882
CSV 001553	EDINGTON, H F	01/04/1882
CSV 001554	PURYEAR, J B	12/27/1881
CSV 001555	EVERETT, NANCY	09/09/1881
CSV 001556	CROWDER, G H	01/04/1882
CSV 001557	DAY, W C	08/24/1881
CSV 001558	LASATER, JAS H	01/04/1882
CSV 001559	SPANGENBERG, HENRY	04/09/1881
CSV 001560	PFEIFER, JOHANN	12/05/1881
CSV 001561	WEICHOLD, HENRY	12/05/1881
CSV 001562	MINGS, MARTHA	01/04/1882
CSV 001563	WILSON, W F	01/04/1882
CSV 001564	GOSETT, F A	11/14/1881
CSV 001565	ENKE, AUGUST	01/05/1882
CSV 001566	ACKER, AMOS	09/12/1881
CSV 001567	TISON, E J	TYSON, WILLIAM, 12/21/1881
CSV 001568	BENKILBACH, GEORGE	01/06/1882
CSV 001569	BARTON, ELIZA C	BARTON, WILSON P, 01/06/1882
CSV 001570	SMITH, MARY	SMITH, J R, 01/09/1882
CSV 001571	BAXTER, S H	BAXTER, J, 12/31/1881
CSV 001572	SMITH, W K	11/14/1881
CSV 001573	ROBINSON, MATILDA	01/09/1882
CSV 001574	MILLER, VICTORIA	MILLER, THEOPHILIUS, 07/07/1881
CSV 001575	BORDEN, GEORGE	11/14/1881
CSV 001576	ALLEN, W W	12/17/1881
CSV 001577	WILSON, L F	01/10/1882
CSV 001578	BISHOP, M	07/13/1881
CSV 001579	DAWSON, JOHN	08/31/1881
CSV 001580	SAVAGE, JOSEPH	01/10/1882
CSV 001581	FRANKLIN, R L	01/10/1882
CSV 001582	BRAGG, W T	01/10/1882

CSV 001583	SURRATT, J M	01/10/1882
CSV 001584	SANDERS, PHILIP	01/10/1882
CSV 001585	BENNETT, R O	01/10/1882
CSV 001586	PEEBLES, S P	11/15/1881
CSV 001587	THOMPSON, W H	04/09/1881
CSV 001588	MC KINLEY, L L	04/09/1881
CSV 001589	HEATH, W C	11/14/1881
CSV 001590	BREWER, T E	07/10/1881
CSV 001591	ADARE, WILLIAM	11/14/1881
CSV 001592	CALVIN, THOMAS	01/12/1882
CSV 001593	SCHAFFER, JAMES	01/12/1882
CSV 001594	MILLER, CARL	01/12/1882
CSV 001595	LOPEZ, IGNACIO	01/12/1882
CSV 001596	TOWNSEND, THOMAS	01/12/1882
CSV 001597	COX, JOHN C	01/12/1882
CSV 001598	STEPHENS, D C	01/16/1882
CSV 001599	ESQUIVEL, LUIS	01/14/1882
CSV 001600	THOMPSON, JULIA A	THOMPSON, JOHN, 01/17/1882
CSV 001601	HOFFMAN, F M	01/17/1882
CSV 001602	JAMES, AGNES	01/20/1882
CSV 001603	CARTWRIGHT, SANFORD	12/17/1881
CSV 001604	MASON, J G	01/02/1882
CSV 001605	VICKENY, VANCE	01/02/1882
CSV 001606	BRACE, JAMES	12/21/1881
CSV 001607	HINES, JAMES	01/02/1882
CSV 001608	BRISTER, F M	01/20/1882
CSV 001609	MOORE, NANCY	01/20/1882
CSV 001610	PRICE, LUCINDA	12/14/1881
CSV 001611	BALL, KENEDY W	01/23/1882
CSV 001612	CORLEY, GEORGE	01/23/1882
CSV 001613	MC CRIGHT, F P	01/23/1882
CSV 001614	ELLIS, JOHN R	01/23/1882
CSV 001615	BECKHAM, R E	01/23/1882
CSV 001616	PAIN, W D	11/14/1881
CSV 001617	CADLE, M A	01/26/1882
CSV 001618	JACKSON, D Y	11/14/1881
CSV 001619	TUNNELL, W B	01/28/1882
CSV 001620	BEASLEY, F	01/28/1882
CSV 001621	TRANT, MARSHALL	01/30/1882
CSV 001622	COOPER, TENABY	01/31/1882
CSV 001623	NORMAN, M M	01/31/1882
CSV 001624	NEWLAND, W W	12/31/1881
CSV 001625	PRICE, MORGAN	12/31/1881
CSV 001626	WILLIAMS, JAMES	02/02/1882
CSV 001627	DABNEY, JAMES A	02/13/1882
CSV 001628	GEE, LEONARD G	02/01/1882
CSV 001629	DENNIH, DAVID	01/03/1882
CSV 001630	BLESSINGTON, J P	02/13/1882
CSV 001631	MINGS, LAVINIA	02/09/1882

Confederate Scrip Vouchers-Numerical Listing

CSV 001632	PARKS, A B	02/13/1882
CSV 001633	LYTTE, JNO J	08/08/1882
CSV 001634	WRIGHT, DAVE	08/22/1882
CSV 001635	FULTON, D W	02/13/1882
CSV 001636	MC CLAIN, JOHN	02/13/1882
CSV 001637	BLAKELY, S T	12/31/1881
CSV 001638	VINSON, A H	12/31/1881
CSV 001639	SHROPSHIRE, WILLIAM	02/13/1882
CSV 001640	CORDOVA, MARY A	02/13/1882
CSV 001641	TURNER, JESSE	07/13/1881
CSV 001642	FOWLER, A W	02/13/1882
CSV 001643	RANDOLPH, E J	02/14/1882
CSV 001644	AYER, DAVID	11/15/1881
CSV 001645	ALLAN, CHARLES	02/14/1882
CSV 001646	ATTAWAY, JOSEPH	02/15/1882
CSV 001647	COULSON, O G	02/14/1881
CSV 001648	ROWLETT, JAMES	02/14/1881
CSV 001649	SIMMONS, B P	02/14/1881
CSV 001650	WEST, ALFRED	02/16/1882
CSV 001651	GILLIAND, SAM	02/17/1882
CSV 001652	WREN, W C	02/17/1882
CSV 001653	JONES, M P	02/13/1882
CSV 001654	CLARK, J M	02/13/1882
CSV 001655	CARPENTER, W L	02/13/1882
CSV 001656	RUSSELL, J J	02/17/1882
CSV 001657	MC CLENDON, L M	02/17/1882
CSV 001658	TERRY, JOHN W	11/15/1881
CSV 001659	HENSON, W L	02/17/1882
CSV 001660	BURNS, J J	02/18/1882
CSV 001661	STEPHENSON, L	02/18/1882
CSV 001662	CUDE, W J	02/18/1882
CSV 001663	ROBERTS, G R	02/18/1882
CSV 001664	JACKSON, IKE	02/18/1882
CSV 001665	WALLACE, AMANDA	02/13/1882
CSV 001666	FOUNTAIN, J B	02/13/1882
CSV 001667	VALDEZ, JUAN ANTONIO	02/15/1882
CSV 001668	BERNAL, LEONARDO	02/15/1882
CSV 001669	CARDENAS, NICANOR	02/15/1882
CSV 001670	ANDREWS, A C	ANDREWS, HARRY, 02/13/1882
CSV 001671	HAMILTON, J W W	02/18/1882
CSV 001672	DE BLANC, ANNA	02/21/1882
CSV 001673	TITUS, E B	02/21/1882
CSV 001674	ANDREWS, MARTHA	02/21/1882
CSV 001675	MANCHACA, JOSE A	02/18/1882
CSV 001676	PHILLIPS, E M	02/18/1882
CSV 001677	TUCKER, G W	02/18/1882
CSV 001678	WORTHY, JANE	02/23/1882
CSV 001679	RODGERS, R M	11/14/1881
CSV 001680	BASS, JAMES H	10/01/1881

CSV	Name	Date
CSV 001681	SMILIE, JACOB	02/24/1882
CSV 001682	WOOD, S M	02/24/1882
CSV 001683	PARLAW, SUSAN	02/24/1882
CSV 001684	STUBBLEFIELD, M M	02/24/1882
CSV 001685	BAILEY, TABITHA	02/25/1882
CSV 001686	SMITH, JOSEPH	02/13/1882
CSV 001687	COOKE, W G	02/13/1882
CSV 001688	CRESS, ALFRED	02/27/1882
CSV 001689	WOODS, ROBERT	12/12/1881
CSV 001690	LE BLANC, OSCAR	02/27/1882
CSV 001691	SMITH, J T	02/27/1882
CSV 001692	SALINAS, VICENTE	02/17/1882
CSV 001693	WILLIYARDS, H C	02/27/1882
CSV 001694	CONROY, ANTHONY	02/15/1882
CSV 001695	LOVE, H B	02/27/1882
CSV 001696	MOULTON, A J	02/21/1882
CSV 001697	EDISON, M T	02/21/1882
CSV 001698	WILLIAMS, D F	02/27/1882
CSV 001699	FINLEY, A T	02/14/1882
CSV 001700	JONES, JOHN G	02/27/1882
CSV 001701	SIMS, J H	02/13/1882
CSV 001702	STAUTS, G W	02/27/1882
CSV 001703	KILLIAN, W L W	02/13/1882
CSV 001704	HATTON, W C	08/08/1881
CSV 001705	HILL, F	02/14/1882
CSV 001706	DIAZ, ALEJOS	02/27/1882
CSV 001707	DOBBS, FRANCES	02/28/1882
CSV 001708	CAGE, BENJAMIN	02/14/1882
CSV 001709	LAMBERT, NATHANIEL	02/15/1882
CSV 001710	ASHLEY, E P	02/28/1882
CSV 001711	BODINE, SARAH A	02/17/1882
CSV 001712	POLK, WILLIAM	02/17/1882
CSV 001713	SKEETERS, DAVID C	02/28/1882
CSV 001714	KNOX, JAMES A	02/28/1882
CSV 001715	RUE, W B	02/28/1882
CSV 001716	MAHAN, J J W	02/28/1882
CSV 001717	MILLER, JOSHUA	02/28/1882
CSV 001718	EAVES, W R	02/28/1882
CSV 001719	ADAMS, A M	02/18/1882
CSV 001720	JONES, WILLIAM	02/13/1882
CSV 001721	DAVIDSON, JNO	03/01/1882
CSV 001722	PARKER, J P	02/15/1882
CSV 001723	CROSBY, MARY	03/03/1882
CSV 001724	SKINNER, J E	03/04/1882
CSV 001725	KENNEDY, J D	08/09/1881
CSV 001726	JACKSON, J H	03/04/1882
CSV 001727	RHODES, MARTHA	02/13/1882
CSV 001728	GILES, MARY	03/06/1882
CSV 001729	LAY, JOHN R	11/14/1881

CSV 001730..... CLEVELAND, WILLIAM 03/16/1882
CSV 001731..... SNOW, EMILY 03/07/1882
CSV 001732..... MATA, ANDRES 02/18/1882
CSV 001733..... COWTHORN, M E....................................... 03/08/1882
CSV 001734..... DWYER, WALIA.. 03/08/1882
CSV 001735..... DAVIS, H H... 02/17/1882
CSV 001736..... BISHOP, J B.. 02/17/1882
CSV 001737..... STEPHENSON, C E....................................... 02/17/1882
CSV 001738..... ALSTON, JAMES NOAH............................. 03/08/1882
CSV 001739..... BIDWELL, E B... 02/17/1882
CSV 001740..... LOGAN, M T.. 03/08/1882
CSV 001741..... TERRY, JOHN K 03/10/1882
CSV 001742..... EDWARDS, J H 03/11/1882
CSV 001743..... TIGERT, J M 03/11/1882
CSV 001744..... FILE EMPTY
CSV 001745..... FILE EMPTY
CSV 001746..... FARIAS, JOSE MARIA 02/16/1882
CSV 001747..... DIXON, JOHN.. 03/11/1882
CSV 001748..... LAWSON, HARRIET 03/14/1882
CSV 001749..... DOOLEY, JOHN E.. 03/14/1882
CSV 001750..... HANCOCK, JOHN P 03/14/1882
CSV 001751..... REASONER, J W 03/14/1882
CSV 001752..... HODGIN, H S.. 08/31/1882
CSV 001753..... WALKER, JOHN W..................................... 03/14/1882
CSV 001754..... BANKSTON, MARY J 03/14/1882
CSV 001755..... RHENDASIL, J C... 03/14/1882
CSV 001756..... CLIFTON, S R... 08/09/1881
CSV 001757..... DAY, N R 03/16/1882
CSV 001758..... MC KINNEY, W A 11/14/1881
CSV 001759..... COCKBURN, CLARK 03/21/1882
CSV 001760..... GRUBBS, B R... 03/21/1882
CSV 001761..... RIPLEY, J W 03/21/1882
CSV 001762..... RUSSELL, LAS E 03/21/1882
CSV 001763..... GREEN, JOHN A 03/21/1882
CSV 001764..... WHITE, R M... 03/21/1882
CSV 001765..... GREEAR, WILLIAM B 03/21/1882
CSV 001766..... MOON, R E 10/22/1882
CSV 001767..... DUNKAN, JOHN 03/21/1882
CSV 001768..... EATON, J R.. 03/22/1882
CSV 001769..... SHELTON, F E 02/13/1882
CSV 001770..... JOHNSTONE, L A 03/23/1882
CSV 001771..... RODRIGUEZ, GREGORIA.......................... 01/14/1882
CSV 001772..... FINNERTY, JOHN....................................... 03/24/1882
CSV 001773..... GIBBS, GEORGE... 01/14/1882
CSV 001774..... KIZER, ENOCH 03/24/1882
CSV 001775..... JONES, MARY ANN 02/15/1882
CSV 001776..... ATWELL, JAMES.. 03/28/1882
CSV 001777..... MYRES, D D 03/29/1882
CSV 001778..... LIVINGSTON, MITT................................... 08/08/1881

CSV	Name	Date
CSV 001779	WORD, R J	03/31/1882
CSV 001780	CULLISON, J G	03/31/1882
CSV 001781	GOODWIN, JULIETTE	03/13/1882
CSV 001782	ROBBINS, LOUISA	12/17/1881
CSV 001783	RIVERSON, C N	02/13/1882
CSV 001784	GARRISON, H H	04/05/1882
CSV 001785	HAMMOND, J M	03/30/1882
CSV 001786	PIERCE, ROBERT	02/18/1882
CSV 001787	WHITE, ELIZA	04/07/1882
CSV 001788	LEDGELY, J T	11/15/1882
CSV 001789	ROLAND, M A	11/25/1881
CSV 001790	NORFORD, Z W	02/17/1882
CSV 001791	BLACK, SIMEON	08/09/1881
CSV 001792	WALKER, E L	11/14/1881
CSV 001793	MC KENZIE, JULIA	04/10/1882
CSV 001794	LITTLETON, ELIZA J	04/10/1882
CSV 001795	SANDERS, JOHN A	12/21/1881
CSV 001796	LINDLEY, R	08/08/1881
CSV 001797	JONES, GEORGE	11/28/1881
CSV 001798	ROBERTSON, J F	11/28/1881
CSV 001799	REED, WARRAN	04/13/1882
CSV 001800	CORNELIAS, DANIEL	04/10/1882
CSV 001801	JOHNSON, A G	04/10/1882
CSV 001802	LOGAN, JAMES	03/13/1882
CSV 001803	WARD, THOMAS	04/13/1882
CSV 001804	MANGNES, LUCIANNO	02/17/1882
CSV 001805	ROMERO, JUAN	03/13/1882
CSV 001806	ONEY, JOHN	04/14/1882
CSV 001807	GARNER, W J	02/15/1882
CSV 001808	GILMORE, MARGARET	11/15/1881
CSV 001809	KUYKENDALL, S C	04/14/1882
CSV 001810	STANSBERRY, MARY	04/14/1882
CSV 001811	MATHEWS, THOS R	04/14/1882
CSV 001812	SIMMONS, CARRIE	04/14/1882
CSV 001813	LATHAM, HOUSTON	04/14/1882
CSV 001814	COTTON, J T	11/15/1881
CSV 001815	GREEN, MARY	04/15/1882
CSV 001816	GREER, J T	04/15/1882
CSV 001817	PHIFER, MARTHA	PHIFER, MATHEW, 08/08/1881
CSV 001818	JONES, WILLIAM	04/15/1882
CSV 001819	MAFFETT, S B	08/12/1881
CSV 001820	HORTON, EMILY C	08/08/1881
CSV 001821	STOKES, ELVIRA	08/08/1881
CSV 001822	GIPSON, LEROY	11/14/1881
CSV 001823	THOMTON, W J	1/15/1881
CSV 001824	DAWSON, JOHN	09/19/1881
CSV 001825	ROBERTSON, W H	08/08/1881
CSV 001826	BRONAGH, WILLIAM	04/15/1882
CSV 001827	HARPER, MARY J	HARPER, J P, 04/15/1882

CSV 001828	CULBERSON, D E	CULBERSON, J W, 07/22/1881
CSV 001829	HOOVER, E M	HOOVER, PORTER, 04/17/1882
CSV 001830	DAVIS, H F	02/14/1882
CSV 001831	CASTELBERRY, ELIZABETH	CASTELBERRY, JOSHUA, 07/21/1881
CSV 001832	AIKIN, J M	07/12/1881
CSV 001833	ROACH, J F G	07/21/1881
CSV 001834	PRIEST, LUCINDA	PRIEST, JAMES, 11/14/1881
CSV 001835	FULLER, ALHMUND	08/08/1881
CSV 001836	BITTICK, MARY ANN	BITTICK, GEORGE C, 04/17/1882
CSV 001837	REED, J A	08/09/1881
CSV 001838	WILEY, MARY ANN	11/14/1881
CSV 001839	DUFFY, CLEMINTINE	07/21/1881
CSV 001840	STANLEY, J K	08/08/1881
CSV 001841	WILLIAMS, LOUISA	04/17/1882
CSV 001842	NIXON, W T	07/21/1881
CSV 001843	NIXON, SARAH	07/21/1881
CSV 001844	WRIGHT, JOHN L	04/17/1882
CSV 001845	HANDY, J H	04/17/1882
CSV 001846	PRIDE, ANGELINA	PRIDE, JOHN, 07/21/1881
CSV 001847	HAGGARD, SARAH	04/17/1882
CSV 001848	ROGERS, LOUISA	07/07/1881
CSV 001849	HANCOCK, J J	08/10/1881
CSV 001850	WHEELER, M M	04/17/1872
CSV 001851	PARISH, J L	04/17/1882
CSV 001852	PARISH, JOHN D	04/17/1882
CSV 001853	LITTLEJOHN, J T	07/21/1881
CSV 001854	WHEELER, A	04/17/1882
CSV 001855	NIXON, REBECCA	04/17/1882
CSV 001856	CLUCK, R J	04/17/1882
CSV 001857	ODOM, JOSEPH	12/27/1881
CSV 001858	ARNOLD, ELI	04/17/1882
CSV 001859	MC KINLEY, D M	04/17/1882
CSV 001860	HUBERMACHER, STEPHEN	04/18/1882
CSV 001861	CRAIG, S	CRAIG, S R, 03/31/1882
CSV 001862	SWEATT, EMALINE	04/18/1882
CSV 001863	OGLESBEE, B H	04/20/1882
CSV 001864	BRONLEE, C H	04/20/1882
CSV 001865	BOWMAN, W H	04/20/1882
CSV 001866	DANIELS, JACK	04/20/1882
CSV 001867	DOUGLASS, DAVID	04/20/1882
CSV 001868	FISCHER, H E	04/22/1822
CSV 001869	ROGERS, DAVE	04/22/1822
CSV 001870	WORTHINGTON, MARY	04/22/1882
CSV 001871	KING, M S	04/25/1882
CSV 001872	KIETH, JOHN	04/25/1882
CSV 001873	STORY, R D	04/25/1882
CSV 001874	STORY, THOMAS F	08/08/1881

CSV 001875	HOLBERT, R M	08/08/1881
CSV 001876	MYER, JOHN	11/28/1881
CSV 001877	DEBORD, R	11/28/1881
CSV 001878	BOYAKIN, L R	04/29/1882
CSV 001879	ANDERSON, T T C	04/29/1882
CSV 001880	SUBLETT, W C	04/29/1882
CSV 001881	BOOTHE, MARY	03/14/1882
CSV 001882	MC ANELY, LAURA	08/01/1882
CSV 001883	FINN, DENNIS	08/01/1882
CSV 001884	CHISUM, ELIJAH	05/03/1882
CSV 001885	HARRIS, ALFORD	08/02/1881
CSV 001886	GOMEZ, MANUEL	03/16/1882
CSV 001887	DIAZ, EMILIA	02/11/1882
CSV 001888	ALDEREHE, JOSE	01/16/1882
CSV 001889	SCHMIT, HENRY	03/13/1882
CSV 001890	GUERERA, ANTONIO	03/13/1882
CSV 001891	GONZALES, MANUEL	03/13/1882
CSV 001892	BAKER, FRANKLIN	03/13/1882
CSV 001893	PARKER, CHARLES	03/13/1882
CSV 001894	MC MICHAEL, J B	05/08/1882
CSV 001895	SEBASTIAN, SARAH	05/06/1882
CSV 001896	FRAZIER, SARAH	05/06/1882
CSV 001897	MAYS, J W	05/08/1882
CSV 001898	ROGERS, NANCY	ROGERS, JAMES, 05/09/1882
CSV 001899	MULLINS, JANE	MULLINS, A B, 05/08/1882
CSV 001900	MC RAE, W R	05/11/1882
CSV 001901	JONES, H W	05/11/1882
CSV 001902	ROBINSON, JOHN H	05/04/1882
CSV 001903	BIRDWELL, B F	05/04/1882
CSV 001904	GREER, ARMINDA	05/04/1882
CSV 001905	WHITE, MARY	05/12/1882
CSV 001906	ELSON, M A	05/12/1882
CSV 001907	ANDERSON, J M	05/12/1882
CSV 001908	MARTIN, M C	05/15/1882
CSV 001909	PEEVEY, W D	05/15/1882
CSV 001910	BASS, JAMES	05/15/1882
CSV 001911	STUBBELFIELD, S S	05/15/1882
CSV 001912	HAMBLETON, JAMES	05/15/1882
CSV 001913	MC CANN, R H	05/15/1882
CSV 001914	GOOLSBY, IRA H	05/15/1882
CSV 001915	DICKEY, JONATHAN	05/15/1882
CSV 001916	EVERETT, MARY	05/08/1882
CSV 001917	GRIGSBEL, J M	05/16/1882
CSV 001918	PIERCE, W M	05/16/1882
CSV 001919	MC DOUGAL, MARY	05/16/1882
CSV 001920	AILLS, THOMAS	08/09/1881
CSV 001921	ANISWORTH, D G	05/16/1882
CSV 001922	COLE, HENRY	COLE, FRANCIS, 05/16/1882
CSV 001923	SCHAEFER, DORIS	SCHAEFER, LOUIS, 05/09/1882

Voucher	Name	Date
CSV 001924	SUTTON, HUGH	08/10/1881
CSV 001925	MILLER, THOMAS	05/10/1882
CSV 001926	STORY, ISAAC	05/09/1882
CSV 001927	WILKES, A H	05/18/1882
CSV 001928	DIXON, WILLIAM N	05/08/1882
CSV 001929	AUSLEY, J T	05/18/1882
CSV 001930	SESSIONS, J M	05/20/1882
CSV 001931	EVANS, C C	05/10/1882
CSV 001932	O GUINN, E J	05/11/1882
CSV 001933	TURLEY, G W	05/22/1882
CSV 001934	PRICE, JOHN ALLEN	05/24/1882
CSV 001935	ROBERTS, ELIJAH	03/24/1882
CSV 001936	KREUTZER, CARL	05/08/1882
CSV 001937	RUSHOU, JOHN	05/08/1882
CSV 001938	BURCH, B D	05/09/1882
CSV 001939	BURCH, S M	05/09/1881
CSV 001940	HEARN, SEREPTA	HEARN, J M, 09/20/1881
CSV 001941	DEFEE, J J	05/09/1882
CSV 001942	BRYANT, C C	05/09/1882
CSV 001943	MORRISON, SUSAN	05/30/1882
CSV 001944	HOLLBROOK, G M	05/30/1882
CSV 001945	WOOD, CAMPBELL	05/24/1882
CSV 001946	GLENN, RHODA	05/08/1882
CSV 001947	SHARP, W C	05/08/1882
CSV 001948	MACHOST, HENRY	06/09/1882
CSV 001949	TURNER, E P	06/12/1882
CSV 001950	HOLT, J M	06/12/1882
CSV 001951	UMPHREY, JOHN H	06/12/1882
CSV 001952	MC AFEE, JOHN M	06/12/1882
CSV 001953	LANIER, C W	06/17/1882
CSV 001954	WAKEFIELD, J H	06/20/1882
CSV 001955	DUKE, JAMES W	06/20/1882
CSV 001956	TALIAFERRO, LOUIS	06/20/1882
CSV 001957	BARTON, N A	02/15/1882
CSV 001958	TAYLOR, MARTHA	06/12/1882
CSV 001959	NEWMAN, SIMPSON	06/25/1882
CSV 001960	TYER, JOHN	06/20/1882
CSV 001961	GROUNDS, JOHN	06/27/1882
CSV 001962	GRIESE, ADAM	04/09/1881
CSV 001963	WILLIFORD, C J	06/28/1882
CSV 001964	CROUCH, W H	07/07/1882
CSV 001965	STEUBING, FRED	11/14/1881
CSV 001966	YEARY, J K	07/08/1882
CSV 001967	ICE, GEORGE	06/19/1882
CSV 001968	THOMPSON, MARY	07/10/1882
CSV 001969	NEFF, JOHN	07/08/1882
CSV 001970	GARRETT, JOHN	06/26/1882
CSV 001971	STALCUP, J M	07/18/1882
CSV 001972	CECIL, WILLIAM	07/21/1882

Voucher	Name	Date
CSV 001973	CALLEY, JOHN T	07/071882
CSV 001974	THOMPSON, GEORGE	07/28/1882
CSV 001975	BUTLER, JACOB	06/26/1882
CSV 001976	CROSS, V A	08/11/1882
CSV 001977	HULLUM, E J	08/11/1882
CSV 001978	GARDINER, C B	08/14/1882
CSV 001979	WOODARD, TYER	08/14/1882
CSV 001980	FOSTER, G R	02/17/1882
CSV 001981	MARSH, N B	08/17/1882
CSV 001982	SHARP, WILLIAM	08/18/1882
CSV 001983	SMITH, JOHN	08/16/1882
CSV 001984	HENRY, WILLIAM	08/18/1882
CSV 001985	WALLACE, SARAH	08/18/1882
CSV 001986	GLASS, B F	08/21/1882
CSV 001987	EVERETT, SAM	08/16/1882
CSV 001988	SQUIER, E	08/20/1882
CSV 001989	SPURLIER, W A	08/24/1882
CSV 001990	DARDEN, E	08/25/1882
CSV 001991	METCALF, L R	08/25/1882
CSV 001992	LANVENDER, E K	08/25/1882
CSV 001993	HARVEY, W H H	08/25/1882
CSV 001994	STEWART, J D	08/25/1882
CSV 001995	GRUN, WILLIAM	11/07/1881
CSV 001996	DONAVAN, JAMES	08/25/1882
CSV 001997	TURNER, JOHN	08/25/1882
CSV 001998	NIEDERHOFER, CHARLES	08/12/1881
CSV 001999	CATE, D H	06/13/1882
CSV 002000	CRAVY, A J	08/25/1882
CSV 002001	SMITH, S C	08/25/1882
CSV 002002	CELLUM, E J	07/11/1882
CSV 002003	HAVARD, C	08/25/1882
CSV 002004	FLETCHER, G W	08/28/1882
CSV 002005	MOORE, ROBERT	08/22/1882
CSV 002006	CASEY, HUGH	09/11/1882
CSV 002007	GROOMS, E C	08/08/1882
CSV 002008	REESE, E M	03/23/1882
CSV 002009	HENRY, JOHN	02/13/1882
CSV 002010	MUREY, HARVEY	09/18/1882
CSV 002011	CRISWELL, D E	09/12/1882
CSV 002012	BAILEY, W G	09/27/1882
CSV 002013	BRADFORD, POWELL	11/15/1881
CSV 002014	PROTHRO, J M	10/11/1882
CSV 002015	PARRIM, G W	10/05/1882
CSV 002016	MC GAHEY, NARCISSA	10/07/1882
CSV 002017	WALKER, S C	12/17/1881
CSV 002018	HODGES, SAMUEL	10/11/1882
CSV 002019	MONTGOMERY, JAMES M	10/12/1882
CSV 002020	NORTH, SARAH	NORTH, R R, 08/15/1882
CSV 002021	BURNS, T E	10/16/1882

Confederate Scrip Vouchers-Numerical Listing

CSV 002022..... CULVER, MARTHA 10/16/1882
CSV 002023..... GRIMES, GEORGIA............................ GRMES, DANIEL, 10/23/1882
CSV 002024..... WAKALEE, AUGUSTINE 10/24/1882
CSV 002025..... STAPLETON, SAM 10/24/1882
CSV 002026..... WHEAT, JOHN 10/24/1882
CSV 002027..... WEBB, MARY J..................................... 11/09/1882
CSV 002028..... KIRKBRIDE, F H.................................. 08/29/1882
CSV 002029..... MAIN, M J.. 08/09/1882
CSV 002030..... STEWART, JAMES 11/13/1882
CSV 002031..... PATTERSON, W A 11/17/1882
CSV 002032..... HOBBS, ISAAC 11/18/1882
CSV 002033..... WHITE, W K.. 11/20/1882
CSV 002034..... HIGH, R M 11/20/1882
CSV 002035..... HOPKINS, JOSLIN 11/20/1882
CSV 002036..... WOOTAN, A A 11/20/1882
CSV 002037..... MORGAN, G W 11/14/1882
CSV 002038..... COPELAND, SUSAN 11/21/1882
CSV 002039..... WILSON, A J....................................... 11/21/1882
CSV 002040..... ST JOHN, H L 11/21/1882
CSV 002041..... PRATER 11/21/1882
CSV 002042..... MC CORGUALDALE, E A 12/19/1883
CSV 002043..... FLORES, JESUS 11/23/1882
CSV 002044..... BATES, WILLIAM 11/14/1882
CSV 002045..... CRAWEN, JOE 11/18/1882
CSV 002046..... DESKIN, AMERICA.............................. 04/08/1882
CSV 002047..... GIBBONS, AUSTIN 11/20/1882
CSV 002048..... BARTLETT, L...................................... 06/12/1882
CSV 002049..... GEE, J B.. 12/12/1882
CSV 002050..... ROGERS, J B....................................... 12/12/1882
CSV 002051..... WOOLVERTON, E H 11/08/1882
CSV 002052..... ALLEN, E T... 12/11/1882
CSV 002053..... ALLEN, J E.. 12/11/1882
CSV 002054..... CODY, J W.. 12/13/1882
CSV 002055..... ALLISON, S P 11/14/1882
CSV 002056..... HEILL, JOHN W 12/16/1882
CSV 002057..... HARRIS, MARY JANE 09/02/1882
CSV 002058..... HARLESS, F G..................................... 09/02/1882
CSV 002059..... TEMPLETON, JOHN S 09/02/1882
CSV 002060..... DANIEL, JOHN W 09/02/1882

www.ingramcontent.com/pod-product-compliance
Lightning Source LLC
Chambersburg PA
CBHW080248170426
43192CB00014BA/2602